SO-CFN-861

geology trails
of
northern california

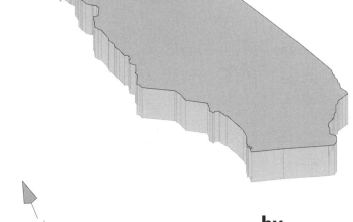

by

Robin C. Johnson
and
Dot Lofstrom

Gem Guides Book Co.
Baldwin Park, CA

Copyright © 2005
Gem Guides Book Company
315 Cloverleaf Drive, Suite F
Baldwin Park, CA 91706

This publication is a creative work fully protected by all applicable rights. All rights reserved. No portion of this book may be reproduced or transmitted in any form or by any means, electronic or mechanical, including fax, photocopy, recording, or any information storage or retrieval system without permission in writing from the publisher, except for inclusions or brief quotations in a review.

Cover Design:	Scott Roberts
Maps:	Dot Lofstrom
Photo Credits:	Authors, unless otherwise noted

ISBN 1-889786-31-4
Library of Congress Card Number 2004114996

Manufactured in the United States of America

NOTE:
Due to possibility of personal error, typographical error, misinterpretation of information and the many changes due to man or nature, *Geology Trails of Northern California*, its publisher and all other persons directly or indirectly associated with this publication assume no responsibility for accidents, injury or any losses by individuals or groups using this publication. In rough terrain and hazardous areas we advise that all persons be aware of possible changes due to the elements or those hazards which may be mad-made that can occur along any of the hiking trails, and make all efforts possible to evaluate any hazard which may be present or anticipated.

DEDICATIONS

To my father, in memory, who successfully instilled in me his great love and respect for the natural world.

—Robin Johnson

To my instructors at Southwest Missouri State University. Thank you for so graciously inviting me into this wonderful world of geology.

—Dot Lofstrom

CONTENTS

INTRODUCTION

In the context of the everyday, it seems as though we are standing on fairly solid footing and that the earth beneath us is stable and immutable. And, except for the occasional significant earthquake, the ground really is a reliable perch. However, taken in a larger context, speeded up significantly, like a time-lapse photography sequence, the earth's crust is a constantly changing and evolving system. In the course of millions of years, land masses have split and merged, oceans have encroached on the land and receded again, mountains have grown and diminished, and masses of living creatures have arisen and returned to the dust.

It is easy to forget about all this activity that the earth is busily engaged in while we scurry to and from work each day. And although we cannot speed the process up enough to see it in any tangible sense, the earth's busyness is visible to those who go looking for it. That is the purpose of this book, to help you explore the hundreds of millions of years of the earth's evolution up until now.

Thinking about all that has come before, most of which had nothing to do with humans, is one of the most humbling experiences we can imagine. Walking through evidence of past geologic processes is the means to achieving that experience. All over the globe there are pieces of the puzzle of the earth's story. Collecting and fitting together those pieces is the job of geologists. Our job, or rather recreation, is to understand and marvel at the resulting composite. One of the best ways to do that is to strap on our boots and go for a walk on that deceptively still surface of the earth. And one of the best places to do that, for both geology and hiking in general, is California.

There are many hiking guides for California, most of them presenting trails to beautiful alpine lakes, stately redwood forests, bird-choked marshes, lush fern canyons, and palm oases. Although we love those hikes, we have noticed an absence of guides to California's geology trails, that is, trails leading to something of geologic interest. Since California occupies one of the most geologically entertaining settings on the Earth's surface, we think that a guide to those sites is in order.

This is not a rockhounding or fossil collecting guide, nor is this an in-depth study of geology. This is a walking and hiking guide, focusing on trails that showcase the natural history of California. If you thrill at caves, want to climb a cinder cone, are awed by the power of time to sculpt natural works of art in stone, you will find many great trails in this guide throughout Northern and Central California. Just as California boasts habitats ranging from alpine forests to low desert, so it can offer us just about every type of geology lesson there is. There is tectonic action of monumental proportions, major earthquake faulting, fascinating volcanoes, glacially-carved peaks and valleys, geysers, bubbling mud pots, lava flows, mines, caves, fossils, and more. The problem in compiling trails for this guide was not finding them, but the unhappy process of eliminating many.

If you sometimes think of the world's biota as getting in the way of seeing the good stuff, you will be overjoyed with the trails in this guide. But there are enough beautiful plants and animals to satisfy your hiking buddies as well. Quite frequently, a geology trail is just as interesting historically and biologically as it is mineralogically. We have certainly taken these other attractions into account in assembling this collection.

For geologists, the earth is divided into naturally-occurring sections based on the type of material and topography found on its surface. These are called geomorphic provinces (see Figure 1), and, because of the convoluted and dynamic history of the West Coast, California has more of them than any other U. S. state. The provinces do not obey our artificial boundaries, of course, so they range where they will, crossing county, state and even national boundaries. The Basin and Range, for instance, is a large province which includes parts of California, Nevada, Colorado, Utah, and Arizona. The Klamath Mountains province, found in the far north of California, continues on into Oregon. We will be taking advantage of these divisions in the arrangement of this guide. Beginning with the Klamath Mountains in the northwest corner of the state, each chapter will represent one of the six geomorphic provinces of Northern California.

Major Geologic Features of California

What are these earthly glories that spring up along our hiking trails? Here's a short overview of the kinds of attractions we are about to see.

Tectonism

A cursory glance at a topographic map of California will show that it is bounded on the west and east by mountain ranges enclosing a huge central valley. These features dominate the way in which the geomorphic provinces are assigned. Several mountain ranges occupy the state, almost all of them oriented in a north-south pattern, such as the Coast Ranges and the Sierra Nevadas. Around San Luis Obispo, though, a different mountain system appears, the Transverse Ranges, which run generally east-west.

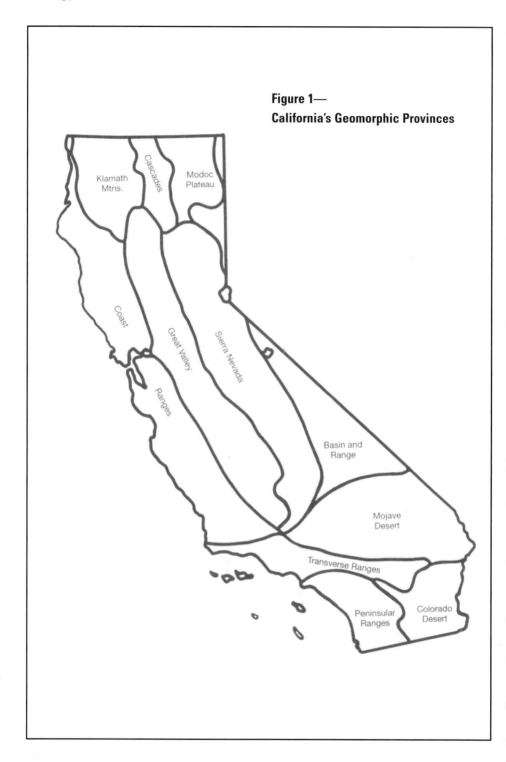

Figure 1—
California's Geomorphic Provinces

In the case of the California mountain ranges and mountains in general, the force at work is tectonism. Plate tectonics, once thought of among the scientific community as just a well-coddled egg in the mind of a half-baked German geophysicist Alfred Wegener, is now accepted as the fundamental explanation about how the earth got to look as it does today. When Wegener first proposed his idea of continental drift in the early twentieth century, it was met with widespread ridicule. What could he expect from a species still reeling from the idea that the earth was not the center of the universe? But the evidence began to stack up, and the notion that vast land masses moved and shifted around the globe grew and gathered momentum. Today, the moving plates have been mapped and named, and are known to be responsible for making mountains on land, the deep basins of the oceans, the ring of fire in the Pacific Ocean, and the Mid-Atlantic Ridge in the Atlantic Ocean. Without them, we would be living on a very flat, uniform, and boring ball, probably standing in ankle-deep water.

There are seven major plates and several minor ones on the Earth. They are rigid pieces of crust and upper mantle, together known as the lithosphere, which move over a softer cushion beneath them called the asthenosphere. Depending on where you live in California, you are either moving westward or northward at this very moment.

The movement of the tectonic plates is responsible for many of the dramatic features of California, including rugged mountain ranges and low deserts. There are also even more obvious bits of evidence to be found in the Golden State. At Pinnacles National Monument, for instance, a bit of southern California now sits displaced in central California, far from home. How did it get there? This is one of the mysteries we will explore.

Glaciation

As in much of North America, ice ages brought vast quantities of ice down into California at various times throughout the history of the earth. Evidence of the scraping action of the ice is visible in the Sierra Nevada mountains and elsewhere. Where the glaciers moved through, they carved lakes and deep gorges and polished hard bedrock. They left "islands" of resistant rock in place, and carried huge boulders far from their origin. They have given us alluring formations such as the turrets of Castle Crags. And they have given us the breathtaking beauty of Yosemite National Park.

At the highest elevations in the Sierras and Cascades, remnants of old glaciers still exist, such as the one on the northern side of Mt. Lyell in Yosemite, or the several glaciers fringing the top of Mt. Shasta. However, most of the trails showcasing glaciation travel to places where the ice receded long ago, leaving tracks on the faces of the rocks.

Mineral Deposits

Without gold, California's human history would be dramatically altered. In 1848, gold was discovered in Coloma, on the South Fork of the American River. A park marks this spot today. This event sparked the 1849 Gold Rush, a sudden and dramatic influx of people from all over the world; miners arrived, of course, and an entire support system geared towards serving their needs. Bars, brothels, hotels, bookstores, supply stores, legal offices, laundries, merchants of every type, shipping, railroads—an entire civilization sprang up wherever there was gold being coaxed from the rivers or pried out of the mountains.

The gold originated primarily in vast quartz veins in the Sierra Nevadas, and was discovered in the many waterways washing eroded particles down into all parts west of the mountains. Many who came for gold settled in California and plied the trades they brought along, such as farming, ranching, and many more.

When the gold fever ran down, the state had been transformed. Gold mining has continued to the present day, but is an entirely different kind of operation now. In the area where gold was first discovered, along the American River, you will still see people panning today. And on public land throughout the state, you will see the rock cairns marking someone's mining claim. There is still some gold in them thar hills.

In addition to gold, other minerals have been successfully mined in the state, including silver, tungsten, borax, salt, and chromium, to name a few. We will visit several historic mining sites and even venture into some of the abandoned mines.

Earthquake Faults

California is well known for its earthquakes, a fact of life that leaves natives almost apathetic, but creates tremors in the bones of visitors riding the trains of Bay Area Rapid Transit (BART) under the San Francisco Bay. Earthquakes are nothing to be blasé about, to be sure, but as is customary, people tend not to fear the familiar. California has dozens of earthquakes daily, most of them so small that no one notices except geologists and seismologists monitoring the undulations of the earth. Occasionally, however, such as in the Loma Prieta quake of 1989 and the Northridge quake of 1994, the earth delivers a major jolt, and then all of us pay attention.

It is no mystery to scientists why we have this activity. The most interesting geology worldwide occurs along tectonic plate boundaries, and California is a perfect example.

California is where the North American and Pacific Plates meet, a dynamic boundary that runs roughly along the San Andreas Fault. This collision is responsible for the mountainous coastal terrain and most of the earthquake activity throughout the state. We will explore how this plate boundary affects the topography of California in more depth as we proceed into the distinct provinces.

Volcanoes

The numerous volcanoes of California have been quiet for a long time now, so much so that those of us living here almost never think about the possibility of an eruption. But evidence of past volcanic activity is easily observed, particularly in the northeast section of the state, where huge volcanoes poured lava over the landscape as recently as 1917. Even today, there is enough geothermal activity just under the surface to create the fascinating spectacles in Lassen National Park—bubbling mud pots, steam shooting out of holes in the ground, and hot springs and creeks. In the Cascades, there are several volcanoes that are considered dormant, but not extinct, including Medicine Lake, Mt. Shasta, and Lassen Peak. The Long Valley Caldera and the Mammoth Lake area are also active volcanic regions.

All over the state, we see evidence of our volcanic past. There are cinder cones dotting the Mojave Desert, and the entire Sierra Nevada range is made of granite that was once molten material underground. There are lava flows so pristine that they look as though they happened yesterday, but actually occurred a few thousand years ago (which in the geologic time scale, is comparable to a few seconds for us).

We will be exploring numerous remnants of this activity, as well as many surface features that hint at the turmoil still brewing just below the surface.

Caves

In California, caves are generally one of two types, either lava tubes or dissolved limestone. Many limestone caves are located in the Sierra Nevada Range and feature typical cave formations, such as stalactites, stalagmites, flowstone, draperies, etc. One of the caves, Black Chasm, also has large collections of rare crystal formations called helictites. These caves have been created by ground water dissolving the calcium carbonate over a long period of time. A cave is considered living if it is still being formed, if water is still present. A dry cave is a dead one.

Lava tubes are an entirely different sort of cave. They are created by highly liquid lava flowing downhill in such a way that the outer area cools and forms a crust while insulating the liquid lava within. The still-liquid lava flows through the hardened crust, eventually draining out when the eruption ceases, leaving a hollow tube behind. Lava tubes are often found when a portion of the ceiling caves in and exposes an opening. Hundreds of these tubes are located in Lava Beds National Monument. They are common in other areas as well, and we will visit several. There are no crystalline formations in these caves, but they have their own particular charms. They are not quite so daunting

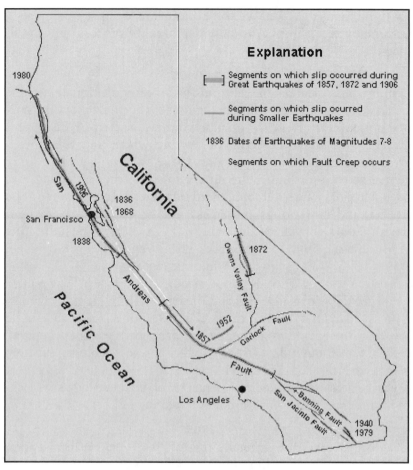

Figure 2—Major California Faults

as other caves to explore because they are often a single tube or limited branching tubes, and difficult to get lost in.

Fossils

Because California contains huge tracts of land that were once at the bottom of ancient seas, a good percentage of the known fossil beds contain remnants of sea creatures, with some notable exceptions such as the La Brea tar pits in southern California. There are several ammonite sites, and many places where clam shells and the like can be viewed. In the round old hills south of Tracy, the gigantic marine reptile, ichthyosaurus, has been found. Many important Miocene mammal fossils have been discovered in the Blackhawk area of Mount Diablo.

Most of the fossil sites we will visit are protected in parklands, so you will only be able to look, but there are places where collecting is allowed. There are few things more exciting than holding something in your hand that was living millions of years ago.

Rules of the Trail

For those of us attracted to rocks and fossils, it is natural to want to take some home. It is important, however, that you know the rules regarding the taking of natural objects. Collecting is prohibited in national and state parks, with occasional exceptions. Leave your rock hammer at home when visiting these places, but bring your hand lens. You can usually collect rocks and fossils on land overseen by the Bureau of Land Management. Make sure you check with the local BLM office, however. Most sites have a 25-pound collecting limit. As an example, these guidelines are issued by the Barstow Field Office for rock collecting:

> Part 8365 of Title 43 CFR (Code of Federal Regulations) provide for the collecting of "reasonable" quantities of rocks, minerals, semiprecious gemstones, and invertebrate and plant fossils of non-scientific importance, for personal use. With respect to rockhound material, the Field Office considers a "reasonable quantity" to be not more than can be carried in a daypack. Regulations do not allow collecting on "developed recreation sites and areas," or where otherwise prohibited or posted. Care should be exercised not to collect minerals on mining claims.

There are other rules regarding collecting of fossils and other objects. Some protected wilderness areas are completely off limits for collecting of any kind, and some allow personal collecting. Check with the agency overseeing the area. Contact information is provided in the Resource List at the end of this book. As always while visiting nature's wonderland, stay on established trails, respect wildlife, bring out everything you take in, and leave no trace.

Hazards of the Trail

By far the most hazardous of animals you will likely encounter is the rattlesnake. Most animals will stay away from you, including snakes, but be careful where you put your hands among rocks. Mountain lions live in the areas you will enter, but you will not normally see one. Bears are mostly interested in your food, so, if you camp, keep your food items locked up or tied high out of the way. Some of the animals living in Northern California are very large, such as elk and elephant seals, and can be dangerous just because of their size, not because they are especially ferocious. Give wild animals plenty of space and don't ever try to corner them.

Poison oak is very common along these trails. Learn to recognize it and stay away from it. In spring, it has glossy, three-part leaves. The best defense is to stay on the trail. The same advice applies for avoiding ticks. Wearing long pants and sleeves can also help protect you from ticks. Mosquitoes can be a problem in wetter areas. It's a good idea to take an insect repellent along in your pack. And to avoid accidents, wear sturdy boots and always watch your footing.

Always carry water, plus a first-aid kit, snacks, matches in a waterproof container, a mirror for signaling, a map, an extra jacket or sweatshirt, and your cell phone, turned off. Forest Service maps, which can be purchased at ranger stations, through the mail, or from the Forest Service web sites, are a valuable resource.

Using This Guide

The trails here are ordered by geomorphic province so you can locate those in your neighborhood or can target a particular area for a hiking trip. There is a thematic cross-reference in Appendix A to let you easily locate your particular favorite attraction. So if you're just wild about volcanoes, for instance, flip to the back of the book to find the trails that satisfy your passion.

Each section begins with an overview of the geology of the area, a description of the forces that shaped it, and what sort of landscape dominates as a result. To help you understand and put these events into perspective, a glossary of technical terms used and a chart of the geologic time scale are included as appendices.

The trails are described in detail, including the round-trip distance, the difficulty level, what you will see on the trail, and directions to parking and the trailhead. Most of these hikes are easy to moderate and last no more than a few hours. The goal is to see interesting geology, not navigate the outback. With your kids, on a Sunday afternoon, you can hike these trails and have a healthy, educational, and joyful outing. Another bonus is that a lot of them are free. If you pack sandwiches, it's almost always cheaper than a movie.

Spotting maps show the distribution of the trails. They are keyed to the numbered hikes in each section. We hope you enjoy traversing these paths as much as we have.

The northwest corner of the state is known primarily for its magnificent, ancient redwood forests. Not only can you not see the forest for the trees, you can't see the rocks either. So geology trails are a little scarce in this province. But there is geology, of course, underneath it all.

The rocks of the Klamath Mountains puzzled geologists for a long time. They seemed to be out of place, as if they had just been dumped here at the edge of the continent. In a sense, that is exactly what happened. Eventually, a new theory had to be developed to explain the origin of these particular rocks. The explanation is known as the theory of accreted terrane, or more poetically, suspect terrane, where pieces of other continents or ocean crust are sutured onto the continent as a result of tectonic plate movement.

When you walk in the Klamath Mountains, chances are that you are not walking on original North American continental crust at all. Instead, the rocks you are walking on began as oceanic crust and underlying mantle material, which first formed as part of an oceanic plate in another part of the world, far out to sea.

This particular sequence of rocks is known as an "ophiolite suite." An ophiolite suite is a series of igneous rocks topped by deep-sea sedimentary rocks that have been squeezed and altered during plate movement. At the base of the suite is basalt, which started out as magma extruded beneath the ocean at a mid-oceanic spreading center, a place where the oceanic plates diverged and moved away from each other, thus providing a conduit for mantle material to rise to the surface. When the lava was extruded onto the ocean floor, the material was rolled around and cooled by the waters of the sea. The result is a rounded glob of basalt that reminds many geologists of pillows, and is therefore called pillow basalt. Whenever you see pillow basalt, you know you are at the base of an ophiolite sequence.

Deep-sea sedimentary rocks overlie the igneous rocks in an ophiolite sequence. One of the more interesting formations in the Klamath Mountains is the McCloud limestone, made of calcium carbonate and full of fossils from the Permian ocean. The fossils include corals, brachiopods (which resemble clams), and fusulinids, small one-celled organisms which go by the nickname of "footballs" because of their shape. Limestone is easily dissolved by groundwater into caverns and sinkholes, a characteristic observable at magnificent Shasta Caverns. The limestone was originally a coral reef surrounding the volcanic mid-oceanic islands of the early Klamath Mountains

How did the igneous rocks from the mid-oceanic spreading center and the deep-sea sedimentary rocks end up in an area called the Klamath Mountains? Think of the oceanic plate as a sort of conveyer belt. As the new molten rock erupts from the mantle to the surface, it becomes part of the existing oceanic plate. At the other end of the plate, where it is probably interacting with a continental plate, the oceanic material that makes up the leading edge of the plate is being subducted underneath the continental plate (See Figure 2). As that is happening, the newly formed material at the spreading center moves a little bit closer to the subduction zone. The time it takes for material at the spreading center to reach the subduction zone is approximately 180 million years. So oceanic plates are all 180 million years old or less.

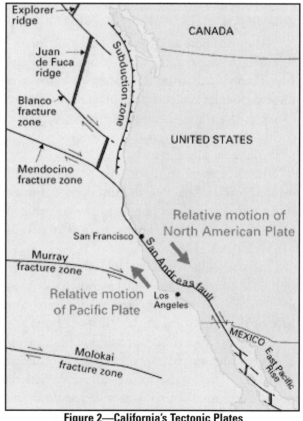

Figure 2—California's Tectonic Plates

In this manner, the oceanic plate moved towards the North American Plate, eventually colliding with the North American continent and subducting (diving) beneath it. As the cold, oceanic plate dove under the North American Plate, some of the material broke off and sutured on to the edge of the continent. Geologists believe that oceanic material was plastered onto the edge of continental crust at least five separate times in the Klamath Mountains province. Each sequence is known as a terrane, and the terranes get increasingly younger as you move from east to west. So the land that scraped off of the oceanic plate accreted here over vast stretches of time. The subduction of the oceanic plate is still occurring, creating an unstable coast where earthquakes and landslides are common. We will be seeing some evidence of that on the coastal trails.

If you are interested in reading more about this process, celebrated writer John McPhee wrote an entire book about it called *In Suspect Terrain*.

The Klamath province includes several mountain ranges, including the Trinity Alps, Siskiyou Mountains, Marble Mountains, and Salmon Mountains. There are many places in these mountains where evidence of glaciation is on view. Along the eastern edge of the province is a unique and dramatic outcrop of eroded granite spires called Castle Crags. We will be visiting Castle Crags State Park for three hikes. From that eastern edge of the province, traveling west, you enter lusher and more densely forested areas as you go. The Klamath River is the major river artery, but several other large rivers course through the northwest part of the state; rainfall is plentiful, and wildlife abounds.

Redwood National Park is located here, as are five state parks, all featuring dense coastal redwood forests. When the Hudson Bay Company fur traders came to this stretch of California, they were astounded at the abundance of beaver. Unlike those earlier visitors, we will be taking photos instead of pelts. Among other early visitors here was the famous mountain man Jedediah Smith in 1828. The Smith River and a state park are named after him. Russian fur traders also made their way through the north coast area, establishing camps and villages. Their presence has been preserved in place names such as Russian Wilderness, Russian Gulch, and further south, Russian River.

As in the rest of northern California, gold was found in the Klamath area as well. The town of Happy Camp was founded in 1851 by miners who were happy with the local pickings. Today, Happy Camp is a base for a variety of recreational activities in the extreme north of the state. But even such pivotal

BIGFOOT

Almost everyone has heard of Bigfoot, or Sasquatch, or Yeti, or the Abominable Snowman, the huge primate who walks on two feet and lives in the forests of the American Northwest, Canada, or the Himalayas. Legends of the creature's existence go back hundreds of years, and even in modern times, thousands of sightings have been reported. But, so far, no firm evidence has been found to prove its existence. No bones have turned up, and no bodies have ever been seen. Footprints have been found, but some appear to have been faked and there is no definitive test of authenticity for the rest.

Descriptions of Bigfoot all over the world are fairly consistent – an ape-like creature walking bipedally with a loping gate, covered in dark, often reddish hair, standing between 8 and 11 feet tall. This description is remarkably close to a known animal thought to be extinct. *Gigantopithecus* lived between 1 and 9 million years ago in central and southeast Asia. Its closest modern relative is the orangutan. Some scientists postulate that this ancient ape migrated to North America the same way humans did, over temporary land bridges, and somehow has survived in North America to this day.

With all of the interest in Bigfoot, however, many people believe that it could not have remained hidden from us for so long. Skeptics suspect that well-intentioned people who report sightings have actually seen a bear standing on its hind legs.

No doubt the legend, if not the actual animal, will remain alive for a long time to come.

destinations in the Klamath are still small towns in this minimally populated region.

There are three wilderness areas located here, the Russian Wilderness Area, located along a major ridge dividing the Scott and Salmon River watersheds, Siskiyou Wilderness between Happy Camp and the coast, and the Marble Mountain Wilderness Area, 250,000 acres of thick forests, tall peaks, glacial lakes, and plenty of solitude. It is probably because of all this wilderness that Bigfoot has managed to hang on here, in legend at least [see inset]. In California, there have been reports of Bigfoot on Mt. Shasta, but his (or her) real domain is in the forests around the Klamath and Trinity Rivers. There is even a road named after the elusive creature, The Bigfoot Scenic Byway, 85 miles along Highway 96. As you might expect, there is always someone looking for a promotional angle, so the tiny California town of Willow Creek (Highway 96 and Highway 299) has declared itself "the Bigfoot capital of the world." You can visit the Willow Creek-China Flat Museum there to see casts of Bigfoot footprints and photos, as well as a *Gigantopithecus* (Bigfoot?) skull. And don't forget to take your camera when you go hiking in the Klamath Mountains. What a shame it would be if you ran into Bigfoot and had no proof.

Trails of the Klamath Mountains:

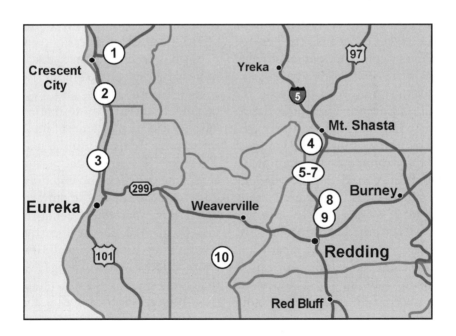

1. Myrtle Creek Trail

EFFORT:..Minimal
LENGTH: ....2.0 miles
GEOLOGICAL FEATURE(S): ....Mining
LOCATION: ....Smith River National Recreation Area

Description: This is a 15-stop self-guiding interpretive trail along Myrtle Creek, a site of intense mining activity during the latter half of the nineteenth century. The creek marks a boundary between typical local soils supporting the redwood and Douglas fir forest, and serpentine soils, rich in iron and magnesium, and therefore reddish in color. This area is designated as a special Botanical Area to protect its unique environment. Because serpentine soils are uncommon, plants growing in them are often of rare types.

On this trail you will visit the remains of mining operations dating from 1853 when gold was discovered here by Louis Gallise. The gold was mined for some time by panning. In 1890, a huge gold nugget weighing 47 ounces was discovered here. Around 1894, a group of investors from Crescent City formed the Myrtle Creek Mining Company and constructed a ditch to allow hydraulic mining. Gold and silver were successfully mined here until the 1920s.

The different plant communities on either side of the creek, and the different soils supporting them, provide clues that this is the location of a fault. Faults are often not very obvious on the surface, so geologists study aerial photographs for suggestions of "lines," called "lineations." Like the name suggests, lineations are an alignment of surface features as a result of a fault. People are usually too close to the earth to be able to see the lineations on the surface, which is why aerial photographs are needed. Even on the photographs, though, the shadowy suggestion of lineations often aren't easily seen.

It's not a coincidence that this mine had been situated in the area of a fault. Both faults and cooling magma result in the formation of deep cracks that go deep into the earth, possibly even into the mantle. These are very small cracks, from a centimeter to a few inches, and they don't come out on the surface, so don't worry that you're going to fall into them. Nor do they go straight down. They usually branch, one to another, like a series of twigs. When the cracks occur, hydrothermal fluid (hot, mineral-laden water) is able to move through them, first as steam and later as water. As the fluid moves upward through the cracks, minerals (including gold and silver) begin to precipitate out on the walls of the cracks, gradually filling them in. Usually, the last mineral to crystallize out is quartz. You've seen evidence of these cracks all the time when you've seen quartz veins in boulders or in road cuts. Mines cannot be located just anywhere it's convenient. They have to be located in an area where the minerals were deposited, and that means an area of volcanic or tectonic activity.

Pick up a trail guide at the Forest Service office in Eureka or at the Smith River National Recreation Area office in Gasquet. The well-established trail will bring you through the ditch system dug by the miners, and remnants of a ground sluicing operation. It will also explain how the surrounding flora was affected by the mining activity. In addition to the diversion of the creek, downing of timber for construction, and moving of soil, the miners also burned the vegetation down to get a better look at the geology (a temptation generally avoided by modern geologists). The landscape still shows scars from the intensive and long-term mining, but healing is ongoing.

Start out on an easy trail through a forest of coast redwood, tan oak, rhododendron, azalea, evergreen huckleberry, redwood sorrel, wild ginger, California hazel, milkmaids, thimbleberry, sword fern, five-finger fern, maidenhair fern, licorice fern, and Port-Orford cedar. Also making an appearance is the Oregon myrtle, for which the creek is named. We usually call this tree a California bay or laurel. Break one of its leaves to smell the distinctive aroma. Near the creek, big leaf maples and alders enjoy the water provided by the year-round stream.

The trail follows the old mining ditch. It was used to transport large amounts of water for washing soil through sluice boxes. Next you will come to a footbridge, a wooden gate, and one of the metal pipes used to divert the water into the ditch. This system could discharge up to 15,000 gallons per minute.

At stop five you will be able to see the different plant communities of the serpentine soils. The reddish soil across the creek supports manzanita, labrador tea, California coffee berry, huckleberry, oak, bear grass, silk tassel bush, and the rare Bolander's lily.

The carnivorous California pitcher plant can be found in the boggy areas along the creek. The brochure brings them to your attention at stop seven. The rare pitcher plants (Darlingtonia californica) are able to live in wet, serpentine soils devoid of nitrogen and phosphorous because they obtain these nutrients from the insects and other small organisms they trap in their cobra-like hoods. They are sometimes called "cobra plants." They produce an abundance of nectar to attract insects inside their single leaf (pitcher). The insects drown in the nectar and decay through bacterial action. These plants are protected and it is illegal to pick them. The pitcher plant grows in marshy areas along the California and Oregon coast where cold, moving water is present. Since it is almost always found in poor quality soils where the parent rock is serpentine, it is considered a serpentine indicator.

Other rare, beautiful flowers growing here are the California lady's slipper and the Vollmer's lily.

You will come to a place where the serpentine is exposed alongside the trail. It is gray-green in color and feels somewhat waxy or soapy to the touch. Since serpentine is unstable, ditches were not dug through it. Instead, the miners built flumes to carry the water over it. Remnants of these flumes can be seen below the trail.

Continue through the moist riparian environment along the creek. Ferns dominate the understory as you approach the trail's end at the creek bed. You might want to stop here for a while to enjoy the serenity of the cool forest and running stream before heading back. Return along the same path.

Directions: On Highway 101 in Crescent City, go 3 miles north to Highway 199, then turn east and go 7 miles across the Myrtle Creek Bridge to the parking area on the river side of the road. Cross the road to the trailhead. Access is free.

2. Coastal Trail – Enderts Beach Segment

EFFORT ....Minimal
LENGTH ....2.0 miles
GEOLOGICAL FEATURE(S).................................Erosional Features
LOCATION ....Redwood National Park

Description: Take binoculars, your camera, and a picnic on this short seaside stroll through Monterey cypress and wildflowers to Enderts Beach and then to the Hidden Beach tidepools. Everyone will love this sweet trail, even if your hiking buddies are indifferent to the erosion on display here. Between the geology, flowers, animals, and surf, there is something to entertain everyone and plenty for us to describe.

The intense seismic activity and rapid uplift of the North Coast leads to frequent landslides, shifting rivers, and dramatic coastal erosion. In the 1990s, at least nine magnitude 6.0-plus earthquakes jolted the North Coast. This incidence of large quakes was higher than in any other decade within the last century. We have already discussed the causes of this activity, the tectonic plate subduction ongoing along California's coast. Now, let's take a look at the results.

22

The Coastal Trail runs up and down the length of this coastline through Redwood National Park and the state parks contained within it. The trail's north end can be found here at Crescent Beach in a short section leading to Enderts Beach where Little Nickel Creek runs into the ocean. The trail to Enderts Beach is only a half mile, but we are going to take a short side trip along the way and extend the hike by walking on to the tidepools.

From the beginning of this trail, there is ample evidence of the powerful forces chewing into the landscape. Near the first parking area you will see a dramatic landslide, an obvious indicator of how wave action is cutting into the shoreline. Follow the old road south, noting how it has been partially reclaimed by the sea and is no longer usable. This sort of action is occurring all along the ocean edge to varying degrees. But it is especially pronounced here because of the type of rock underlying the park. Later, down on the beach, we will get a close-up view of that unstable foundation.

As you walk, enjoy the lovely seascapes and excellent wildlife viewing. Among the birds you may see here are brown pelicans, murres, cormorants, and, of course, gulls. Dolphins, killer whales, and gray whales may be passing by offshore. Gray whale watching is best from March to May during the spring migration. Harbor seals may be frolicking closer in.

The path is wide and gently slopes downhill, routing you between hedges of greenery and a profusion of wildflowers. Towards the beginning of the trail, we walked between a feast of white daisies. It reminded us of the yellow brick road and made us want to skip.

Views out to sea are good in clear weather from the upper trail. In any weather, your walk will be accompanied by a distant foghorn. Looking back, you will see the long sweeping curve of Crescent Beach leading out to Battery Point and Crescent City. As you drop down from the high points, you will become enclosed by arbors of dense vegetation and lose the views. These sections are brief, but quite enjoyable.

Continue the easy walk downhill to a junction. Left is a nature trail along Nickel Creek and right is the path to Enderts Beach. Going south, the Coastal Trail continues. If you want to, detour to the nature trail (recommended). It is only a quarter mile long and displays licorice ferns overwhelming the trunks and branches of the trees. It's sort of eerie, especially for those of us more accustomed to looking at rocks, with all these vines and ferns reaching towards you. The trail follows Nickel Creek inland through a very dense forest, smothered in green moss and ferns. You can hear the creek beside you, but can't see much of it. Be

23

careful not to step on banana slugs here on the moist creekside trail.

After you've covered over half of this little side trip, you will begin to see the licorice ferns growing on the trees. As you go further, you will come to a huge branch across the trail, high enough for you to walk under. It is overwhelmed with ferns. Look up and around you to see how the ferns are colonizing the trees. From here, it is only a few steps to a broken bench. The legs of the bench rusted through in this damp spot, and the bench is now sitting directly on the ground. The bench marks the end of the trail.

Returning to the junction, go straight towards the beach. From the grassy cliff top, head down the steep slope on a narrow, rocky path. You will pass a trail to the left when you reach the toilets. That trail leads to the campground. You want to continue straight towards the beach. Going steeply down between walls of thick plants, you will come out on a sandy platform above the beach. Clamber down the rocks to the beach and turn left to reach the spot where the Nickel Creek carves a narrow channel through the sand on its way into the ocean.

Facing the eroded cliff face, you can see the different layers of the Franciscan mélange. Notice that the bottom visible layer is very dark with much lighter layers above it. This is an excellent opportunity to observe the Franciscan formation, one of the most complex and famous rock formations in the United States. The Franciscan mélange includes fine-grained, deep-sea sedimentary rocks (greywacke) with large blocks of oceanic crust along with blue and green schist metamorphic facies. This type of conglomerate forms at a convergent plate boundary, where the deep-sea sediments are dragged down with the oceanic crust as it is subducted beneath the continental crust. The result is a complicated mixture of Jurassic and Cretaceous sedimentary, metamorphic, and igneous rocks. You can see fine examples of the Franciscan formation around San Francisco, where it has been bent into lovely chevron folds, made starkly visible by the alternating beds of chert and shale. Here in the North Coast, this formation underlies most of Redwood National Park, and is composed primarily of sandstones and mudstones, with some serpentinite and greenstone, sheared and altered and highly fractured.

Generally, the Franciscan formation is highly unstable, largely because of the presence of faults, both small and very large, and shear zones often hundreds of feet wide. These inherently weak structural features, combined with high rainfall and prolonged storms on the north coast, account for the instability and erodibility of this shoreline. As you observed at the start of this trail, catastrophic landslides, stream bank erosion, and soil creep are common.

Hop the creek and continue walking southward. Notice the many black stones in the sand. These have washed out of the dark layer visible at the base of the cliff. Many of these rocks have white stripes in them, which are quartz veins. Some are crisscrossed many times with these veins, creating quite interesting black and white striped rocks. The high stresses at the plate boundary create a lot of highly fractured rock. Facing the cliff wall, notice that the rocks exhibit obvious bending patterns, yet more evidence of the forces at work here. Notice how the separate layers of sandstone, siltstone, and shale are easy to distinguish.

We are heading to where the sandy beach gives way to jagged black rocks which jut out and appear to form a barrier between this beach and the next. Climb among the rocky shoreline to take advantage of some of the most fertile tidepools we have ever seen. They are teeming with green and pink anemones, acorn barnacles, snails, sea urchins, limpets, sea stars, and sea palms. Be careful to step only on the rock, which is difficult here. Every little crevice in the surfaces is a home to small sea creatures.

It is most rewarding to find a good tidepool and sit still and look into it. The details of its contents will reveal themselves slowly. Hundreds of sea stars can be seen here, including the brilliant orange leather star.

Make your way across the rocks to the incipient arches (arches in the making). You are witnessing a particular stage in the process of coastal arch formation. At this stage, the resistant rock you are climbing on has remained in place while the softer

cliff of Enderts Beach has eroded further inland. But even this material will eventually succumb. For now, the ocean has managed to punch a couple of holes into it. Over time, the waves will work the walls and ceilings of these caves, increasing the size of the hole. Someday, a delicate arch may result. And then, further into the future, the center of the arch will collapse, leaving behind a couple of sea stacks. As we visit more coastal trails, we will observe these other stages of arch formation.

You can pass through the first cave, which is somewhat narrow and partially blocked by a large branch, but easily maneuvered. Coming out the other side, you will find a treasure trove of tidepools and another beach, Hidden Beach. No doubt the rich abundance of sea creatures here will hold your interest for a while.

Okay, it looks like your friends are impatient to break out the sandwiches. Back on Enderts Beach, you will find some nice big smooth logs to perch on. After your picnic, return by the same path.

Directions: From Crescent City, take Highway 101 south two miles. Turn right on Enderts Beach Road and proceed to the end of the road and a parking lot overlooking Crescent Beach. Access is free. There are picnic tables, but no other facilities.

3. Rim Trail

EFFORT	Moderate
LENGTH	4+ miles
GEOLOGICAL FEATURE(S)	Rock Collecting, Erosional Features
LOCATION	Patrick's Point State Park

Description: In addition to dramatic shorelines, sandy beaches, sea stacks, and tidepools, this park offers a reconstructed Yurok village to investigate, Sumeg Village. Consider walking that trail near the visitor center before or after this one and spend the entire day in the park.

The Rim Trail runs for two miles along the ocean bluffs, connecting several of the popular stops and terminating at Agate Beach where we will do some poking about for pretty rocks. If your time is limited, you can pick up the trail at Patrick's Point or Mussel Rock to shorten the hike. Be forewarned that the coastline is often fogbound in summer. Sometimes beach hikes are best done in winter when other places may be less hospitable.

At the edge of the Palmer's Point parking area, you will find an interpretive panel explaining the gruesome discovery of over 1,000 sea lion skulls on offshore Cone Rock, each with a hole drilled in it. Archeologists deduce these to be the remnants of hunting rituals. One of the skulls is mounted inside the case.

Before hiking the featured trail, you may want to wander out to Palmer's Point for a look-see. It is doubtful that you will hike only the length of the Rim Trail, so your hike will be determined by how many side trips you take.

To find the beginning of the Rim Trail, walk back down the road a short distance. It is signed and located on the left of the road. The trail heads north, following the coastal bluff, giving you commanding views of the rugged coast and Trinidad Head to the south. Offshore, sea stacks provide resting places for sea lions, seals, cormorants, gulls, brown pelicans, black oystercatchers, and pigeon guillemots.

Sea stacks are isolated resistant rocks that are located near shore and project above sea level. They are sometimes the remnants of an arch or natural bridge. A natural bridge occurs when the waves erode softer sediments away from more resistant rock in such a way as to wear right through the middle. As the process continues over a long time, wearing the "legs" of the bridge thinner, the top collapses under its own weight, leaving two sea stacks. This evolution is well demonstrated at Natural Bridges State Park near Santa Cruz. When the park was established, there were bridges, but today there are none.

Vegetation along the bluff includes alder, spruce, Douglas fir, pine, Douglas iris, salal, trillium, rhododendrons, and azaleas. Ferns line the trails, and berry vines and wildflowers are prolific in summer. Vegetation piles up on itself in places, so don't be surprised if you start to imagine yourself in Jurassic Park on some stretches of this trail.

As you hike, you will encounter many spur trails leading to overlooks and beaches. Enrich your experience by taking these side trips. The windy trails down to Abalone Point, Patrick's Point, Wedding Rock, and Mussel Rocks make for a delightfully varied hike.

This park was once underwater. When the seas receded, the huge rocks just offshore emerged into view. Abalone Point is just 0.4 miles from the trailhead. Next will be Lookout Rock and Patrick's Point. After 1.5 miles, you come up to the spur trail leading to Mussel Rock. Go out towards it, through a natural arbor, and notice that a huge fracture has developed on the left side. Imagine that massive chunk of rock breaking free and falling into the sea. Someday, that is exactly what will happen. Erosion can be an extremely slow process, but moments do occur where a great change takes place instantaneously, like when an arch collapses or rocks break off and fall.

Clamber around the stone steps of Mussel Rock where stone walls have been erected to keep visitors from plummeting off. If you train your binoculars on the large sharp rock to the left, you will probably see pelicans or cormorants roosting there.

Return to the Rim Trail and continue. You will reach the end of the trail at Agate Beach Campground after two miles. There is a parking lot here, so if you came just to look for agates, you can park here and skip the Rim Trail.

From the parking area, take the steep trail down to a staircase that leads to Agate Beach. Once you are on the beach, look back at the cliff face. You can easily see the various bedding layers revealed there. On the bottom is the dark greenstone layer, and then Tertiary gravel above it. The top layer is sandstone.

Allow some time to search for agates, jade, and red jasper in the gravel bars. Most people do find agates if they have a little patience. You can walk along in the surf and look for them where the rough gravel lies, or you can sift through the dry sand up higher on the beach. The agates are glassy, translucent, and nearly white. They vary in size, but are normally about the size of a dime or smaller. There are plenty of quartz pieces here as well. You can distinguish the agates from them easily enough, as you cannot see into the quartz.

Agates and banded chalcedony are semi-precious gemstones which vary greatly in form and color and historically were highly prized. Chalcedony is a type of cryptocrystalline quartz, which means that the crystals are too small to be seen even with a microscope. Agates are formed in vesicular volcanic rocks by a process that is not completely understood. The volcanic rocks have cavities (vesicles) because of escaping gases. The agate forms when groundwater percolates through the volcanic rock, leaving behind a micro layer of precipitated silica in the vesicle. The vesicles in the host rock are often round; thus, the precipitated layers will be seen as concentric bands. Although the agates found here are generally white, agates occur in many different colors, depending on what dissolved chemicals happened to be in the groundwater.

Time your visit to coincide with low tide, so you will be able to find the newly deposited stones. Agate collecting is best after a winter storm. Some people suggest looking for discarded agates at the base of the stairs leading to the beach. After a day at the beach picking up rocks, some folks toss them out before they leave.

Agate Beach has many pretty surf-polished stones in addition to agates. If you are a rockhound, you will find this a rewarding spot to visit.

When you're ready, head back the way you came.

Directions: From Eureka, proceed 30 miles north on Highway 101 (Redwood Highway), to just north of the town of Trinidad. Exit on Patrick's Point Drive and follow it to the park entrance. Follow the signs to Palmer Point, about 0.25 miles past the entrance. There is a day-use fee. Restrooms are available.

4. Heart Lake Trail

EFFORT ....Difficult
LENGTH ....2.2 miles
GEOLOGICAL FEATURE(S) ....Glaciation
LOCATION ....Shasta-Trinity National Forest

Description: This is a short, gratifying trail in the Eddy Mountains with magnificent alpine views and great swimming opportunities. For many people, this will be an easy trail, but for those of us who are acclimated to sea level, the continual climb here was tiring and required several stops to catch our breath. Wear good boots and bring swimming suits. Most of the trail courses through open sun, so wear a hat and sunscreen.

Even if you don't make it all the way to Heart Lake, the surrounding views are gorgeous and well worth climbing up part of the way.

Castle Lake sits within a glacial cirque with a high granite cliff at its southern end, something like a castle wall, one supposes. Look up to the top of that wall and over it. Somewhere up there is your destination on this trail. Castle Lake itself is a lovely and popular canoeing, kayaking, and swimming destination.

From the parking lot, head to the edge of Castle Lake where interpretive panels stand on the shore. Follow the trail across Castle Lake's outlet, boulder hopping, and climb along the lake's east side among glacially carved granite and sparse conifers. You will be taking the Little Castle Lake Trail to start.

Views of Castle Lake are inspiring as you continue climbing to a better vantage point for taking it all in. Watch your footing, as this is a rocky, uneven path. With the continuous climbing, this narrow section of trail will get your heart pumping.

This is a popular trail, and you will probably find yourself greeting several other hikers on the way. Seeing small children scampering back along the trail, we were lulled into a false feeling that it would be smooth going. We later discovered that not everyone on the trail had the same destination. For families, the large beautiful meadows above Castle Lake seemed to be the draw. For a couple looking for a more secluded spot, Little Castle Lake was their choice.

Climbing higher, you will reach more open areas with full sun. We sampled some wild raspberries along the way, and thoroughly enjoyed the blooming wild roses and Indian paintbrush.

When you reach a ridgetop saddle and trail junction, bear right uphill. This junction is difficult to find, and the trail is indistinct over the ridge because the landscape is dominated by boulders and bare rock. Since we missed the trail ourselves, we positioned some cairns here on the way back. If you can't find the trail, just climb up on the ridge ahead and keep climbing in a southwest direction. Then, from a high point, turn around and look back. The trail is quite visible from the other direction, looking back down on it.

If you miss the junction and continue on the trail to Little Castle Lake, you will be heading east instead and will pass by a lovely grassy meadow on your right. The Little Castle Lake Trail will descend beyond the meadow. Our trail climbs the entire way, so you will have no doubt if you heed this description about whether or not you are on the right trail. You don't have to worry much about getting lost, even if you do miss the turn. There are plenty of people around and, as a last resort, you can just head back down to Castle Lake.

Having made it over the ridgetop, walk the rocky path in the open sun, enjoying a profusion of wildflowers in spring and summer. Along this section of trail, it is easy to spot the glacial striations in the flat surfaces of the rocks. Look for patches of green, and then examine them closely to see the polished, scratched surfaces where moving ice with its load of gravel scraped along. Make sure to run your hand over the surface of this polished rock to marvel at its smoothness. Remember, striations point in the direction of glacial movement.

You will want to stop (maybe you will have to) often to look around you in every direction to take in the breathtaking views. Mt. Shasta is over to the northeast, a companion along most of this hike.

Still climbing steeply, you will finally come up over another ridgetop to see tiny Heart Lake below you. It is hard to believe that it's only been a mile to get here. The lake is small and warm in summer, and shaped like a heart.

Drop down to the lake and proceed to its northern edge. From here, look north to enjoy the highlight of this trail, the fine expansive view. All at once you can see Castle Lake shimmering below you, Mt. Shasta, Black Butte, and, in the distance to the northeast, The Whaleback, a huge cinder cone. Taking in this view, you have no doubt you are in the midst of a fairly young volcanic region.

Around the shore of Heart Lake you will find a few nice boulders to perch on after you take a dip. This is a perfect spot to spend some time, so bring a picnic lunch. If you are lucky, you will have some solitude here in this special place which reminds us of the idyllic swimming holes frequently seen in Tarzan movies. No, there is no waterfall tumbling down to the lake, but it is blissful up here anyway.

Return the way you came, all downhill, sometimes steeply, but with great views spreading out ahead of you all the way.

Directions: From Interstate 5, take the Central Mt. Shasta exit and turn left onto N. Old Stage Road. Turn onto W.A. Barr Road, following the signs to Lake Siskiyou. Cross the Box Canyon Dam at Lake Siskiyou and turn left 0.2 miles further onto the paved road to Castle Lake, 7.2 miles along. At the 6-mile point where the road turns sharply right, there is a pullout on the left with a magnificent view of Mt. Shasta. It's worth a stop. Park in Castle Lake parking lot at the end of the road. There are restrooms. Access is free.

Castle Crags

Castle Crags State Park

The Crags, easily viewed from Interstate 5 between Dunsmuir and Castella as they jut up to 6,000 feet high, are dramatic granite spires named for their likeness to the turrets of a castle. The pluton that formed the Crags about 170 million years ago resulted from magma welling up underground and cooling slowly. It was later forced upward through a layer of serpentine. Later, glaciers moved through the area, carving the rock into the interesting jagged forms we see today. Exhibited here at the Crags is the result of all three agents of erosion: wind, water, and ice. During the nineteenth century, this formation was called *Castle del Diablo*, Spanish for Castle of the Devil. Earlier than that, however, the local Indian legends identified the Crags as home to an evil spirit.

The earliest European visitors to this area were fur traders, including Michael La Framboise, who led parties of Hudson Bay Company trappers through the Shasta Valley and Sacramento River Valley from 1830 to 1843. He founded the base of French Camp near present-day Stockton, and established a well-used trail through the area leading north into Oregon, known as Michael's Trail. The trails followed by the fur trappers would later be used by immigrants and miners pouring in from the east, and cattle ranchers in the Great Valley. La Framboise mapped the area to some extent and named some of the features. One such map has been found, in which he named Castle Crags the "Needles," and Mt. Shasta, "Sasty Peak."

After the Gold Rush brought a large influx of white men, relationships with the locals became strained. In 1855, the Battle of Castle Crags broke out, marking the beginning of the long and disastrous Modoc War. The primary site of fighting was at the northwest end of the Crags between Battle Rock and Castle Lake.

In 1886, the Southern Pacific Railroad was built through the Sacramento River canyon, opening up vast areas for mining and lumber operations. Chromium mines were operated in the area of Castle Crags as late as the 1950's. In the Castella area, you will find a few historic buildings dating from the days when Castle Crags was a flourishing resort area. The mineral springs attracted many visitors in the late 1800's and early 1900's.

In 1933, Castle Crags State Park was established with the acquisition of 925 acres. Today, it consists of 4,500 acres. In addition to the distinctive rock formations, the park includes two miles of the upper Sacramento River and Castle Creek. A 10-mile segment of the Pacific Crest Trail runs through the park, and there are 18 miles of improved hiking trails.

The trees, shrubs, and flowering plants include Jeffrey and Ponderosa pine, Douglas fir, incense cedar, pacific yew, western yew, live, black and valley oaks, white fir, azalea, pitcher plant, and several kinds of ceanothus and manzanita, red fir, weeping spruce, western ledum, vine maple, and dogwoods. There are over 300 varieties of wildflowers found here, including Indian rhubarb, tiger lily, yellow monkey flower, yarrow, aster, and the Castle Crags harebell, a flower found only in the Crags.

Wildlife includes Stellar's jays, robins, Brewer's blackbirds, western meadowlarks, common ravens, western bluebirds, great horned owl, Northern spotted owl, long-eared owl, red-tailed hawks, Cooper's hawks, turkey vultures, peregrine falcons, and the occasional bald eagle. Mammals include the chipmunk, coyote, gray fox, bobcat, black bear, black-tailed deer, raccoon, California ground squirrel, gray squirrel, mink, marten, river otter, ermine, and, in the higher elevations of the park, the mountain lion.

Elevation within the park ranges from 2,000 feet to over 6,000 feet at the top of the Crags. High elevations cannot be hiked during winter. The Crags themselves have no trail, but they are popular with rock climbers. We will be walking on well-developed, signed trails, all of them beginning from the main trailhead in the park at Vista Point. For this reason, directions are given here for all trails at Castle Crags.

Directions: From Redding, go north 50 miles on Interstate 5 to the Castella exit. Or go south about six miles from Dunsmuir. Follow the signs to the park and pay a day-use fee. Just past the entrance kiosk, turn right towards the campground and continue past the campground until the road becomes a single lane winding up the side of the mountain. Honk when you come to blind corners, as traffic goes both directions, and proceed slowly. Park in the Vista Point parking area at the end of the road. There is a toilet adjacent to the parking area and a couple of picnic tables at Vista Point above the parking area.

5. Vista Point Trail

EFFORT...Minimal
LENGTH..0.3 miles
GEOLOGICAL FEATURE(S).................................Erosional Features
LOCATION.......................................Castle Crags State Park

Description: If you want a fantastic view of the Crags, but don't have time for a real hike, you can walk up this steep trail to a picnic area and one of the best views you will find in this park. From this lookout, you see the cream of the landmark crop—Mt. Shasta to the north, Castle Crags to the west, and Grey Rocks to the southwest. Grey Rocks are metamorphic greenstone and slate which has been thrust upward at quite an angle. The Crags, as we noted earlier, are granite. We will explore Mt. Shasta at some length in the next chapter, as it is California's most beautiful Cascade-range volcano. This is a real photo opportunity, and visited by enough people that you can probably find someone to snap your picture with the Crags in the background.

This is also an inspiring place for lunch, but be prepared for sweat bees if you have food. They were particularly infuriating and persistent when we were here in August.

You can also hike to the Vista Point from the park's campground instead of driving, but we suggest saving yourself for hiking one of the other park trails described below.

Directions: Vista Point Trailhead. The trail begins on the east side of the parking lot.

6. Crags Trail

EFFORT	Difficult
LENGTH	5.4 miles
GEOLOGICAL FEATURE(S)	Erosional Features
LOCATION	Castle Crags State Park

Description: This trail goes up steeply to Castle Dome to a height of 4,900 feet with an elevation gain of 2,250 feet. The trail starts at the south side of the Dome and follows a crack up along the east side. You must be strong and sure-footed for this climb. Allow about 4 hours for the trip.

From the parking area, look up at the crags and locate the tall, dominant, rounded spire, that's Castle Dome. Walk back up the road about 40 yards to the trailhead. Begin in a shady forest of Douglas fir, giant incense cedar, and a few oaks on a needle-carpeted path. In spring, you may pass blooming shooting stars and Indian warrior. After a quarter mile, you will reach a trail junction. The trail heading dramatically upward is your path, the Crags Trail.

Continue through the forest. After 1.3 miles, you come upon a sudden view of the Crags. From here an optional quarter mile spur trail on the left leads to Indian Springs at the southern edge of Castle Crags. There, a cool spring provides some relief among big leaf maples and dogwoods.

If you take the side trip, return to the main trail and continue climbing up above the tree line. Enjoy breathtaking mountain views along this trail, dominated by Mt. Shasta. As you climb into the Crags, you will leave the shade behind and enter switchbacks up the stark granite cliffs. Finally you will reach the base of Castle Dome and gaze triumphantly out over your dominion, with a fine view of Mt. Shasta to the north.

Return by the same path.

Directions: Vista Point Trailhead.

7. Pacific Crest Trail – Castle Crags Segment

EFFORT	Moderate
LENGTH	4.0 miles
GEOLOGICAL FEATURE(S)	Erosional Features
LOCATION	Castle Crags State Park

Description: Ten miles of the Pacific Crest Trail (PCT) runs through the park. You can hike a fairly easy section with great views of Grey Rocks and the Crags from Vista Point to Winton Canyon, the route we have chosen to describe here. It's a tame two miles to our destination. There are no good picnic spots on the trail, so we recommend leaving your lunch behind to enjoy at Vista Point upon your return.

Walk back down the road about 40 yards to the trailhead. Walk through the forest for 0.25 miles on a smooth, shady trail. At the junction where Crags Trail veers off up and left, turn onto it and climb some steep switchbacks. You will soon reach a four-way junction. Turn left onto the Pacific Crest Trail. Right, the PCT continues on down to Interstate 5.

Generally uphill, steadily, but not too steeply, this trail takes you through a mixed conifer and oak forest. After a while, views open up on the left, giving you a sweeping panorama of the surrounding mountains to the south. Reaching a junction with Bob's Hat Trail at about a mile, continue on the PCT. Bob's Hat joins you for a moment, and then veers off to the right. At about this point, you will be able to see Interstate 5 down below. The traffic hum from that major artery will be noticeable on this trail for a while as you walk parallel to it.

Round a bend and get an eyeful of Grey Rocks at 1.5 miles. Continuing on, you get your first view of Castle Crags. The trail curves around a bend, turning to head north. You will notice that the dirt underfoot and on the hill to your right turns red at this point. Along this red dirt trail you will have some of your best views of the crags. With intermittent views of the granite spires through the trees, you will notice the sound of rushing water nearing.

At 1.5 miles, enter the Castle Crags Wilderness (signed). A few more feet brings you the edge of a creek, amusingly signed "No Name Creek." If you need to take a break, this is a good spot to sit on a log in the shade and rest.

Continuing on the trail, you will notice that the path is getting rockier and hotter as you traipse past manzanita on an open hillside. This open area gives good views of Grey Rocks. Notice the granite outcrop beside the trail just before you reach a wooden bridge at 1.7 miles. This is the same rock that comprises Castle

Crags. The bridge spans Winton Canyon, which is flanked by blackberry bushes. A thin ribbon of water falls down a sheer bank here before ducking under the bridge through a narrow channel on its way down the hill.

Soon you will cross a creekbed, which is usually dry in summer, and arrive at pretty Indian Creek at just under 2.0 miles. Rest a moment and enjoy this lovely spot. The creek is clear and cool. Picturesque leafy plants growing among the rocks in the creek make it seem more like a landscaper's creation than a natural stream.

You can turn around here if you have gone far enough, but if you continue for just a short distance further, you will get one last good view of the Crags from a different angle than you normally see them. Just past the creek, you emerge into the open sun on a granite cliff. Turning to look behind you, take in the Crags high above.

You can continue further if you like, but we turned back here after two miles. For the duration of this hike, we met no one else until we were on our way back and passed a PCT hiker on his way into the wilderness.

Directions: Vista Point Trailhead.

8. Samwel Cave Nature Trail

EFFORT	Minimal
LENGTH	1.5 miles (trail only)
GEOLOGICAL FEATURE(S)	Caves
LOCATION	Shasta-Trinity National Forest

Description: Samwel Cave is a limestone cave once visited as a holy place by the Wintu Indians who believed the cave was inhabited by bear spirits. They knew it as "Sa-Wal" (Grizzly Bear Cave). Artifacts have been found here that are even older than the Wintun occupation, from an unknown prehistoric culture. The remains of a prehistoric giant ground sloth, cave bear, and eagle bones were found at the bottom of a 75-foot pit in the cave. Also found there was the skeleton of a girl. One of the Wintu legends tells of three girls who went into the cave to bathe in the pool on advice of an old woman who promised they would find strong, brave husbands if they did so. One of the girls fell to her death in the dark. Considering the skeleton, perhaps there is some truth to this tale.

You can walk the trail to the entrance of the cave, or you can extend the adventure into an actual spelunking experience. If you choose to enter and explore the cave, make sure you are prepared with the proper equipment and a couple of companions. Never go caving alone.

This is a self-guiding interpretive trail explaining the Wintu legends surrounding the cave. The trail starts at the lakeshore. Keep in mind that in historical times, the McCloud River ran through this canyon, and there was no Lake Shasta. The cave entrance lies 355 feet above the original riverbed in a limestone cliff, making it a little harder to get to in earlier times.

Take the steep trail from the parking area down to the interpretive trail. You will alight shortly before the trail reaches the cave, but to do the trail as intended, you need to walk back to its start. Walk southeast towards the cave, reading the signs as you go. The trail ends at a locked gate inside the cave antechamber, open enough to the outside to explore without a flashlight. The sign here tells of the archaeological finds deeper in the cave. This is the end of the interpretive trail.

If you want to explore the cave, you can do so by checking out the gate key from the Shasta Lake Visitor Center. A $10 deposit is required, which is returned when you bring the key back. Wear helmets with headlamps, carry flashlights, and be prepared to get dirty. You may want to wear kneepads and leather gloves. You will have to squeeze through a narrow opening which may be muddy and slippery. The fissure leads you down into the first chamber where you will find yourself in an attractive room with typical limestone cave formations.

Unfortunately, many of the stalactites and stalagmites have been removed by souvenir collectors.

There are four levels in the cave, connected by crawlways. On the first level, you will be in Putnam Hall. The second level contains the Upper Magic Pool, the Pleistocene Room, Corridor of the Past, Merriam's Chamber, Sloth Hall, and Sinclair's Hall, at the end of which is the long pit down to the fourth level, called Furlong's Room. Be very careful around the pit and in Sinclair's Hall. The floor is muddy and slippery. Most people will want to avoid this area altogether. There is another pool on the third level, the Lower Magic Pool.

Descend as far as you want into the cave. The air will get cooler as you go, and you may have to deal with mud. Some of the passages are tight for large people. You decide how much squeezing you want to do. After emerging from the cave, lock the gate.

Return to the spot where you first reached the trail and climb back up to the parking area. If you checked out the key, return it.

Directions: From Interstate 5, exit at Gilman Road 18 miles north of Redding. Go east 16 miles to McCloud River Bridge. Cross the bridge and continue on gravel Fenders Ferry Road 2.8 miles to a turnout on the right. There is no sign and no facilities.

9. Lake Shasta Caverns

EFFORT..Moderate
LENGTH ....N/A
GEOLOGICAL FEATURE(S)..Caves
LOCATION ....Shasta-Trinity National Forest

Description: For the price of admission to the beautiful limestone caverns, you get a boat trip across Lake Shasta and a bus ride up the steep mountainside with scenic lake views along the way. These caverns were first opened to the public as a show cave on May 30, 1964. Prior to that, around the turn of the century, this cave and Samwel Cave were studied extensively by the Department of Anthropology of the University of California. Those interested in the human history of the area will want to visit Samwel Cave (previous hike) as well.

In summer (Memorial Day to Labor Day), tours depart every half hour, 9:00 am to 3:00 pm and take about two hours. The rest of the year, daily but fewer tours are conducted. Bring your camera, as photos are allowed inside the cave. Purchase tickets in the visitor center and then walk downhill on a dusty road to the boat dock. You will be rafted across the lake on a short cruise amid the roar of the boat engine. On the other side, walk up a steep hill to the staging area and bus stop. There is a picnic area here. We decided that these short, steep hikes are designed to get you ready for the stairways in the cave.

The bus ride takes you up a precipitous one-lane road overlooking the McCloud arm of Lake Shasta. You are dropped off in a waiting room with information about the caverns and area wildlife. There are restrooms here. A tour guide will take charge of your group and lead you to the cavern entrance to a doorway into the lower levels of the cave. During the tour, you will climb through the caverns and exit up above.

The cave is quite wet and has a humidity level of 95%, so it is not very comfortable. Wear light clothing and anticipate perspiring. Even though the cave is cool, you will not need a jacket. Normally, you can expect to have a diverse mix of people on a cave tour, with varying levels of fitness, so the pace is usually driven by the slower folks. Our particular group turned out to be quite spry, racing up the narrow staircases, so we got a workout and had time to spare at the end of the tour.

As you are led through the cave, you will see gorgeous examples of flowstone and draperies. The typical cave formations are here—stalactites, stalagmites, soda straws, angel wings, cave bacon—along with a small group of the rare crystalline formations known as helictites (see Black Chasm) in the Discovery Room. As always, you are warned against touching any of the crystals. This is a living cave and they are still forming. The guide will point out the different types of crystal structures and explain how they are formed, and will also shine a light on the formations which resemble Santa Claus, animals, etc., to entertain the kids.

On one wall you will see where the first white man in the cave signed his name, James A. Richardson, November 3, 1878, with the carbide from his lamp.

The tour proceeds through several rooms and up lots of stairs to the final chamber, which is magnificent and a fitting climax for the tour. Quite large, this room houses huge formations which you can admire from benches as you rest up after the climb.

After exiting the cave, you will make your way down many flights of stairs with a view of Lake Shasta below to the left. The trail ends back at the waiting room. From here, a bus takes you back down the hill, and then you walk down to the boat dock. After another boat excursion across the lake, a bus takes you up the steep dirt road to the visitor center.

Directions: From Interstate 5 in Redding, drive north across Lake Shasta to the Lake Shasta Caverns exit. Turn off and proceed east, past Bailey Cove and Holiday Harbor to the large parking lot outside the visitor center. There are restrooms, a gift shop, and a tour fee is charged.

10. Natural Bridge Interpretive Trail

EFFORT	Minimal
LENGTH	0.5 miles
GEOLOGICAL FEATURE(S)	Erosional Features
LOCATION	Shasta-Trinity National Forest

Description: This is an interpretive trail to a natural limestone arch, something of a rarity in California. Pick up a pamphlet at the trailhead, which will explain the natural and human history of the area.

The native Wintu Indians tell of a man with a huge bundle of hides coming along, tired and hungry, and slipping off the bundle. It rolled into Hayfork Creek and formed the natural bridge, or "bundle of hides," "Kok-Chee-Shup-Chee" to the Wintu. The color and texture of the bridge inspired this legend.

Names and dates etched into the limestone tell of early pioneers passing by. The ravine over which the arch stands has also given its name to a bloody confrontation between local law enforcement and a band of Wintu Indians. The Bridge Gulch Massacre took place in 1852 after a group of Wintu murdered a local rancher. The sheriff and his party traveled through this canyon to the Indian camp and shot everyone they found there, including women and children. According to the story, only three children survived the massacre.

The arch has a span of over 200 feet across the narrow ravine. Its opening is about 50 feet high. Over time, water has carved out the soft limestone below the arch to form this bridge. The trail brochure covers the geological, mythical, and historical aspects of the arch area.

You begin the trail at the picnic area and continue straight at the fork. You reach the arch almost immediately. Continuing up Bridge Gulch, you will come to the site of the historic massacre. This is halfway along. The trail then loops back on the other side of the canyon. You will come to a place where a scout from the sheriff's party stood on the arch and spotted the Indian encampment. Past this, you will encounter a steep section of the trail, and then be returned to the trailhead.

Directions: From Hayfork, travel about 4 miles east on Highway 3 to its intersection with County Road 302 (Wildwood Road). Turn south onto County Road 302 and travel about 4 miles to Forest Service Road 31N11 and on to the Natural Bridge Picnic Area one mile farther. Parking, toilets, and picnicking are available at either end of the arch. Both parking areas are reached off of the same road. Access is free. This site is open from May 20 through November 1.

CHAPTER 2
THE CASCADES

The Cascade Range is a string of volcanoes extending from Mt. Garibaldi in British Columbia to Mt. Lassen in Northern California. These volcanoes are the distinguishing characteristic of the Cascade Province, which is mostly located in Oregon and Washington. Only the southern tip of the chain is present in California. However, of the twelve major volcanoes within the range, California's beloved Mt. Shasta, at 14,162 feet, is the second highest, coming in second only to Mt. Rainier in Washington. The two major California cones, Mt. Shasta and Mt. Lassen, are spectacularly beautiful landmarks visible from many miles around.

Visible geology is everywhere in this province, primarily in the form of relatively recent volcanic activity and glaciation. Mt. Shasta has been a very active volcano, erupting about every 600 years. Four of its major eruptive episodes have occurred since the last glaciers retreated, during the last 10,000 to 12,000 years. The most recent eruption occurred 200 years ago. Lassen has the distinction of being one of only two volcanoes in the continental United States to erupt during the twentieth century with a series of eruptions between 1914 and 1917. The other eruption was Mt. St. Helens in Washington, of course, which many of us remember. Figure 3 illustrates the eruptive history of the Cascades.

The source of the Cascade Range activity lies deep beneath the mountains and is a continuation of the story of plate tectonics we introduced in the previous chapter. The geology throughout California is dominated by the stressful meeting of the Pacific and North American Plates. As the dense oceanic plate dives beneath the lighter, more buoyant continental plate, the oceanic material begins to melt. This buoyant, melted rock material then

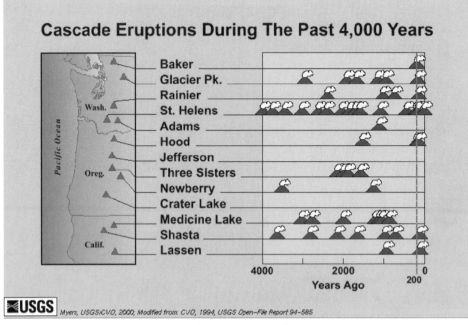

Figure 3—Cascade Range Eruptions

begins to rise to the surface, making its way through the cold, brittle continental crust. The result on the surface is a volcano.

As the molten rock rises to the surface, it may interact with the preexisting continental rocks, producing different magmas with varying chemical compositions. The ultimate result of this interaction are different types of rocks. If the molten rock finds its way to the surface with very little interaction with preexisting rocks, the rock formed at the surface will be the same composition as the original melt, basalt. You've probably used basalt in your backyard grill, and may have referred to it as "lava rock."

A different type of rock is formed if the oceanic crustal melt interacts with preexisting continental rock. The composition of the magma changes as the preexisting continental rock partially melts and mixes with the oceanic magma. Molecules of seawater, carried deep into the earth by the subducting plates, are released from the minerals in which they are trapped, lowering the melting point of the continental rocks, and helping the melting action along. The resulting rock type from this sort of interaction is called andesite, named for the Andes Mountains. Andesite is commonly light gray in color, lighter than basalt, because of a higher silica content, which results in the formation of light colored minerals such as quartz and potassium feldspar. Andesite is the most common volcanic rock in the Cascades.

Mt. Shasta and Shastina

A third type of rock results when the original melt is formed strictly from continental crust. This melt does not involve oceanic crust at all, and there is so much silica in the rocks that free quartz may form. This type of rock is called rhyolite. If it cools very quickly, too quickly for individual minerals to form, the rock is obsidian, a type of volcanic glass. Glass Mountain and Little Glass Mountain in the nearby Modoc Plateau are examples of obsidian lava flows. If the magma never reaches the surface but stays deep underground, it will cool slowly and large minerals will form, resulting in the familiar rock granite, the type of rock that forms the bulk of the Sierra Nevadas, as well as Castle Crags on the border of the Cascade and Klamath provinces.

The major volcanoes in the California Cascades are called stratovolcanoes, also known as composite cones. Stratovolcanoes are classic steep-side volcanoes, such as Mt. Shasta and Mt. Fuji in Japan. A sequence of eruptions over thousands of years results in layers building from the lava flows and pyroclastic debris. Also visible within the Cascade region are cinder cones, small cone-shaped landforms composed of fragments thrown from a central or secondary vent. You can easily see two of these in wide vistas of the region—Black Butte near Mt. Shasta and the Whaleback to the north. A third type of volcano, a shield volcano, forms a broad, gently sloping mountain. A well-known California example is the Medicine Lake volcano, which is discussed in the Modoc Plateau chapter.

Mt. Shasta is a huge stratovolcano built by eruptions from four main volcanic events issuing from four separate vents. It has taken approximately

200,000 years for the present-day Shasta to form, with major cone building, including the summit, taking place within the last 10,000 years. But this site has been volcanically active for much longer. Shasta sits atop much older basalts and andesites, indicating that lava has been flowing here for at least 600,000 years. The two most active volcanic cones on Mount Shasta have resulted in two distinct and easily visible peaks—Shastina, on the western flank, and Hotlum Cone at the summit. The main rock type is andesite, although Shastina is composed primarily of dacite, a rock with a higher silica content than andesite.

You can't travel anywhere in the Cascades of northern California without noticing Shasta. It dominates every view and has a revered history among California's human inhabitants.

Because of Shasta's immensity and height, it is home to several glaciers, the Wintun, Konwakiton, Bolam, Whitney, Hotlum, Mud Creek, and Watkins. Above the timberline, you will find stark rock, few plants, ice, rugged canyons, and cold winds. The mountain also offers an astoundingly beautiful wild landscape of colorful volcanic rock, delicate wildflowers, sheltered green valleys, waterfalls, pure, natural springs, and the best views you could dream of. Even if you are not interested in climbing into the glaciers' domain, many of these wonders are also available with just a couple of hours investment for the day-hiker.

If peaks are your thing, there are also plenty of striking cinder cones in this region, and since it is human nature to want to climb every mountain, those who came before you have blazed trails to the tops of them all. There are flat trails as well, so everyone will be happy walking in the beautiful Cascades.

Trails of the Cascades:

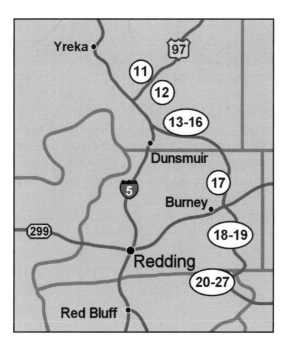

11. Pluto Caves

EFFORT:..Minimal
LENGTH:..1+ miles
GEOLOGICAL FEATURE(S):......................................Volcanism, Caves
LOCATION:...Klamath National Forest

Description: Pluto Caves are large lava tubes created by Mt. Shasta's eruptions. You will find a discussion of lava tube formation in the introduction to this guide. The main tube has collapsed in three places to provide portals into the tunnel. If you are in the area and don't have time to detour out to Lava Beds National Monument, this is a good example of a lava tube that is more easily reached.

Whenever you go caving, bring more than one light source and don't go alone. From the parking area, you will see a rock-edged walkway leading to the cave entrance. It's about a half-mile to the cave. The trail is level and easy. The cave entrance will appear before you, fifteen feet high, no stooping required.

Walk into the cave on a sandy floor and notice right away that the temperature is much cooler than outside. Where the ceiling has collapsed, you will have to climb over rocky debris. Wear sturdy shoes.

The tube is extremely large, sometimes as wide as 90 feet and as high as 50 feet. Marvel at this lava channel as you proceed about 250 yards into it. You may encounter bats, and will no doubt see graffiti. When you reach a wall of rock, you have gone as far as you can. Turn around and go back.

Directions: From Weed, take Highway 97 north and drive 12 miles to County Road A12. Turn left and drive 3 more miles, and turn left. There is a telephone post signed for Pluto Caves to mark the road. Drive down the dirt road about 0.2 miles to the parking area. Access is free. Note: While you are in the area, the imposing metal sculptures of the Living Memorial Sculpture Garden are worth a visit. You will find the garden one mile beyond where you turned off Highway 97 on Road A12.

12. The Whaleback

EFFORT:	Difficult
LENGTH:	3.0 miles
GEOLOGICAL FEATURE(S):	Volcanism
LOCATION:	Klamath National Forest

Description: This is a hike up to the top of the Whaleback, an 8,528 foot high volcano, a cinder cone with a collapsed center that sits prominently in the high desert landscape just south of the Oregon border. It is located north of Mt. Shasta, so the views of that majestic peak from the summit are unrivaled. And because the Whaleback stands alone, looming high over its territory, the views in all directions are unobscured from the summit. The higher you go, the better they get.

Cinder cones around the world look very similar, especially if they are recent enough that vegetation has not had time to gain a foothold. The cone is created when the lava explodes into the air and solidifies into cinders before reaching the ground. The cinders fall back down around the central vent, building a conical mass of loose material. It grows higher and steeper as the cinders rain down, eventually causing the slopes to slide under the weight of the new material. The debris comes to rest when the sides of the cone reach a stable angle of steepness. This angle, usually about 35 degrees, is called the angle of repose. Most cinder cones have that same angle of repose, since they are composed of the same type of material, which is why they all look more or less the same, varying mainly in size.

The cinder cones in this area are extremely symmetrical and relatively young. They have sparse vegetation and are covered with loose debris. There is no maintained trail, but you basically just go up 1.5 miles and then back down when you're ready.

Directions: From Interstate 5 in Weed, take Highway 97 for 15 miles. Turn right on Deer Mountain Road and drive 4 miles to Deer Mountain Snowmobile Park. Drive 3 miles east on Deer Mountain Road and turn right on Forest Service Road 42N24. Drive 3 miles to a gate and park. Access is free.

13. Avalanche Gulch Trail

EFFORT:..Difficult
LENGTH:...10.0 miles
GEOLOGICAL FEATURE(S):..............................Glaciation, Volcanism
LOCATION:..Shasta-Trinity National Forest

Description: Alternately known as the John Muir Route or Sisson Trail, this is a climb to the 14,162-foot summit of magnificent Mt. Shasta, leaving from the 6,900-foot high Bunny Flat trailhead, the most frequently used starting point for Shasta climbers. Mt. Shasta, dominating the landscape from all over northern California, is an irresistible challenge to many, and an inspiration to many more. Since prehistoric times, its remote grandeur has encouraged fanciful legends in the human mind, and continues to do so in modern times. It has supposedly served, among other things, as the birthplace of humanity, residence of fairies and dwarves, home to Bigfoot, and a popular alien landing site. Harmonic Convergence festivals are held here, and a race of magical people from the lost continent of Lemuria are said to live inside the mountain [see inset].

Although we doubt that you will get a glimpse of any of the unusual creatures rumored to be present, we think that the mountain's natural charms are enough of an attraction for anyone. You don't have to climb all the way to the summit. Climbing even a couple of miles up Mt. Shasta is a magical experience.

LEMURIA

The Lemurian-Shasta connection began with the puzzle of how lemurs ended up in India. Lemuria was a term coined to describe a hypothetical continent, which was later submerged, bridging the Indian Ocean and allowing migration of lemurs from Madagascar to India.

One tale inspired by this hypothesis claims that the people of Lemuria were highly advanced and that they escaped their doomed land. Towards the end of the nineteenth century and continuing into the early twentieth century, a few articles and books appeared suggesting the Lemurians had settled inside Mount Shasta. The story really gained speed in 1925 when a writer named Selvius published an article in which he claimed that a respected scientist, Edgar Lucian Larkin, had seen a Lemurian village on Shasta through a telescope on several occasions. The legend has been built upon over the years and has persisted into the present day.

Before we get to the trail description, let's get all the warnings out of the way. Sign in at the registry station before setting out. Hike this route in early summer, and take an ice axe, crampons, insulating layers, and a windproof parka if you are going all the way to the summit. Also, to hike above 10,000 feet in the Mt. Shasta Wilderness area, you must have a permit. The permit requires that you pack out everything, including your fecal matter. Helmets are recommended to protect against falling rocks, a common hazard on this route. Wear sunscreen at all times, and carry lots of water. The weather is highly variable, depending on the wind conditions. Check conditions at a ranger station before setting out. Do not make this trip alone. It is best to go with someone who has already done it and knows the ropes. Finally, for one reason or another, plenty of people turn back, as should you if you are feeling unsure about your abilities.

If the rewards of the trail are commensurate with the effort, you know this is going to be an awesome experience. Along the way, you can stop at the Sierra Club's Horse Camp, a cabin built in the 1920's, where there is spring water and sanitation facilities. This is about 1.5 miles along. Just beyond the cabin, you are above the treeline, walking through talus slopes and pumice.

From Horse Camp, continue on the trail up Avalanche Gulch to Lake Helen near 10,400 feet. This is a popular campsite for hikers spending the night. Don't be surprised if there are dozens of other tents pitched around you. Melt snow and filter the water here for the next day's ascent, and try to get an early start.

Leaving Lake Helen, the route becomes steeper and heads over the snow filling Avalanche Gulch. Crampons will be required from this point onward. Later in summer, you can hike up to Red Banks without crampons, but the danger from falling rocks is more serious. The rocks along the gulch will provide a sort of staircase when the snow has melted. Along the way, you will have the Red Banks up above as an enduring landmark.

Veer to the right towards Thumb Rock and climb through one of the passages in the Red Banks (prominent red rocks above the snow field). The red pumice here is dated from a 9,600 to 9,700 year old eruption. If you prefer, you can go around the Red Banks and over the saddle above Thumb Rock. On the way back, some people slide down the snow, so consider bringing along some waterproof pants. It is quicker to slide, but this may not be possible after May or early June when the snow is melting and rocks begin to protrude.

Once you are past the Red Banks and up Misery Hill, you will be on the summit plateau. Look to your left for stunning views into Shastina. You can also see Whitney Glacier, named after geologist Josiah Dwight Whitney, and first written about by Clarence King after an 1870 expedition. It is the longest glacier in California and resembles glaciers found in the Alps. Whitney Glacier flows from just below the peak of Shasta in a northwesterly direction through the valley between Mt. Shasta and Shastina. The ice has been measured at 126 feet thick.

Because this volcano is isolated and surrounded by much lower terrain, you can see for vast distances. If the air is clear, all of the Sacramento Valley will be visible south. You also get quite an overview of the Modoc Plateau and its expansive lava fields from up here.

Follow Misery Hill to the Summit Ballfield and on up to high point to the north. Evidence of present-day thermal activity exists only in these highest places on the mountain. Just to the west is a cluster of small hot springs. On top of the Hotlum-Bolam Ridge are sulfurous fumaroles. This volcano is definitely not extinct.

The climb will take an average of 12 hours, and most people take two days to do it. Spending a night on the mountain at Helen Lake may help to acclimate you to the elevation before you finish the climb the following day.

There are guided climbs to the summit offered by local commercial outfitters if you are insecure about trying it on your own.

Directions: From Mt. Shasta City, drive east on Lake Street. Turn left onto Everitt Memorial Highway and follow it up the flank of Mt. Shasta as it winds towards the trailhead at Bunny Flat about 11 miles from town. The road is open year round up to this point. Access is free. Restrooms are available.

14. Brewer Creek Trail

EFFORT:	Difficult
LENGTH:	6.0 miles
GEOLOGICAL FEATURE(S):	Glaciation, Volcanism
LOCATION:	Shasta-Trinity National Forest

Description: There are not many places in California that you can walk on a glacier, but Mount Shasta has seven permanent ice fields. A glacier is a mass of ice so large that it flows downhill under its own weight. Glaciers develop in places where some of the snowfall never melts and eventually the pressure of the overlying snow converts the snow into ice. As it moves, the glacier tears off hunks of the underlying mountain, and grinds up rock beneath it. A glacier is an effective eroding force carrying tons of rubble, where it comes into contact with bedrock, the glacier grinds and polishes the rock it passes over.

The movement of glaciers is not as slow and methodic as it may appear, and there is always a possibility of devastation on and below Mount Shasta. If the ice melts rapidly, lots of water coming down the mountain could turn into a huge debris flow, bringing down rocks and soil and creating quite a danger to the communities below. Avalanches do happen on the mountain as well, and a sufficiently large one could bring massive amounts of debris to the valley below. Such a huge debris flow is known to have occurred on Shasta's northern flank in the distant past.

In places where there were once glaciers that have long since melted, scientists can see the distinctive footprints that remain. Mountain valleys shaped by glacial erosion are U-shaped rather than the V-shaped valleys carved by rivers. Other features that are left behind are moraines, cirques, and arêtes. On other trails in this guide, we visit many of these features where no ice remains today, but during colder climate cycles vast sheets of ice covered North America. These former glaciers would dwarf those now covering the high valleys of Mount Shasta many times over. Nevertheless, the sheets of ice we will be visiting are big and powerful enough to dwarf us.

This trail takes you to Hotlum, Bolam, and Wintun glaciers on the northeast side of the mountain. Hotlum is the largest glacier on Shasta, containing some 1.3 billion cubic feet of ice.

Some people use this as a route to the summit of the mountain, but you don't have to go that far to enjoy the majesty of Shasta. It is 6 miles to the top, with a gain of almost 7,000 feet! For our hike, we will be going as far as the glaciers to get close-up views of them, but will not go to the top of the mountain. On this side of Shasta, above a certain height, it isn't really hiking any more, but mountain climbing.

The trail is easy to follow up to the timberline. After the snow melts in summer, rangers mark the trails above that with bamboo wands. Hike the switchbacks up the forested slopes, enjoying the view from on high. For the first two miles, the trail heads south and southwest, and then turns to head west. After 2.5 miles, the trail will be harder to follow. If you want, you can turn back here for a 5-mile trek.

If you want to get closer to the glaciers, continue into the harsher elevations and the low-growing trees. Climb up to the saddle between the Wintun and Hotlum Glaciers. From here, you have excellent summit views, as well as intimate views of the glaciers. Stay off of the ice unless you are properly equipped. The return route is the same.

Directions: From Mount Shasta City, take Highway 89 east to McCloud. Continue east 3.5 miles and turn left on Pilgrim Creek Road. Proceed 7.1 miles to Sugar Pine Butte Road (Forest Road 19) and turn left. Follow the signs to Brewer Creek Trailhead, turning left on Forest Road 42N02 and then left again on 42N10 to the end. Access is free.

15. Black Butte Trail

EFFORT:..Moderate
LENGTH:...5.2 miles
GEOLOGICAL FEATURE(S):..Volcanism
LOCATION:..Shasta-Trinity National Forest

Description: Black Butte, once known as Muir Peak, is the big, brassy cone sitting beside Mt. Shasta, a prominent landmark visible from several of the other trails in this area. This well-defined trail takes you up about 2,000 feet to the 6,325-foot summit, where you will have fantastic 360-degree views. Black Butte formed about 9,500 years ago through a series of eruptions, leaving this cluster of hornblende dacite plug domes. Compare it to Shastina, Mt. Shasta's second peak, which formed about the same time.

This trail was built by the Civilian Conservation Corps in the late 1930's to access a Forest Service fire lookout at the summit. Pack animals were used to bring supplies to the lookout. You will see why the site was chosen once you get to the top.

Head out through a conifer forest, climbing steadily. There are some steep and rocky stretches, and your total climb will be 1,845 feet. Bring plenty of water, and a hat, as there is not much shade. As the trees thin, views open up before you of the Shasta Valley and surrounding peaks.

Mt. Shasta itself looms right there beside you all the way. The trail swings wide around the mountain, eventually reaching tighter switchbacks up to the summit.

Relax and enjoy views in all directions, including the commanding and massive Mt. Shasta, Mt. Eddy, Shasta Valley, Castle Crags, and the Sacramento River Canyon. Return the way you came when you are done playing king of the world.

Directions: From Interstate 5, take the Central Mt. Shasta exit and head east for 0.7 miles on Lake Street. Go left onto Everitt Memorial Highway. Proceed 2.2 miles, and turn left on a dirt road signed for Black Butte Trail. Stay on the main dirt road for approximately 2.5 miles. Where the dirt road crosses under the overhead power line, take the dirt road to the left. Go approximately 0.5 miles on this road to the trailhead. Parking is very limited. Please park off the access road and turn around loop. Access is free.

16. Squaw Meadows Trail

EFFORT:	.............Moderate
LENGTH:	.............Up to 8.0 miles
GEOLOGICAL FEATURE(S):	.............Glaciation, Volcanism
LOCATION:	.............Shasta-Trinity National Forest

Description: One of the best things about this hike is that most of the climbing is done in the car before you set out, and you can climb up the mountain a short or long distance and still have an adventure. The trailhead is at 7,800 feet high. Still, it's a steep climb with a gain of nearly 2,000 feet. But the scenery is fabulous and weirdly intriguing, and worth the attempt even if you only go a half mile up.

In the Ski Bowl parking lot, fill out your wilderness permit and take a moment to examine the map on display. You will see a rock-lined trail leading up the bowl to the right. This trail crosses the saddle above Green Butte and skirts the north side of Red Butte with its strange volcanic landscape. These colorful names are not misnomers. Because you are above the timberline on this trail, you'll have great views along its entire route. Watch for a natural spring along the way.

Wildflowers grow among the rocks, including the western anemone. But there are no trees in this harsh environment. It is cool and windy up here and the rocks are the main inhabitants. There are large boulders all around you, and ahead your view is of the colorful, highly altered green, yellow, red, and purple ridges. The rocks along the trail are colorful too, black, red, light gray, and pink. The vivid colors are a result of alteration of the original rocks by steam. Porous red lava rock like that used for landscaping is abundant. Evidence of the mountain's origin lies at your feet. There is flow banding apparent in the rocks— bands of different types and colors of rock indicating liquid flow patterns.

As the trail winds upward, it becomes rougher, more rocky. Even if you are tired, you will want to keep going because the landscape is so strange and wonderful. And just up above you Mud Creek Glacier is calling.

There are places where the trail becomes indistinct. Below Red Butte, enter the natural passage called The Gate, which takes you between Red Butte and Sargents Ridge. Through the Gate, you will drop down into a canyon and an entirely different environment of mountain hemlocks and Shasta red fir. The trail is easier to follow now, taking you less than a mile to the upper meadow with its running streams and blooming flowers.

From the lush meadow, look up for a view of Konwakiton Glacier. Return the way you came when you are rested.

Directions: From Mt. Shasta City, drive east on Lake Street. Turn left onto Everitt Memorial Highway and follow it up the flank of Mt. Shasta as it winds towards the trailhead at the old Ski Bowl parking lot at the end of the road. Access is free.

17. Burney Falls Loop

EFFORT:...Minimal
LENGTH:...1.2 miles
GEOLOGICAL FEATURE(S):..Volcanism
LOCATION:...........................McArthur Burney Falls Memorial State Park

Description: Located in the fascinating geological wonderland of northeastern California, a magnificent waterfall, Burney Falls, drops 129 feet in a wide and breathtaking tumult. One hundred million gallons of water fall daily into a deep mist-filled basin below it. The falls, sacred to native peoples, runs year-round, as it is fed from underground springs. Save this one for autumn when the other waterfalls are puny trickles. The waterfall was named after pioneer settler Samuel Burney who lived in the area in the 1850s. The parkland, including the falls, was given to the state in the 1920s by another pioneer family named McArthur, hence the name of the park.

A self-guiding loop trail takes you around the falls and past several numbered stops illustrating the park's geology and flora. The trail is paved for a couple hundred yards.

From the parking lot, walk over to the walled overlook for your first look at the magnificent waterfall. Besides its volume, what you will notice from this vantage point is the fascinating turquoise blue color of the water in the pool. We have never seen water quite this color before. You can also readily see how the two main torrents split around a hard cap of basalt at the top of the cliff. This volcanic layer lies beneath a layer of Pliocene lake sediments, which the water has eroded at the top of the falls. Under the basalt is a layer of volcanic lake bed sediments of ash and pumice mixed with sand from ancient Lake Britton. Layers of diatomaceous earth or diatomite are sandwiched in the cliff as well. Burney Creek has found several cracks and holes to spring out of along the porous clifftop. Much of the water comes pouring out of the wall below the main falls, seeping

Burney Falls

trail, switchbacking wide to take you gently downhill. As you descend, notice the drop in temperature. On the last leg of the trail, you will feel the spray. Once you reach the base of the falls, you have already had the best experience you can have of this waterfall. If you have limited time, you can turn around here and walk back up to the parking lot.

If you want to hike more, follow the trail to the right downstream along the bank of Burney Creek. On your left the creek runs robustly. On the right is a hillside covered with mossy basalt blocks, a talus slope. When you come to a bridge over the creek, turn right onto it. The trail continuing straight is Burney Creek Trail on its way to Lake Britton, another option if you have time. Across the wooden bridge, turn right at the bench, and then turn left to climb up to an overlook. A sign here tells you that you are now level with the top of Burney Falls, which you can see up ahead.

From here, turn right and climb up a rock stairway away from the falls through a forest of Douglas fir, white and black oak, cedar, and Ponderosa pine. Switchback up a hill with a split-rail fence on the right. A bench has been provided at the high point if you need to catch your breath.

down through the basalt before emptying into the pool below. The pool is between 18 and 24 feet deep.

From the overlook, you will also be able to see darting birds around the falls. The aptly-named black swift nests in the cliff, catching insects on the wing and alighting only in its nest.

When you are ready, take the trail downhill to the edge of the pool at the base of the falls. The route is lined with rock walls and contains benches and water fountains. This is a very civilized

The view from here is across the canyon to the paved trail you started on. Continuing on, the trail now turns south to follow the bank of the creek above the falls, leading you to a bridge. Turn left onto it and cross over Burney Creek. A sign on the other bank informs you that a half-mile upstream the creek is completely underground. We did not investigate that oddity, although it was tempting. To continue with the loop, turn right and then left to go up the paved trail to a road. There are trails along the shore of the creek as well, but they are used by fishermen, and are not part of this loop.

Once you gain the road, turn left onto a gravel trail and walk towards the park's entrance station. There are two benches positioned here to allow you a last look at the falls. The trail loops back towards the parking lot. Interpretive panels are positioned along this section of the trail, explaining the geology of the creek and falls.

Directions: Located in McArthur-Burney Falls Memorial State Park, from Redding take Highway 299 east to Burney. Go five miles further east to Highway 89, then north 5.8 miles to the park entrance on the left. Restrooms and picnic tables are adjacent to the parking area. There is a small day-use fee.

18. Subway Cave

EFFORT:..Minimal
LENGTH:...0.3 miles
GEOLOGICAL FEATURE(S):......................................Volcanism, Caves
LOCATION:..Lassen National Forest

Description: If you've never been in a lava tube, this will be a thrilling experience, but be advised that small children may be frightened. This cave is easy to get to and takes only a few minutes to traverse. Bring a flashlight, preferably two, or battery-operated lantern and go through one of the largest lava tubes open to the public. You will be able to stand upright through the entire length of the tube. At 46 degrees, it's a little chilly, so wear long sleeves.

From the parking area, find the trailhead on the northeast side. Walk a short distance on a dirt trail to the cave mouth. The tube is short, but typical, with its smooth walls and ceiling drip features. The floor is very rough, so wear sturdy shoes and watch your footing. Near the end of the tube, there is a gas bubble in the floor, an interesting remnant. The

56

loop trail leads you up and over the tube once you have passed through, but we recommend going back through the way you came. There is nothing of special interest on the path back to the parking lot.

When touring a lava tube or any cave, it is requisite that you stop about midway and turn off your flashlight. Total darkness is something we rarely experience above ground, so it does leave an impression on most people.

Directions: The parking lot is located about a quarter-mile north of the junction of Highway 44 and Highway 89 near Old Station, across the road from Cave Campground. There is a prominent sign on the highway. Access is free. There are no facilities at the trailhead.

Subway Cave *(Courtesy USDA Forest Service)*

19. Spattercone Nature Trail

EFFORT:...Moderate
LENGTH:...3.0 miles
GEOLOGICAL FEATURE(S):...........................Volcanism
LOCATION:.............................Lassen National Forest

Description: This is a sandy, sometimes rocky trail. Wear boots. Lava rocks are rough. This trail is hot and dry and will remind you of the desert. Hike it in early morning or late afternoon. You will walk through manzanita bushes to observe several different sizes of lava tubes and the main feature of the trail, spatter cones. They are fascinating remnants of lava fountains, and there are several of them here to see.

From the parking area, find the trailhead on the south side. The trail signs are confusing. Follow the numbered guide available at the trailhead, which helps quite a bit when the signs are pointing you in opposite directions. We saw a snake and a lizard along the way. The snake, although small and harmless, was rather aggressive, lunging out at us when we tried to examine the rocks comprising the threshold of its den. Oh, well, you've seen one lava rock, you've seen them all.

The trail winds through the basalt, taking you from one spatter cone to the next. Observe the melt features preserved in the now solid lava flows. It is easy to imagine this rock in its liquid form. Climb up to the spatter cone necks and look inside. This is where the lava came bubbling up from. As it cooled, it piled on top of itself to form the cone around the spout. As is typical of spatter cones, the inside is choked with solid rock, so you can't see very far down. As the lava flow loses energy, it settles into the cone and cools there, plugging the opening.

You will climb gently for much of the first half of the trail, gaining the top of a ridge where the views south, east, and west are amazing.

In addition to the cones, you will also see some collapsed lava tubes in the ground. These are much smaller than the Subway Cave tube in the previous hike. Nevertheless, they were formed by the same process. Most of these tubes are discovered only when their ceilings collapse.

The trail makes a wide loop over the volcanic landscape and back to the parking area. The dry vegetation was especially beautiful as the sun rode low in the west on its way to sunset. The sagebrush seemed to be outlined in gold dust.

Directions: The trailhead can be found on Highway 89 at the Sanitary Dump Station across from Hat Creek Campground in Old Station. Access is free. There are no facilities.

LASSEN VOLCANIC NATIONAL PARK

Hiking is definitely the way to see this park. There is one road going through it north/south, Highway 89, but most of the more interesting features of the park can only be reached on foot. There is also an access road on the southeast side from Chester, but it does not go through the park, nor does it take you to any roadside points of interest. A short, unpaved road brings you to the extreme northeast corner of the park. To visit all the trailheads in the park will take quite a bit of driving.

The sights you will visit here are what remains of ancient Mt. Tahama, a volcano that was almost completely destroyed about 400,000 years ago. Evidence of past eruptions and present geothermal activity are all around you, most noticeably in the form of Mt. Lassen at 10,457 feet, which began as a vent on Tahama and last erupted in May, 1914. This eruption was recent enough that it was captured on film. Lassen Peak is the world's largest plug dome volcano. That 1914 eruption began a 7-year cycle of outbursts.

You will have no doubt that there is still plenty of activity just below the ground as you walk past steam shooting up from the earth, boiling water, bubbling mud pots, and warm streams and lakes. Some of these areas are getting hotter, which makes Lassen a likely candidate for future eruptions. This is the best place in California for observing geothermal activity by virtue of the variety and number of surface features.

When we went, it was early October, which is off-season. Most of the campgrounds and services close after Labor Day in preparation for snow season. We were lucky, though, as the first storm of the season arrived the day we were leaving, so we had warm, sunny days to explore with a minimum of company. This park opens as soon as the roads can be cleared of snow, so the window of opportunity varies, but is generally July, August, and September. You can visit the park all year, however, if you want to ski or tromp about in snowshoes.

There are 150 miles of trails in Lassen, leading through pine forests, remnants of lava flows and volcanoes, cinder cones, active geothermal areas, a dwarf forest, and many wonderful and unusual offerings. It is a beautiful park with plenty of opportunity for solitude. There are places here that will make you feel like you're on another planet, where water runs milky gray and hills are yellow and pink. Fortunately, Lassen is easier to get to than another planet. Just an hour east of Interstate 5 from Red Bluff, this amazing geological fantasyland awaits.

Directions: From Red Bluff, take Highway 36 east to the town of Mineral. Continue past it to the junction with Highway 89, and turn left (north). Proceed to the park entrance. An entrance fee is charged.

20. Cinder Cone Trail

EFFORT:..Difficult
LENGTH:..3.0 miles
GEOLOGICAL FEATURE(S):..Volcanism
LOCATION:......................................Lassen Volcanic National Park

Description: The best evidence available suggests that this volcano erupted in the 18th century. It is a classic cinder cone resembling those we have already encountered near Mt. Shasta, the Whaleback and Black Butte.

The trail starts by the boat launch. Take a brochure from the box at the trailhead. Take Nobles Emigrant Trail, a historic pioneer route, past black basalt hills bordering the Fantastic Lava Beds. At 0.4 miles, bear left at the fork and go another mile and bear left again.

The climb up Cinder Cone is steep, gaining 750 feet, and there is no shade. Its lava flows created the weird and wonderful Fantastic Lava Beds, and the colorful Painted Dunes to the south. You get a good view of these from the top of the cone. When you've caught your breath, descend the cone and head back the way you came.

Directions: From Highway 44, 11 miles east of its junction with Highway 89, turn right at the sign for Butte Lake. Proceed 6 miles to Butte Lake Campground, and park in the lot by the lake's north shore.

21. Lassen Peak Summit Trail

EFFORT:..Moderate
LENGTH:..5.0 miles
GEOLOGICAL FEATURE(S):..Volcanism
LOCATION:......................................Lassen Volcanic National Park

Description: In May, 1914, Lassen Peak erupted, beginning a seven-year period of volcanic outbursts. In 1915, this activity climaxed in a huge explosion which pushed a seven-mile high mushroom cloud into the atmosphere. The mountain continued to rumble until 1921, after which it quieted down. This was the most recent episode in the long history of this volcano, which was originally a vent on the now extinct, much larger Tahama volcano. Tahama and its progeny are responsible for the landscape of the park. Lassen Peak is visible from all over northeastern California, a major landmark, diminished only by its cousin, Mt. Shasta, another of the Cascade Range volcanoes. But Mt. Shasta has not erupted for about 200 years, and no other volcano in California can beat Lassen in terms of activity. To find a Cascade volcano more recently active, you have to go to Washington's Mt. St. Helens, whose eruption many of us can remember from contemporary news broadcasts in 1980.

So, if you want to climb a volcano, this is a good one to choose. The trailhead is at 8,512 feet, culminating at the peak at 10,457 feet. Guess what? It's uphill all the way. This sounds daunting, but lots of people manage it, including whole families with young children. Most people make the climb slowly and have to stop frequently to catch their breath in the thin air.

It is a well-graded trail and easy to follow. From the parking area, the trail will be highly visible. Take plenty of water and be prepared for cooler temperatures as you near the peak. Also, sunscreen and a hat are recommended. Avoid this trail when rain clouds are present, as lightning frequently strikes the summit. There is very little shade, as you can see at the trailhead. The landscape before you is stark. A few pines have gained a foothold on the mountain, but its loose talus slopes are mainly barren.

Other than the thrill of hiking to the top of a big mountain, which is quite a high in several senses, the attraction of this trail is the view. The higher you go, the better it gets. If you are lucky, you'll have a clear day, with distant views in all directions. Head out on the trail towards the jagged outcrop you can see from the trailhead.

As you gain altitude, beautiful Lake Helen appears below. The volcanic rocks alongside vary in color from light gray to dark red. Patches of snow remain on the mountain year round. The trail switchbacks up the side of the mountain. In some places, it narrows with dramatic drop-offs on either side.

Once you reach the summit, you will look out over other park landmarks, including Chaos Crags, the Devastated Area, Prospect Peak, Cinder Cone, Butte Lake, and Brokeoff Mountain. Outside the park, you will be able to see the Sierra Nevada mountains to the southeast, Blue Lake Canyon southwest, the Sacramento Valley and the Coast Range mountains to the west, the Klamath Mountains and the Trinity Alps, as well as Mt. Shasta to the northwest.

Return by the same path, downhill all the way.

Directions: The trailhead is located on the main park road, Highway 89, heading north and climbing from Lake Helen, on the left side of the road.

22. Bumpass Hell Trail

EFFORT:...Minimal
LENGTH:...3.0 miles
GEOLOGICAL FEATURE(S):.......................Geothermal Activity
LOCATION:...............................Lassen Volcanic National Park

Description: Poor Mr. Bumpass gave his name to this trail after losing his leg in one of the boiling pools. Make sure you heed the warning signs to avoid the same fate. This trail leads to one of the most popular destinations in the park, and one of the best spots to view the geothermal activity present here. It is a gentle climb to the lookout, and then a steeper descent to the boardwalk area, which winds through the bubbling mud pots and fumaroles.

The colors here are gorgeous and otherworldly.

Here's a tip if you want to cut the trail shorter: pass the main trail parking lot and park across from Lake Helen in a pullout. There's another trailhead here that starts you a bit further along the trail. Lunch at the picnic area at the trailhead, or beside Lake Helen where there are a few picnic tables set up.

Head out through a forested area walking on a nearly level trail. Before

Bumpass Hell Mudpot

long, you come to an overlook of the geothermal area. Look down to see steam rising up from the ground below. The smell of sulfur will reach up at you. From this vantage point, you can also observe the discoloration of the soils caused by the minerals in the water and steam. If anyone in your group is unable to negotiate climbs and descents, this is where you will leave them. But we hope you are up to it because down below is where the party really shakes.

Follow the trail down steeply to reach an open area beside a creek. Heed the warning signs and stay on the trail and away from steam and hot water. Somewhere beneath the ground, water is being heated enough by magma to produce this continuous display of steam wherever the pressure can escape through fissures. These spots are known as fumaroles. In some places, the heat source is near enough to make the ground itself hot. Right beside the trail you will find a couple of mud pots full of a grayish green ooze, heated to a slow boil. As the bubbles of steam escape, the mud issues burbling noises. Between this ongoing sound effect, varying in degree with the size of the bubbles, and the hissing of steam, there is quite a little concert going on down here. And the various colors of the surrounding soils (red, orange, yellow, white, and purple) present an artistic backdrop to this music.

The trail winds its way to all of the primary geothermal features here and then returns you to the place where the trail heads steeply back up to the overlook. Make the climb and take one last look down at Bumpass Hell before returning the same way you came out to the parking area.

Directions: From the southwest park entrance, head north past Sulphur Works and continue on the main park road past Emerald Lake to the trailhead parking on the right. There is a restroom.

23. Cold Boiling Lake Trail

EFFORT:..Minimal
LENGTH:..1.4 miles
GEOLOGICAL FEATURE(S):.............................Geothermal Activity
LOCATION:...Lassen Volcanic National Park

Description: This is an easy walk to the edge of a small lake where you can see bubbles coming up to the water's surface, evidence of underground gases escaping. The lake's name inspired some excitement in us, so we didn't want to pass it up, but the fact is that the lake was a disappointment. You will probably want to pass on this one unless you have finished with all the other trails in the park and have time left for a short walk in the woods.

From the parking area, walk southwest. One of the high points of this trail is how easy it is. After a short, pleasant walk on a level trail through the forest, you emerge at the edge of Cold Boiling Lake. There is a muddy place at the shore where you can step out to the edge of water and observe the little gas bubbles coming up. Admittedly, you would have to be quite the science aficionado to get excited about this. Other than the bubbling gas, there is just grass, trees, and some water. But it is a tranquil place to sit, and definitely not as crowded as some of the other trail destinations. You might want to spread your picnic lakeside.

Return via the same trail.

Directions: From the main park road, drive east past Lake Helen to the Kings Creek picnic area. There are picnic tables and a restroom.

24. Sulphur Works Trail

EFFORT:..Minimal
LENGTH:...0.6 miles
GEOLOGICAL FEATURE(S):...........................Geothermal Activity
LOCATION:...Lassen Volcanic National Park

Sulphur Works

Description: This is not really a hike, but there is a trail. You park alongside the road and walk along the edge of the road and over boardwalks around the steam vents and smell the sulfur. For some, this is all they see of the park's geothermal activity. It is the only spot on the main road you can glimpse evidence of the massive forces at work beneath the surface. But if you are coming into the park from the south, this is the first major feature you come to, so it is a good place to start. Also, kids will love this spot because it stinks!

Walk over to the boardwalk and start your overview of Sulphur Works. Do not leave the trail. Steam can burn badly.

Scientists propose that this area is the remains of the main vent of ancient Mt. Tehama, the mother of the other geothermal features in the park, including Mt. Lassen itself.

Hot magma comes close to the ground here and causes underground water to boil and issue forth as steam. Mixed in with the escaping gases are minerals that stain the soil around the vents. In the case of Sulphur Works, the main mineral coming out is sulfur. It is deposited on the surrounding rocks, staining them yellow.

The trail is very short, winding around the steam vents. You might also walk just down the road where some more such smelly features can be seen just beside the other side of the road. There is no trail there. You just look from the edge of the road.

Directions: From the southwest entrance station, proceed on the main park road past Lassen Chalet. A short distance further, pull off the road at Sulphur Works, on the left.

25. Devils Kitchen Trail

EFFORT:	Moderate
LENGTH:	4.0 miles
GEOLOGICAL FEATURE(S):	Geothermal Activity
LOCATION:	Lassen Volcanic National Park

Description: Devils Kitchen is one of the most beautiful and fascinating sights in the park, especially if you are here for the hot spots. Do people come to Lassen for the fishing? The bad news about this hike is the trip to the trailhead. If you are visiting the main area of the park, you have to leave it, drive all the way to Chester and then back into the park at the Warner Valley entrance, which requires a drive down a rough, unpaved road. If you are staying at Drakesbad Guest Ranch, you have a trailhead of your own, and it is a half mile shorter, located behind the

Devils Kitchen

saw woodpeckers and deer along the trail, a serene forest walk leading to a place of unexpected volatility. After a short climb, you will come to a ridgetop and look down into Devils Kitchen, its swirling mists rising up to meet you. It reminded us of a scene out of MacBeth, but if you see three old women with a big black pot down there, you'd better make tracks.

Drop down from the ridge on a steep trail into the "kitchen." As interesting a place as this is, we were alone the entire time we were here. That made the place stranger yet, and only added to its allure.

Once you reach the bottom of the descent, you will follow a half-mile loop trail through the fumaroles and warm streams. Mineral deposits have turned the landscape pink, yellow, and orange. Sulfide crystals line the paths. Heat emanates from small dark fissures all around you. Be very careful, as they are sometimes very small and not immediately apparent. Jockeying for a good place to snap a picture, one of us stepped nearly on top of one of these tiny fissures and immediately felt the heat and moved. You will be okay if you stay on the path, but some of these vents are within inches of the trail and are not marked or barricaded in any way.

ranch house. Otherwise, your trailhead is just before the entrance to the Guest Ranch.

From the parking pullout, take the trail south, crossing over Hot Springs Creek and heading southwest. This route follows the Pacific Crest Trail for a short distance. At the junction with Boiling Springs Lake Trail, turn right, leaving the PCT.

The trail traverses a meadow north of Dream Lake, and then enters a tranquil forest, following a wide, dusty path frequented by horses. We

When we were there in fall, the ferns were turning yellow, and the brilliance of the colors of soils and plants was inspiring. From the stream, follow the trail up to the most active part of the area where the large fumaroles are belching steam near the trail's high point. From here, you look down and across to where you entered the kitchen where the stream flows. The colors down there are particularly appealing from this vantage point. It is a good place to get an overview. The trail descends from here and starts winding back to the loop junction.

Climb back up the slope out of the kitchen, return to the forest trail, and retrace your steps to the trailhead.

Directions: From Chester, drive north on Warner Valley Road for 17 miles. The road turns to dirt just before you enter the park, and then leads to Warner Valley Campground and to Drakesbad Guest Ranch at the end of the road. The road is rough, but is passable for a passenger car. Just before you get to the ranch, there is a pullout for trailhead parking on the left side of the road. There are no facilities.

26. Boiling Springs Lake Trail

EFFORT:..Minimal
LENGTH:..3.0 miles
GEOLOGICAL FEATURE(S):......................................Geothermal Activity
LOCATION:..Lassen Volcanic National Park

Description: After the rather grand promise of Cold Boiling Lake, which turned out to be a bust, you might be a little skeptical about this one. So if you must choose between Boiling Springs Lake and Devils Kitchen at this trailhead, we'd choose Devils Kitchen. But if you can do both, take the plunge (not literally). Both of these destinations are remarkably active geothermal areas. The area bordering the lake features fumaroles and boiling mud pots, and the lake itself maintains an impressively high 125° Fahrenheit.

Starting from the main trailhead in the Warner Valley section of the park, this hike is difficult to get to, but is an easy trail which climbs gradually about 200 feet through the forest to the largest hot lake in the world.

From the road, take the trail south, crossing over Hot Springs Creek and heading southwest. This route follows a section of the Pacific Crest Trail. Head uphill to the junction with

Devils Kitchen Trail in less than half a mile, then turn left and continue to stay on the PCT to Boiling Springs Lake. At the next fork, bear left to stay on the PCT. The trail right goes to Drake Lake. In another half mile, you will reach the lake, which is a murky greenish or brownish color surrounded by milky mud. At the trail fork just at the edge of the lake, go either way and make a loop around the lake, which is 2,000 feet in circumference. The loop portion is 0.7 miles and will take you past the bubbling mud pots. There will be more mud action early in summer than there will be later in the season when the mud dries.

The smell of sulfur is heavy in the air around the steam vents. Be careful to stay away from the steam and the boiling mud. The unusual coloring of the lake is the result of the heavy mineral content of the hot springs.

If you continue past the lake on the PCT, and then take a short side trail left, you will reach Terminal Geyser (Hike #27). When you are ready, return on the same trail.

Directions: From Chester, drive north on Warner Valley Road. The road turns to dirt just before you enter the park, and then leads to Warner Valley Campground and to Drakesbad Guest Ranch at the end of the road. Before you get to the ranch, there is a pullout for trailhead parking on the left side of the road.

27. Terminal Geyser

EFFORT:..Minimal
LENGTH:..6.0 miles
GEOLOGICAL FEATURE(S):....................................Geothermal Activity
LOCATION:..Lassen National Forest

Description: After a peaceful forest hike, you will arrive at a steaming fumarole and two warm pools, about 100 degrees Fahrenheit, in an active geothermal area. Don't expect to see Old Faithful spouting here. There is not really a geyser. These are hot springs arising out of vents in the ground, spouting with plenty of force into a steam cloud. You can approach this destination either from the north within Lassen Volcanic National Park or from the south. Directions to both trailheads are given below. The start of the trail within the park follows the same course as Hike #26 for Boiling Springs Lake. Described here is the trail originating from Willow Lake.

Willow Lake is a unique ecosystem, a floating sphagnum bog hosting rare plants and buzzing with dragonflies. Mats of moss grow on the water's surface and so much grass grows in the water that it at first appears to be a meadow. There too you may find the interesting carnivorous sundew plant. It is reddish-tinged and ensnares insects with sticky "dew" on its tentacles. We wish it happy mosquito hunting.

After leaving the lake, you will enter meadows where wildflowers will be blooming in season. Continuing, you will walk through Lassen National Forest and then the national park. The trail continues, wending its way through the conifers rather uneventfully until you approach the geyser area. In some places you may find the trail chewed up from horse traffic. Before you reach your destination, you will smell sulfur and hear the steam hissing.

When you reach the fumarole, you are greeted by hot steam rising up from fissures in a rocky crevasse. The steam shoots in a continuous spray up to 40 feet high. The soils around the geyser are colorfully stained from minerals within the water. The water at the source is boiling. Be careful to stay safely away from the steam vents, as the steam can cause serious burns. There are many holes where the water emerges, some very tiny, creating billowing clouds of steam. The water issuing from the fumarole runs as a small stream down to the pools which are enclosed in rocks.

The pools are shallow, only a couple of feet deep, and about five to six feet in diameter with muddy bottoms. They are the perfect size and temperature, though, to create inviting personal hot tubs. Because the pools require a hike to reach, they are usually not crowded.

As you would expect, the pool closest to the fumarole is the warmest. People have arranged rocks to create several such pools, each successively cooler as the stream moves away from the hot water source.

A cool summer or fall day or night would be perfect for this trek if you intend to soak in the pools. In early morning before the sun hits the ground, the pools are especially peaceful, and the woods are intriguingly veiled with rising steam. In winter, snow covers the trail. In early summer, the stream will be full and vigorous with snowmelt. By autumn, the fumarole may be the only source of water. Mosquitoes can be a serious problem on this trail, so bring insect repellent.

Directions: This trail departs from Willow Lake. From Chester, go on Feather River Drive and turn right at the sign to Willow Creek. The last several miles to the lake are on a very rough road. The trailhead is at the east side of the lake, where you will also find a toilet. For a slightly shorter trail (5.4 miles round-trip) originating in Lassen Volcanic National Park, from Chester, go northwest on Feather River Drive to Warner Valley Road and go 17 miles to the Drakesbad Guest Ranch on a dirt road. Your trailhead is just before the entrance to the Guest Ranch on the left. This is also the trail for Boiling Springs Lake (Hike #28), which you will pass along the way.

CHAPTER 3

THE MODOC PLATEAU

The Modoc Plateau is a high plain of accumulated lava flows. Here, most notably in Lava Beds National Monument, evidence of geologic activity abounds. There are over 400 lava tubes in the monument, many of them open to visitors. Bring your flashlights, hard hats, and camera, for you are about to see some of the most fascinating geology California has to offer, from massive craters to icy caverns and all manner of delights in between.

In contrast to the dramatic stratovolcanoes that make up the Cascades, the Modoc Plateau consists primarily of wide-ranging lava flows and one broad shield volcano. The Medicine Lake volcano extends throughout the region, and encompasses Lava Beds National Monument.

As defined in the introduction to the Cascades, a stratovolcano is a volcano made of alternating layers of lava and pyroclastic debris. In contrast, a shield volcano is made from successive lava flows across the landscape rather than an explosive eruption. Shield volcanoes are typically broad and much less steep than stratovolcanoes. The size of the lava flow is often obscured, and the Medicine Lake volcanic complex is actually larger in volume than Mt Shasta. The Medicine Lake Highlands area exceeds 200 square miles and has been in the making for over a million years. A major series of eruptions occurred about 100,000 years ago, resulting in the huge crater that now contains Medicine Lake.

Although the Modoc Plateau is a distinct geologic province within the state of California, it is actually the southernmost tip of a much larger geologic province known as the Columbia Plateau. The Columbia Plateau consists of a huge Miocene flow of fluidic basaltic lava that simply poured over the land instead of erupting as a volcano. The resulting "flood basalts" or "plateau basalts" of the Columbia Plateau have an estimated volume of 25,000 cubic miles!

Because this volcano is not a tall mountain like Lassen and Shasta, it is easy to miss it, even when you are driving on top of it. But as you drive along the Modoc Volcanic Scenic Byway, you will begin to glimpse great blocky black rocks through the trees, and as the trees thin, you will see youthful looking basalt all around you. There are many visible remnants of the Medicine Lake eruptions, including lava tube collapses, pumice deposits, craters, cinder cones, obsidian flows, and, of course, the lake itself sitting within the old caldera.

As you might anticipate from this description, the hikes in this province are all about volcanism, but they are by no means all alike. There is a great deal of variety to be seen in the differing ways magma emerges onto the landscape and hardens into surface material. Let's strap on our boots and get to know California's chunk of this volcanic playground.

Trails of the Modoc Plateau:

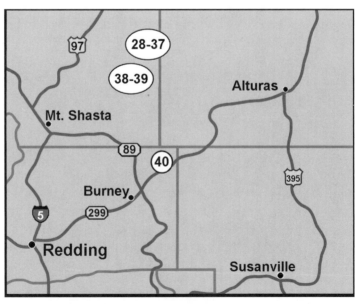

Lava Beds National Monument

Tucked up into the northeastern corner of the state, Lava Beds is in the high desert at 4,000 to 5,000 feet, and is so isolated that it is going to take some effort for most of us to get there. Because of this, it is usually not crowded. The closest town of any size is Tulelake, "the horseradish growing capital of the world." For an unusual souvenir, stop by The Horseradish Factory at 420 Main Street, quenching the American horseradish craving since 1959.

Because Lava Beds National Monument is rife with volcanism, we are going to spend some time describing its history and features before listing the trails. The trails in the monument are just a few of the fantastic attractions you will want to visit on this trip. For geology buffs, even the roads leading to the monument are full of amazing sights.

Over the last 500,000 years, repeated eruptions from the Medicine Lake shield volcano have created a rugged landscape of cinder cones, lava flows, spatter cones, lava tube caves and open pits in the ground. The lava from this volcano had a low viscosity, a term that describes how easily a substance flows. Maple syrup and ketchup are examples of highly viscous liquids, while water and milk have a low viscosity. It is the amount of gas contained within that will determine the viscosity of the lava. Close to the vent, the lava contains a higher amount of gas, and is therefore fairly fluid. The resulting basalt will have a smooth, ropy surface and is called pahoehoe (pronounced pah-ho-ee-ho-ee). Further from the vent, some of the gases have escaped and the lava is less fluid. The resulting rock is more angular and sharp, and is known as "aa" lava (pronounced ah-ah). The volcanic rock types resulting from the Medicine Lake volcano are basalt, andesite, dacite, and rhyolite. Most of the surface rocks in Lava Beds National Monument are basalt.

There is sparse vegetation through most of Lava Beds, primarily consisting of sagebrush and grass. Towards the southern boundary some juniper trees spring up, and as you leave the monument to the south, you enter a pine forest among the fascinating volcanic landscape of the Medicine Lake Highlands (definitely worth driving through).

Perhaps the biggest attraction here is the multitude of lava tubes, over 400 of them, two dozen of which have been developed for public exploration. Development generally consists of some clearing of floor debris, and installing stairs and ladders, as well as the occasional bridge. The monument contains the largest concentration of lava tube caves in North America.

Lava tubes are created during an eruption of low viscosity lava flowing downhill. As the lava comes into contact with air, it begins to cool, and forms a crust on the outside of the still-fluid lava inside, insulating it from the cool air. You have probably observed this process when a bowl of hot pudding is left sitting long enough to form a top skin. When you peel the skin off, the pudding beneath is still hot. The outer walls of the lava tube continue to solidify, becoming permanent rock, but the flow inside tapers off when the eruption is over, and the molten lava drains out of the tube. Most of the tubes in the monument are from the Mammoth Crater flow and are approximately 30,000 years old.

There are all kinds of caves available in the monument, developed and "wild," some where you walk in standing up, and some where you must crawl around through crevices. There are smooth tubes and rough tubes, straight and curving tubes. There is a cave containing a fern grotto and Native American pictographs. There are caves containing permanent ice. You can choose your level of difficulty. It is easy to lose your sense of direction underground, but in most of the tubes, you can't be lost for long. Find out all the details at the Visitor Center, including information about ranger-guided tours. If you stick to the caves on Cave Loop Road, you will probably have company and probably won't get into too much trouble. If you are more experienced at caving, you can opt for some of the less developed options. In any case, never go caving alone.

You can get lanterns for free at the Visitor Center, but we found that our flashlights were more powerful and also allowed for beam adjustment. Helmets are not necessary, but it's hard to avoid hitting your head on the low ceilings when you are looking down, up, ahead, and behind yourself. Since the floors are often rough, you will find yourself concentrating on footing rather than how close your noggin is to the ceiling. Temperatures are much cooler in the caves, so bring a sweatshirt. Wear sturdy boots for caving and for hiking over lava rocks. Surfaces are uneven, and some lava is quite jagged.

If you are planning on exploring any of the wilderness caves in the monument, register at the Visitor Center so someone will know where you are in case of an accident.

In addition to non-stop geological intrigue, the monument is also historically important. It has been occupied by various Native American groups for hundreds, perhaps thousands, of years. Rock art can be seen in several locations in the park, including Painted Cave, Fern Cave, and Petroglyph Point.

More recently, this was the site of the major battles of the Modoc Indian War of 1872 and 1873. Before the arrival of European settlers to the area, the Modoc Indians lived here, hunting, fishing, and fashioning boats and homes from the tules around Tule Lake, which was much larger then. With the arrival of settlers in the 1850s, the lifestyle of the Modoc was changed forever. Numerous confrontations ensued, culminating in a standoff between the Modoc and the U.S. Army when the Modoc left the reservation they had been assigned to and returned to this land.

The Modoc fought numerous battles with the U.S. Army in an effort to resist being returned to the reservation. They were greatly outnumbered, however, and ultimately succumbed. The Modocs were then removed to a reservation in Oklahoma, and their leader, Captain Jack, was hanged. Details of the war will be revealed on the trail through Captain Jack's Stronghold (Hike #35).

Although the land looks stark and forbidding, many animals do live here. There are raptors living in the monument year round, feasting on numerous rodents. Bald eagles spend the winter here in great numbers. Other birds that call this place home are various species of hawk, falcons, and owls. Other wildlife in the park includes mule deer, rattlesnakes, squirrels, kangaroo rats, yellow-bellied marmots, jackrabbits, California quail, and the rare sage grouse. Avoid rodents, which may harbor diseases, and be aware that snakes can be lying in crevices in the rocks.

The Klamath Basin bordering the monument to the northeast is an important stop on the Pacific Flyway for migrating birds, and perhaps you will have an opportunity to stop there as you head out north from the monument on Hill Road and Highway 161. When we drove by the wildlife refuge, we were entranced by a flock of white pelicans. In fall, this area is teeming with millions of migratory geese and ducks, plus grebes, herons, cormorants, gulls, coots, terns, avocets, and many others.

Plan on at least two days to visit the monument. If you are intending to explore the lava tubes in depth, more time will be required. There is a campground, Visitor Center, and restrooms, but no food services or gas stations in the monument.

Directions: From Interstate 5, take Highway 97 north at Weed to Highway 161. Travel east on Highway 161 to Hill Road, turning south, or right, following the Monument signs. From Tulelake, travel north on Highway 139 to Highway 161, turning west to reach Hill Road. Travel south on Hill Road to the north entrance of the Monument. From here, turn right and follow the main park road to the Visitor Center. Or, if you turn left, you can visit Captain Jack's Stronghold and continue on out to Petroglyph Point. A self-registering fee station is available in the parking lot of the Visitor Center.

There are other routes into the monument, but no others with good paved roads. From the south, however, you can plan a good trip along the Modoc Volcanic Scenic Byway (closed in winter) from Bartle on Highway 89. If you have a four-wheel drive vehicle, you can take the gravel side roads to the Burnt Lava Flow (stupendous) and Glass Mountain. Even with a passenger car, you can travel this route and stop at some lava tubes and Medicine Lake along the way. Medicine Lake has picnic tables, restrooms, and is a fine swimming spot in summer (and it's free). *Note:* The little town of Dorris boasts the tallest flagpole west of the Mississippi. Look for it on Highway 97 shortly before you reach Highway 161. The pole is 200 feet tall and flies a flag measuring 30 by 60 feet.

Time to go underground.

28. Mammoth Crater

EFFORT:..Minimal
LENGTH:..0.4 miles
GEOLOGICAL FEATURE(S):..Volcanism
LOCATION:...Lava Beds National Monument

Description: At the south edge of Lava Beds National Monument lies one of its most impressive features. It's a good idea to start your monument tour here because this is the source of almost all of the lava tubes you will explore in the park. Mammoth Crater is the remains of a huge eruption about 30,000 years ago, a deep pit in the earth. The outpouring of lava was so great that it covered the monument from the crater to Tule Lake to the northeast.

The paved trail climbs steeply up to the rim and an overlook into the depths of the crater below. This is an awesome view. There is an interpretive sign here explaining the volcanic event that created this spectacle. When you're ready, continue on the trail down to a lower overlook within the crater, and then climb back out.

Directions: Entering the monument from the south, traveling north on Highway 49, just after the paved road ends, locate the parking area for Mammoth Crater and Hidden Valley on the left. From the Visitor Center, turn left on the main park road and drive about a mile to the graded gravel road leading off to the left. Take it for about 2 miles to the Mammoth Crater/Hidden Valley parking area.

29. Valentine Cave

EFFORT:...Minimal
LENGTH:...Varies
GEOLOGICAL FEATURE(S):.....................Volcanism, Caves
LOCATION:.............................Lava Beds National Monument

Description: This cave has smooth floors and high ceilings, making it easy to navigate, at least in the beginning. It also has some especially notable features. If you are choosing just a few of the tubes, make this one of your choices.

Just inside the mouth of the cave, you will see extraordinary lava shelves along the walls and around the huge column in the center of the cave. The technical term for these features is benches. The benches are about three feet off the floor, six inches wide, and have well-defined lips. They are the remains of small streams of lava flowing after the main chamber emptied out.

The column right in front of you is also remarkable. Go around either side of it deeper into the cave. This is a big, wide cave, navigable for some distance. There is a second column after the first. After passing this, the cave splits and goes two directions, and then tunnels head off taking several paths. Continue if you wish, though the unusual features of this tube are right at the start.

Directions: Valentine Cave is located along the road to the southeast entrance to the park, just north of Caldwell Butte. Heading south, turn left onto the access road.

30. Big Painted Cave & Symbol Bridge Trail

EFFORT:..Minimal
LENGTH:..1.5 miles
GEOLOGICAL FEATURE(S):..Volcanism, Caves
LOCATION:...Lava Beds National Monument

Description: The trail passes many large collapsed lava tubes and other volcanic features as it leads you to a rock art site. Bring flashlights to light up dim recesses in the caves, but they are not necessary to visit these two sites.

The gently ascending trail leads northwest through the open volcanic landscape, generally heading towards Schonchin Butte. The trail is rocky in places, so watch your footing. It is also hot, so wear a hat and carry water. Soon after starting out, you can take a short spur trail on the right to a huge tube collapse. Shortly thereafter, the trail crosses another such collapse, leaving a ravine choked with immense chunks of basalt.

After a half mile, you reach a signed junction. The left arm takes you down to Big Painted Cave, which is a huge chamber accessible as the result of a collapse similar to those you have seen earlier on the trail. Make your way carefully down to the mouth amid the boulders. You will notice as you descend into the cave that the temperature drops dramatically. Take a break in this cool, shady spot before returning to the junction and continuing straight on to Symbol Bridge at 0.8 miles. A narrow path leads down the entrance of the cave.

Around the entrance, the basalt walls contain Modoc pictographs painted over thousands of years. On the left side of the opening are some very clear symbols, which resemble cogwheels. The trail continues just inside the cave, where you will see more pictographs of animals, human figures, and geometric shapes. Also, unfortunately, there is some modern graffiti here. This cave is called a bridge because of another collapse deeper inside which allows the sun to shine in, like a skylight or back door.

When you are ready, retrace your steps to the trailhead.

Directions: Take Skull Cave Road east off the main park road to the parking area and trailhead, on the left.

Symbol Bridge

The Center of the World

Lava Beds National Monument houses a magical underground place that does not appear on the park map. The Modoc Indians believed it was the center of the spiritual and physical world. Is it a myth? No, it's really there, and you can visit it to experience your own spiritual journey. It is Fern Cave, a collapsed lava tube with a dense mat of ferns growing in its mouth. Many artifacts have been discovered here, dating back thousands of years to the ancient ancestors of the Modoc. How strange to see ferns in this semi-arid high desert place. But inside the cave it is cool and moist. The continual condensation of water on the ceiling and walls creates a kind of rain forest, simulating annual rainfall of 100 inches.

The interior of the cave is heavily decorated with rock art. The pictographs are black and white, made with charcoal and a chalk-like substance. There are trails of white dots, circles, man and animal-like figures, and zigzag patterns. There is one unprecedented drawing, a crescent with circles on its top and bottom left side. Some researchers have proposed that this unique drawing is a representation of the Crab Nebula supernova that occurred in July, 1054 AD when the crescent moon was close to Jupiter and the supernova.

For reservations for a ranger-led tour (your only option), call Lava Beds Visitor Center at (530) 667-2282.

Black Crater

31. Black Crater Trail

EFFORT:..Minimal
LENGTH:...1.0 miles
GEOLOGICAL FEATURE(S):...Volcanism
LOCATION:...Lava Beds National Monument

Description: This trail has a lot to offer. It's short, it has great views, and it takes you to what we believe to be the most beautiful spatter cones in the park. Geologically, it's an amazing place.

A spatter cone is a volcanic feature where hot gasses mixed with molten lava escaped through a fissure in the earth's crust. In a way, they are miniature volcanoes. Fleener Chimneys is another collection of spatter cones within the monument. Contrast this sort of eruptive feature with the large cinder cone, Schonchin Butte, and the explosive Mammoth Crater.

You will hike on a flat gravel trail for a short distance, and then turn right towards the cones. The trail continues ahead towards the

Thomas-Wright Battlefield if you want to check that out.

Ascending over rough black lava, with a steep climb at the end, you reach the rim of a large crater at about 0.3 miles. The trail continues inside on a cinder path around the crater's center. Take some time to look closely at the material and you will notice several things. The flow patterns are lovely and obvious. You can easily imagine what it looked like in liquid form. There are many colors in the lava, ranging from bright red to jet-black.

If you can tear your gaze away from the rocks, you will notice that you have a great view of the Klamath Basin to the northeast, and the rest of the monument around you, including the black, chunky Devils Homestead Lava Flow. Off to the west, Mt. Shasta rises up to meet the sky.

On the far side of the cone, the trail leads out over the back of it and down. Perhaps the most interesting part of this hike is found on the backside of the cone. Right away, there is a fine example of pahoehoe, the smooth, ropy type of lava, which is less characteristic of this flow than the sharp and jagged type known as aa. As you look closely at the lava, you will notice metallic colors shimmering there, shades of gold, silver, copper, and bronze. We doubt that lava can get any more beautiful than this. Take some time to enjoy it.

As you continue on the trail, you will see that there are at least four distinct spatter cones here. You can climb up and look into the craters of each one. The trail generally makes a loop around the entire complex, with short spurs around the rocks where people have found interesting views.

Coming back around the front of the formation, you follow the trail through a gully and then back to the flat trail you came out on. Retrace your steps back to the trailhead.

Directions: The trailhead and parking area are on the east side of the main park road north of the Visitor Center.

32. Fleener Chimneys

EFFORT:...Minimal
LENGTH:...0.25 miles
GEOLOGICAL FEATURE(S):...Volcanism
LOCATION:...Lava Beds National Monument

Description: This short trail takes you to two large spatter cones, similar to Black Crater (Hike #31), but not quite as attractive. The main difference here is that the central crater is deep. The cones were created by thick, pasty molten lava burbling up and piling on top of itself. A hole is left in the center where the lava emerged, giving it a chimney-like appearance. The hole inside one of the chimneys is fifty-feet deep. The chimneys are the source of the tremendous aa lava flow called The Devil's Homestead, an eruption which occurred between 2,000 and 8,000 years ago. You will pass over this black, blocky lava field on the main park road. There is a pullout, and it is worth a stop.

There is a picnic area here shaded by western juniper trees. The picnic tables were constructed by members of the CCC; the logs were obtained at Oregon Caves and the rocks were gathered locally. A wheelchair accessible toilet is also available here, and the trail is paved up to the point where it begins to ascend the flanks of the cones. Beyond this, you must walk, but the trail is easy, rising gently to the rim of the craters. They have metal bars placed over them to prevent people from falling in (or climbing down).

From the top of the northern chimney, if you look to the north, you will see a perfectly-shaped dome nearby, the remains of a collapsed lava tube. You can walk down and examine it more closely if you want, but if you have already done the cave loop, you may be a little hard to impress.

The trail makes a circuit around the chimneys and then back to the parking lot.

Wildflowers, such as Indian paintbrush, phacelia, and mariposa lilies can be seen in the area in season. Coyotes, pronghorn, and deer have also been spotted crossing the road at various times.

Directions: On the main park road, from the Visitor Center, go north past the turnoff for Merrill Cave. The access road is on the left before you reach the Black Crater trailhead.

33. Schonchin Butte Trail

EFFORT:..Difficult
LENGTH:...1.8 miles
GEOLOGICAL FEATURE(S):...Volcanism
LOCATION:...Lava Beds National Monument

Description: Some people think the goal of this hike is to see how fast you can make it to the top. It's a steep climb, rising 600 feet, which will leave most people breathless. From just about anywhere in the monument (above ground, that is), you will be able to gauge your position by locating this prominent landmark. It has been said that the entire world of the Modocs can be seen from atop this peak.

Schonchin Butte is a cinder cone, an eruption that occurred more than 30,000 years ago. Today it is a fire lookout, which provides expansive views of the surrounding area. On a clear day, you may be able to see as far as Crater Lake in Oregon. The lookout is staffed from June through September. If you climb this trail in late spring or summer, you will be rewarded with abundant wildflower blooms of penstemon, Mariposa lilies, and sulfur flowers.

Starting at the northeast side of the cone, the trail is signed "Schonchin Butte Trail: Foot Traffic Only." The gravel trail switchbacks up the mountain, making the climb a little easier. There is not much variation as you climb through sagebrush and bunch grass over volcanic soils. As you come around to the north side of the cone, the environment is a little less barren. Juniper trees grow here and more grass covers the ground. When you come upon a bench in the shade of a juniper, you may want to rest a bit. The trees are old, twisted, and stunted, testifying to the severity of life here.

Walking in open sun, you come to a fork. You can go either way here to reach the summit and lookout. Notice that the trail is now covered with red cinders.

Once you make it to the lookout, you will find an inscription in the cement, telling you that you are at 5,293 feet in elevation and that the cement was poured on 8/26/1942. Take a seat and take in the view. To the north, you will be looking into Oregon and may be able to see Crater Lake. To the east, look into Nevada and the Warner Mountains. Closer in, you can see Tule Lake, and between that body of water and the base of this cinder cone, a bare, black lava flow of blocky basalt. West, snow-capped Mt. Shasta rises up to dominate the landscape, and south, you look out over the Medicine Lake Highlands with its pine forest cover. Rest a while, enjoy your perch and then descend via the same route.

Directions: A short side road leads east off the main park road to the trailhead.

34. Heppe Ice Cave

EFFORT:..Minimal
LENGTH:...0.8 miles
GEOLOGICAL FEATURE(S):.....................................Volcanism, Caves
LOCATION:...Lava Beds National Monument

Description: This trail takes you to a large collapsed lava tube which is easily explored. Begin by walking out under pine trees with bitterbrush, yarrow, and buckwheat alongside. Red-tailed hawks, ravens, and turkey vultures can often be seen riding the air currents above.

At the end of this short trail, you will come upon an enormous collapse. Heppe's Bridge is visible at the far end. Continuing along the trail, you pass Heppe's Chimney, a fine example of a hornito, an accumulation of lava drips ejected through the roof of a lava tube, also known as a driplet cone. Follow the trail into Heppe Cave. It has large openings at either end where the ceiling collapsed. At the cave entrance, where it is cooler than the trail you just left, ferns have found a niche to dwell in. Lichen grows on the inside of the cave. At the bottom of the trail is a pool of water on a base of ice.

Swallows nest here in spring, and other animals use this cave as a reliable source of water. In a park visited by few, this is a spot visited by even fewer, being off the beaten path, as it were. So take a few moments to sit and enjoy the solitude before retracing your steps. It will probably be just you and the chipmunks.

Directions: From the Visitor Center, go north to the gravel road for Mammoth Crater, and turn left on that. Pass Mammoth Crater heading south out of the monument. You will see a sign to Heppe Ice Cave. Turn left and proceed to the parking area.

35. Captain Jack's Stronghold Trail

EFFORT:	Minimal
LENGTH:	0.5 or 1.5 miles
GEOLOGICAL FEATURE(S):	Volcanism
LOCATION:	Lava Beds National Monument

Description: There are two self-guiding interpretive trails into this historic site. Take the shorter or longer one; both are fairly level, and include representative volcanic features. When we were here in July, no one else was in the parking lot, and we had a lot of fun on the trail. It lends itself to play-acting as you make your way along, reading the brochure.

During the Modoc War of 1872-1873, the Modoc Indians used these tortuous lava flows to their advantage. Under the leadership of Captain Jack, son of a Modoc chief, the Modocs took refuge here in a natural lava fortress in November, 1872. Their grievance was based on the refusal of the U.S. government to give them a reservation of their own near their ancestral home on the Lost River. They were forced, instead, to share the Klamath reservation with the Klamath and Pit River Indians. The Klamath people were their long-time enemies, and they were not treated well on that reservation.

From this base, a group of 52 Modoc men held off U.S. Army forces numbering up to twenty times their strength for five months. In the end, however, Captain Jack and his followers, vastly outnumbered, were taken into custody. During the war, Captain Jack shot and killed General Edward Canby during peace negotiations. For that act, he and three of his men were hanged on October 3, 1873.

As you walk the trail, you will soon see how defensible this spot would be in a gun battle. There are plenty of places to hide in and behind. You can look out over the rough black landscape and be oblivious to the endless contours it takes beyond your view. You will visit two caves along the trail, home for the first and second in command on the Modoc side. You will also see examples of how the Indians and the U.S. army built fortified walls to enhance their defenses.

Climb around on the rocks and ambush your hiking buddies. Climbing to lookout points, you will notice what fine views you have of the entire area.

This was not only advantageous to the Modocs, but is currently of benefit to the many raptors that live in the monument. Nesting in the rough cliffs roundabout, they have a keen view of anything going on below in the monument and around Tule Lake.

Directions: From the Visitor Center, drive north on the park road and follow it as it turns to head east. After passing the junction with Hill Road, proceed about three miles further to the parking area and trailhead on the right. Restrooms and picnic tables are available.

36. Whitney Butte Trail

EFFORT:..Minimal
LENGTH:...7.0 miles
GEOLOGICAL FEATURE(S):...Volcanism
LOCATION:..Lava Beds National Monument

Description: The trail takes you to the top of Whitney Butte. From the top of this volcano, you can get a good overview of the volcanic landscape in the monument. You will also reach Black Lava Flow, a vast black field of jagged basalt.

Before setting out for Whitney Butte, take the short trail to Merrill Ice Cave with its permanently frozen floor. The trail will take you across the wilderness to the west boundary of the monument, curving around Whitney Butte. As you go, you will see Mt. Shasta on the horizon ahead.

At 2.2 miles, the trail forks. Bear left, walking along the northern flank of the mountain. At 3.3 miles you will see the vast Callahan lava flow, a thick basalt field. The trail ends at the edge of this flow. Just prior to the end of the trail, you may have noticed a spur trail leading up Whitney Butte. If you want to climb it, this is your route. You will see the collapsed center of the volcano and have even better views than those from the trail below.

Return along the same trail.

Directions: From the Visitor Center, proceed north 1.2 miles, then turn left for Merrill Ice Cave and proceed to the trailhead parking area.

37. Cave Loop Road

Beginning at the Visitor Center, this one-way road takes you to most of the explorable caves in the monument, so we are lumping them together for the sake of expediency. You can try them all, of course, if you have the time. If not, we have chosen a few we particularly don't want you to miss. We will not describe the trails through the caves in too much detail, since the route you take and the distance you travel can vary so much. But we will mention the most unique features of each cave. Remember to stop along the way and shine your light on the ceilings and the walls.

Because of the unusual nature of these trails, we are deviating from our customary format and provided the length of the caves in feet rather than miles. This distance represents the total length of the caves in one direction. You will probably make your own route inside the tubes, so time and distance will vary with each spelunker. Also, because the cave loop road is so short, directions are not given to each trailhead, but the caves are listed in the order you will encounter them on the one-way road.

Lava Tube Entrance, *(Photo Courtesy of the Bureau of Land Management)*

Mushpot Cave

EFFORT:	Minimal
LENGTH:	770 feet
GEOLOGICAL FEATURE(S):	Volcanism, Caves
LOCATION:	Lava Beds National Monument

Description: This cave is perfect for beginning spelunkers. It is lighted, with information along the path about various lava formations. The entrance is in the middle of the visitor center parking lot. But don't skip Mushpot because you are looking for a more adventurous encounter. This cave is quite interesting and worth the few minutes it takes to walk through it, especially if you are unfamiliar with the features found in lava tubes. This cave has quite a few of these, so you will learn the jargon here before going out to the unlit and unsigned tubes.

Climb down the stairs into a tube tall enough to walk upright through. The cave will remind you of modern museum displays. The signs along the way have blue buttons to push, which light up the features being explained. Even though the tube is lit, take your flashlights to get a better view of the drip patterns on the walls and ceiling. Drips that hang down from the ceilings are called lavacicles. Depending on how fluid the lava was that formed them, they can be little nubs or thin needle-like features.

The trail ends after a third of a mile where the tube runs out. Turn around and return.

Golden Dome

EFFORT:	Minimal
LENGTH:	2,229 feet
GEOLOGICAL FEATURE(S):	Volcanism, Caves
LOCATION:	Lava Beds National Monument

Description: The most formidable part of this cave is the ladder leading down into it. It is straight down with a narrow passage near the top, so watch your head. The unusual feature of the cave is the yellowish bacteria coating the ceiling. When these are wet, they glimmer with a golden luster in the beam of your light.

Look for the pahoehoe floors and pulloffs as you go.

Blue Grotto

EFFORT:..Minimal
LENGTH:..1,541 feet
GEOLOGICAL FEATURE(S):.....................Volcanism, Caves
LOCATION:.........................Lava Beds National Monument

Description: This is a fairly easy cave to explore. Its name comes from the colors of the ceiling which looks like it's been coated with black, light blue, and white frosting. In the main chamber below the ladder, you can go either direction. Behind the ladder the cave branches into several tunnels, some of which have ceiling collapses to the outside.

Catacombs

EFFORT:...Moderate
LENGTH:..6,903 feet
GEOLOGICAL FEATURE(S):.....................Volcanism, Caves
LOCATION:.........................Lava Beds National Monument

Description: This one is for the thrill-seekers. There are many tunnels and interconnected passageways that remind us of the "twisty passages" maze of that classic adventure game, Colossal Cave. In the game, you never wanted to be there. But plenty of people do want to try exploring this one, and it can be a lot of fun in a scary kind of way. We saw some very serious spelunkers with equipment and protective clothing exiting the cave. If you venture far enough, you will have to crawl and squeeze through the passages, and should be prepared for rough going.

Sunshine Cave

EFFORT:..Minimal
LENGTH:...466 feet
GEOLOGICAL FEATURE(S):.....................Volcanism, Caves
LOCATION:.........................Lava Beds National Monument

Description: This one is short, so you can easily travel the entire length without scaring yourself. Just within the entrance, notice some interesting flow patterns. Large chunks of the ceiling have fallen to form your trail. As you go, you will encounter two collapses in the ceiling where the sun shines in. In one of them, plants have grown around the hole and hang down into the cave. There is a wooden walkway in this cave to make for easier going, but there are a couple of places where you need to duck.

Sentinel Cave

EFFORT:	Minimal
LENGTH:	3,280 feet
GEOLOGICAL FEATURE(S):	Volcanism, Caves
LOCATION:	Lava Beds National Monument

Description: This cave is easily walked, large enough to stand upright through the main tube, if you don't venture into the side tubes. The most unusual feature here is a tube within a tube, and that is why we are including it.

38. Burnt Lava Flow

EFFORT:	Minimal
LENGTH:	Varies
GEOLOGICAL FEATURE(S):	Volcanism
LOCATION:	Modoc National Forest

Description: Located southeast of Medicine Lake and south of Glass Mountain, this is one of the youngest flows in the area, estimated to be only 200 years old. It is one of many flows in the area originating from the Medicine Lake shield volcano.

The landscape is black and jagged for miles around. The lava comes right up to the road on the west side where a smoothed spot near a pullout allows you entry into the field. You can stop at any spot where it is safe to pull off the gravel road. There is not much traffic to contend with.

The only vegetation within the lava field is contained in "islands" that the lava spared. There is no trail over the flow. You just put on some sturdy boots and climb up onto it. It is very rough and difficult to walk on. Gloves will be a tremendous help here, since you will need your hands to steady yourself on the uneven surface. Observe the endless flow structures and bubble holes (vesicles) in the once-fluid lava.

Rising up above the flow is High Hole Crater, a flat-topped cinder cone, providing a dramatic horizon.

Directions: From McCloud, go east on Highway 89 to Harris Spring Road and turn north (left). After a little over 4 miles, you reach a fork. Bear right on Forest Road 49 and proceed about 30 miles. Turn right onto Forest Road 56 and continue on the gravel road 4 miles to the edge of the flow. Access is free. There are no facilities.

39. Medicine Lake Glass Flow

EFFORT:..Minimal
LENGTH:..Varies
GEOLOGICAL FEATURE(S):................................Volcanism
LOCATION:................................Modoc National Forest

Description: A visit to the Glass Mountain Geologic Area is a truly unique and fascinating experience. Plan your trip between July and October, as snow closes the area throughout winter and spring. The "glass" is actually gray dacite and rhyolitic obsidian, a vast 4,000-acre lava flow from the Medicine Lake volcano, which erupted about 950 years ago. More recent eruptions have occurred through over 100 cinder cones located in the highlands. The eruption that created Glass Mountain is about 300 years old.

Obsidian forms when the lava flow cools very quickly, too quickly to allow for the formation of crystals that are present in other volcanic rocks (even in basalt, though they are too small to see). It is called a glass because it is amorphous, and therefore has the same noncrystalline structure that window glass does.

There are several glass flows in the highlands, including Grasshopper Flat, Little Glass Mountain, Glass Mountain, and Sugar Hill. These flows were used as prime obsidian quarries by native peoples making arrowheads and spear points. Obsidian from the Highlands was traded throughout northern California. If you know what you're looking for, you will see evidence of prehistoric mining efforts, as the most highly-favored pieces were below the surface.

You can explore the glass flow at will, enjoying the unusual landscape. Wear gloves to avoid being cut. And avoid walking on the glass, sticking instead to informal pathways among the gray dacite.

Directions: From Interstate 5 north of Redding, take Highway 89 east for about 30 miles. Just past Bartle, turn left on Forest Road 49. Proceed to Forest Road 97. Turn right and go 6 miles north to Forest Road 43N99. Turn left (north) and proceed to the southern edge of the Glass Mountain Geologic Area. Park alongside the road. The glass flow is directly off the road. Access is free. There are no facilities.

40. Spatter Cone Loop

EFFORT:...Moderate
LENGTH:..4.8 miles
GEOLOGICAL FEATURE(S):..Volcanism
LOCATION:...Ahjumawi Lava Springs State Park

Description: If you are looking for a place to satisfy your thirst for adventure, this is it. Ahjumawi is remote and visited by fewer than 2,000 people a year. This park, a wilderness of forest primeval, surrounded by water, is unusual in that you cannot drive to it. You have to take a boat. Make this an all-day adventure or even an overnight adventure and you will be amply rewarded. There are a few primitive campsites lakeside. If you fish, be sure to bring your tackle along. And because of the remoteness of this location, make sure you do not go alone and let someone know your schedule.

Ahjumawi means "where the waters come together" in the native tongue of the Pit River Indians. A series of lakes, rivers, and creeks come together here, forming a huge freshwater system through and around the volcanic island. The park trails explore lava fields, lava tubes, a spatter cone, cold springs, ponderosa pine forests, marshland, bedrock mortars, prehistoric fish traps, and wildflowers.

Over two-thirds of the park is

covered by recent (three to five thousand years) lava flows, so much of the land is rough black basalt. Flowing up through the basalt near the shoreline are cold freshwater springs. The source of these springs is believed to be Tule Lake, fifty miles north. The porosity of the basalt allows the Tule Lake ground-water to move through it.

From the shores of Big Lake, take the trail away from the water. You will soon leave the shade of trees as you cross through the lava field through rabbitbrush and sagebrush. On your walk to the volcanic features, keep an eye out for bald eagles, great blue herons, and mule deer. The spatter cone on this trail is a 5,000 year old lava vent. Examine its steep sides and imagine the lava shooting up through the center.

Heading back to the trailhead, you will be graced with the imposing figures of Mt. Shasta and Mt. Lassen, the two mighty Cascade Range volcanoes that we visited in the previous chapter.

Directions: From Highway 299 in McArthur, turn north on Main Street and pass the Intermountain Fairgrounds. Continue north on a graded dirt road for three miles. Leave from the P.G. & E. boat launch known as "Rat Farm." Cross Big Lake to get to Ahjumawi.

CHAPTER 4
THE COAST RANGES

The extensive ranges of coastal mountains running along the western edge of California reveal the dynamic nature of the earth's surface and tell a fascinating story of what happens where tectonic plates meet. The mountains were largely formed by the Pacific and North American Plates bumping up against each other and by the shearing action of the San Andreas Fault. These ranges are a complex amalgam of sedimentary, metamorphic, and volcanic deposits of differing ages. The hiking trails through these mountains are varied, offering many types of pleasures, including unusual erosional patterns, evidence of powerful earthquakes, rare mineral deposits, abandoned mining operations, marine fossils, and loads of beautiful non-geology stuff as well. We are fortunate to have huge tracts of the coastal mountains enclosed within many state and regional parks, offering endless opportunities for public recreation.

The Coast Ranges, like the Klamath Mountains, played an active role in formulating the theory of plate tectonics. At first, geologists could not understand why so many different rock types representative of completely different depositional environments occurred in juxtaposition. In frustration, geologists coined a term for the whole mess, and the rocks were referred to as "The Franciscan Melange."

Since this province showcases such an important tectonic plate boundary, it seems appropriate to take this opportunity to review plate tectonic theory. When two plates interact at a boundary there are a limited number of responses available. One possibility is that the two plates collide head-on, which is referred to as a *convergent boundary*. If the plates are made out of similar material (that is, two oceanic plates or two continental plates), both plates will crinkle up. The wrinkles are perceived on the earth's surface as mountain chains, such as the Himalayas in India, which came about when the Indian subcontinent crashed into the Eurasia, about 40 to 60 million years ago. It is also possible to have a convergent boundary where one plate over-rides another. This happens when two dissimilar plates collide, an oceanic plate with a continental plate. In that case, the less buoyant, more dense oceanic plate slides down underneath (is *subducted* under) the continental plate.

A second type of collision results when the plates slide past each other in opposite directions, forming a *strike-slip* or *transform fault* boundary. This is the type of boundary that forms the present-day San Andreas Fault.

A third type of boundary interaction, termed a *divergent boundary*, results when two plates are moving away from each other in opposite directions. In the Atlantic Ocean, new oceanic material is being created at the mid-oceanic ridge, which is the divergent boundary between the North American Plate and the African Plate. An example of a well-known divergent boundary on land is the Great African Rift Valley.

Around 30 million years ago, the North American Plate and the oceanic Farallon Plate were colliding at the edge of the continent where California is now. As the more dense, oceanic Farallon Plate dove under the buoyant continental plate, parts of the plate heated up, and the resulting melt gradually made its way back to the surface, where it eventually cooled and became basalt. On the journey to the surface, some of this material encountered continental crust, melting it as well, resulting in a mixture chemically somewhere between the two, typically forming the light colored plutonic rocks diorite and granodiorite. This process continued until most of the oceanic plate was consumed. Bits and pieces of the oceanic plate that were not consumed ended up stuck on the North American Plate as described in the Klamath Mountains chapter.

The subduction of the Farallon Plate brought another, different oceanic plate right up against the North American Plate. This is the Pacific Plate, which is still there today. The division between the Pacific Plate and the North American Plate is California's infamous San Andreas Fault, pictured in Figure 4. San Andreas is the longest fault in California, 750 miles long, with movement along the fault of approximately two inches a year. Of course, that movement is averaged over geologic time. In human time, there may be no observable movement at all. Additionally, the fault is not a single fault but rather a system of faults. Thus, there may be steady movement along one portion of the fault while there is no movement at all along a different portion.

Figure 4 —San Andreas Fault

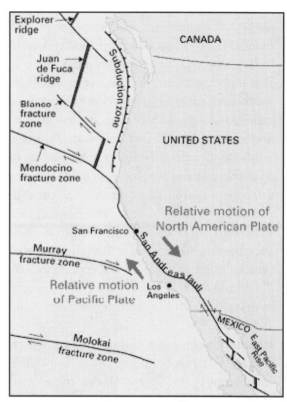

Although geologists talk about plates sliding past each other as if it is a smooth, continuous movement, in reality, the plates do not slide easily past each other at all. Different portions of the plates will be stuck in place, unable to overcome friction and move past each other. This results in the build up of a great deal of stress. The stress builds until there is a sudden release of energy, revealed on the surface as offset and resulting in an earthquake. You can see evidence of this sort of offset on the Earthquake Trail (#43) at Point Reyes National Seashore and The San Andreas Fault Trail (#51) at Los Trancos Open Space Preserve.

The rocks that make up the Coast Ranges reflect their tectonic boundary origin. The largest group of rocks, the Franciscan assemblage (or Franciscan Melange), consists of alternating layers of sandstone, shale, and siltstone, with occasional limestone. The layers formed from underwater ocean currents that carried sediments and deposited them at the mouths of submarine canyons. Over time, the sediments hardened into rock. These rocks were later scraped off the oceanic plate and carried down into the oceanic trench, as the Farallon Plate collided with the North American Plate. Later, after most of the Farallon Plate was consumed and the oceanic trench destroyed, compressive stresses brought about by the collision of the Pacific Plate and the North American Plate caused the buoyant rocks to be raised up and tilted. No longer underwater, they began to erode, with the silt and clay layers eroding faster than the sand layers.

A particular type of erosion-resistant rock, chert, is found in layered rocks that make up the Coast Ranges. Chert is a fine-grained rock formed in the deep ocean from the accumulation of microscopic skeletons of tiny one-celled animals called radiolarians. The radiolarian skeletons are made primarily of silica, and over time, this silica-rich muddy ooze becomes hardened into chert. Chert is also called "flint" and can be used as a fire starter. Arrowheads were frequently made from chert (as well as obsidian). Layers of chert are found alternating with sandstone, siltstone, and shale. Thin, dramatically tilted layers of "ribbon" chert can easily be seen in the outcrops around San Francisco's Golden Gate Bridge.

In the Coast Ranges, whenever you see tilted, layered rocks with some layers sticking out and some layers eroded back, you are seeing an ancient ocean bottom of sand, silt, mud, and muddy ooze.

Metamorphic rocks can also be found in the Coast Ranges. As you can imagine, when the Farallon Plate was subducting under the North American Plate, the existing rocks were subjected to intense pressure. One of the most common of the resulting metamorphic rocks is serpentine. Although serpentine is fairly widespread here in California, it is an unusual rock to encounter in the rest of the United States. It is only because of the unique plate boundary system that rocks such as serpentine are found here. Serpentine is a very weak rock, and is responsible for many of the frequent and sometimes disastrous landslides that occur along the coast.

The province is extremely large, extending from the top of the state in the north all the way down below San Luis Obispo into the Sierra Madre Mountains in the south. It continues inland from the coast over the Santa Cruz Mountains, incorporating the Mount Diablo Range, and then tapering mildly off as it descends into the Great Valley to the east.

Mount Diablo, Mount Tamalpais (known locally as Mt. Tam), and the Santa Cruz Mountains offer extensive developed trail systems within the Coast Ranges. The East Bay Regional Park District has been extremely active in acquiring parklands, and they are much appreciated by Bay Area residents. The Point Reyes National Seashore and Pinnacles National Monument are two geologically important sites which we will visit to glimpse the wonders wrought along the uneasy San Andreas Fault zone. There are so many interesting day hikes in the coastal mountains that it is difficult to choose a handful, but we have tried to present a diverse few with representative geology to get you started.

Trails of the Coast Ranges:

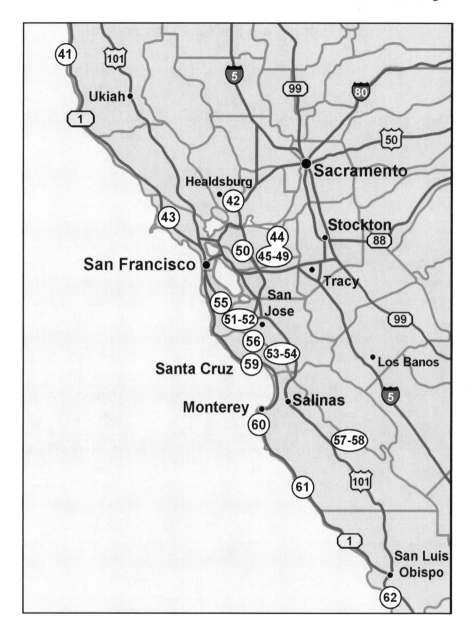

41. Ecological Staircase Nature Trail

EFFORT:...Moderate
LENGTH:..5.0 miles
GEOLOGICAL FEATURE(S):....................................Erosional Features
LOCATION:...Jughandle State Reserve

Description: There are plenty of stairs on the Ecological Staircase Trail, both ecological and manufactured. Jughandle State Reserve is the site of an interesting and important geological process, the creation of marine terraces. There are five distinct terraces here supporting different ecosystems, the youngest at the beach and the oldest in Jackson State Forest. Each "stair" climbs about 100 feet and 100,000 years backward in time proceeding inland for a distance of three miles. Two and a half miles of that trip are covered by this trail.

The reserve is a natural scientific laboratory in which to observe landscape evolution. A terrace is a topographically flat area of ground that was created when a body of water resided for a while at that elevation. Terraces can often be observed carved out in mountains surrounding a valley that used to be filled with a much-larger lake (such as Lake Conneville in Utah or Lake Lahonton in Nevada). The terraces at Jughandle State Park were created by wave action against *graywacke* (pronounced "gray-wacky") sandstone cliffs and subsequent uplift caused by the meeting of tectonic plates. The terraces are unusually well preserved and distinct, making this one of the best places in the world to study terrace formation.

With that said, we have to insert a caveat regarding how "visible" that geologically significant process is to the hiker. Along most of the trail you will be walking through a pretty forest with no visible geology. The trail brochure describes the flora along the way, but not much geology, and that is because the geology is subtle and detected through the differing plant communities. As you walk over an ancient sand dune, for instance, you may not be aware of it. On the headlands loop portion of the trail, and later in the pygmy forest, however, you will have a chance to see something of what lies beneath.

At the trailhead, grab a pamphlet to guide you through 40 numbered stops along the way. Some of the numbers are missing, but usually, the post is still intact. Be sure to take a moment to study the interpretive panel showing the layout of the terraces.

The trail starts by heading west towards the ocean and Jughandle Cove. At the grassy coast you are on terrace #1, and, if it is spring, you are likely to be treated to blooming poppies,

Indian paintbrush, baby blue eyes, wild strawberry, and seaside daisies.

A new terrace is gradually being formed here under the water. Each terrace is flat and was once the beach before a period of uplift raised it above sea level.

As you come around the headlands and turn inland, you will notice that the trees near the coast—fir, pine, and spruce—are bent and twisted by the furious coastal winds. Up ahead you can see the bridge that supports Highway 1 over Jughandle Creek. We will be passing under that bridge shortly and heading uphill through the forest.

Look in the crevices on the cliff to your left to see blooming poppies and other colorful flowers in spring and summer. Across the cove, the soil layers are exposed in the cliff face. Down below is a beach where the creek runs into the sea. From the parking area, there is a trail and steep staircase down to that beach if you want to visit it later.

For now, continue inland, into the coastal scrub where you may very well startle a brush rabbit as we did. They are small, cuddly cottontails and very common here. At stop #6, you will find a fir tree lying on its side and creating a sort of tree cave with its roots and branches. It's fun to duck into this space, especially for kids.

Soon you are routed back near the parking area where a trail goes right to it, or ahead to continue the nature trail. Continue straight to walk under the Highway 1 bridge to the top of a tall staircase. This takes you down to the edge of the creek where willows grow thickly. The post for Stop #10 is at the base of the staircase, but the number is missing.

Cross the bridge to continue the trail on the other side of the creek, climbing out of the ravine. The narrow trail is hemmed in by vegetation on both sides. Be very careful that the leaves brushing your legs are not poison oak. You will enter a forest of Bishop pine, flowering currant, red alder, and wax myrtle. The dark currants hang in brilliant pink blossoms all along the trail. Trees tower high overhead and sway in the breeze. Their creaking and the occasional woodpecker's drumming are the only sounds in the forest.

Finally, after stop #18, you reach the second terrace. The only evidence of this is the changing plant community. Now, the forest is dominated by Sitka spruce and Grand fir. Douglas fir, western hemlock, tan bark oak, hairy manzanita, rhododendron, huckleberry, salal, and sword ferns are also present.

As you head further inland, redwoods begin to appear in numbers. The understory is typical of coastal redwood forests, consisting of shade-loving plants like sword fern, deer fern, red huckleberry, redwood sorrel, and mushrooms. The flowers that may be blooming here in spring are white trillium, calypso orchid, and starflower.

Once you reach the 300,000 year old third terrace at stop #30, you are walking on ancient soil indeed. As you proceed, you will notice a change in the surrounding vegetation as you approach the fascinating pygmy forest where highly-acidic topsoil and near-surface hardpan prevent deep root growth, resulting in extremely stunted plants. The pygmy forest was the main impetus for preserving this land. It was first studied in 1936 by Swiss soil scientist, Dr. Hans Jenny, and was set aside as the Pygmy Forest Reserve in 1968. In 1969 it was declared a National Natural Landmark. Today, it is part of Jughandle State Reserve.

Leaving the state park, you enter Jackson State Forest where a board-walk transports you over the lichen-covered ground to avoid damage to the delicate ecosystem. The lichens help to prevent erosion. Don't leave the trail, as this is a truly unique environment that is extremely sensitive to intrusion. True pygmy forests occur only in isolated patches in northern California where wave-cut terraces have remained flat over hundreds of thousands of years of uplift. Over time, the minerals in the soil leach down to a depth of about 18 inches where the iron particles collect and form a hard, impenetrable layer. The top layer is eventually nearly white, having lost its mineral content. No new soil is created and there is no higher terrace to drain in. This is the environment that these plants struggle with, adapting by growing very slowly and compactly, practicing a sort of extreme energy conservation.

The trees appear even more stunted as you continue. A hundred year old tree will be just a few inches in diameter and reach only a couple of feet tall. Pygmy cypress, Bolander pine, Bishop pine, rhododendron, salal, huckleberry, and manzanita grow here. Notice how all of the plants in the pygmy forest are less robust than the same plants we saw earlier on the trail.

The trail loops around at the end, after which you will retrace your steps to the trailhead, now traveling mainly downhill back to the coast.

Directions: On Highway 1, five miles south of Fort Bragg and five miles north of Mendocino, turn west into the Reserve parking lot. Note: Non-hikers can visit the pygmy forest in Van Damme State Park where a short, wheelchair-accessible boardwalk loops through it. This trailhead can be found on the left on Airport Road three miles off of Highway 1 just south of the main entrance to Van Damme State Park.

42. Petrified Forest Trail

EFFORT:..Minimal
LENGTH:..0.5 miles
GEOLOGICAL FEATURE(S):.......................................Fossils
LOCATION:......................4100 Petrified Forest Road, Calistoga, CA

Description: A level self-guiding interpretive trail winds through a grove of petrified trees, which were felled and buried by debris from a major Pleistocene volcanic explosion. This is a privately owned attraction with a museum and gift shop. It was established in 1910 by Ollie Bockee and her family.

Large redwood trees hundreds of feet high, up to 8 feet in diameter and 3,000 years old, were blown down in the path of a massive volcanic blast coming from the north-east. They were buried in volcanic ash and over time, as groundwater flowed over and through the buried trees, the organic material in the wood was replaced by silica that was dissolved in the groundwater. Silica is the name given to the combination of the rock-forming molecules silicon and oxygen. Quartz is made up of pure silicon, and minerals for which silica is a major component are known collectively as silicates. Check the redwoods beside the trail for sparkling quartz crystals. Some of the quartz may appear reddish from iron staining (rust).

Gradual soil erosion has brought these petrified trees into view, although many remain buried. Some of the fallen trees have been partly excavated and sprayed with water to display their crystalline composition more clearly. The signs along the way help to direct you to points of interest and explain the process of petrifaction.

Start the trail from behind the gift shop with a sampling of petrified logs, mostly light-colored in the characteristic style of the fossilized redwoods here. Head uphill to the left through a shady grove, noting the exposed volcanic tuff among the manzanita bushes. This is the material that fell upon the area, burying and preserving the trees. Examine the rock along the trail for bits of volcanic glass, more evidence of the ancient blast that brought havoc to the forest.

The first petrified tree you come to is a pine. It is called the Pit Tree because it is located in a 15-foot deep pit with light-colored ash walls.

Next you come to the Gulley Tree, which has broken into blocky chunks. Continue on through a meadow.

A plaque dedicated to Petrified Forest Charlie and his mule is located along the trail. He was a sheep rancher who originally owned this land and was friends with local writers Jack London and Robert Louis Stevenson. Charlie discovered the petrified forest in 1870 and generously showed it off to the public.

Visit the Giant Tree and the Queen Tree, checking out their root balls, knots and growth rings. One reason this spot is so interesting is the exceptional size and age of some of these downed redwoods. It is hard to imagine the force that knocked them over. The Queen Tree was about 2,000 years old when the volcanic blast took it out. The Monarch Tree has the distinction of being the largest intact petrified tree in the world. It is 105 feet long and six feet in diameter. The Robert Louis Stevenson Tree is a good spot to look

more closely at how the finer features of the original living tree were preserved.

Complete your stroll by visiting the museum and gift shop.

Directions: From Calistoga on Highway 29/128, take Petrified Forest Road west for four miles to the entrance to the park on the right. From the Redwood Highway (101) in Santa Rosa, go north to Mark West Springs Road. Proceed east to Mark West Springs where the road becomes Porter Creek Road. Continue east to where the road splits. Bear left on Petrified Forest Road and then turn left into the parking area. A fee is charged.

43. Earthquake Trail

EFFORT:..Minimal
LENGTH:...0.6 miles
GEOLOGICAL FEATURE(S):...........................Fault Activity
LOCATION:................................Point Reyes National Seashore

Description: Although the lighthouse and beaches get a lot more attention in this beautiful coastal park, it is well worth walking the little geology trail if you are visiting Point Reyes. It won't take much time and you will get to see visible evidence that the ground moves. Interpretive signs along this short, paved loop

describe plate tectonics, the 1906 earthquake, and related geology that are at work at this tempestuous plate boundary.

From the visitor center parking lot, locate the trailhead between the picnic area and restrooms. Walk out on the trail a short distance to a fork, then bear left to begin the loop. If you are here in spring, a gorgeous blanket of poppies will be blooming trailside. During the 15 minutes we were on this trail, we saw swallowtail butterflies, barn swallows, and a garter snake.

The first stop is a sign telling you that the San Andreas Fault is just in front of you, marked by a string of blue posts. If you look carefully at the hillside along the line made by the posts, you will be able to make out a hint of the offset still visible. Following the posts, you will come to the highlight of this trail. It is an old wooden fence, a rare bit of readily observable evidence of movement produced during a major earthquake. In this case, we are referring to the great 1906 San Francisco earthquake, during which the San Andreas Fault broke the ground for 270 miles and moved two sections of this fence away from one another. The fence on the right side moved northwest with the Pacific Plate. The fence on the left side moved southeast with the North American Plate, creating a remarkable 16-foot offset.

The relative movement for strike-slip faults, such as the San Andreas, is named according to which direction the opposite side seems to move to the viewer. The fence seems to have moved to the right; therefore, this is called a "right lateral" fault. If you walked over the fault, turned around, and looked at it again, you would see the same result: that is, the fence would appear to have moved to the right. So it doesn't matter which side of the fault the viewer is standing on; the result (and hence the name) is the same.

As the two plates grind in opposite directions alongside one another, stress begins to build up at the plate boundaries. Although the plates themselves are moving at a fairly steady pace of one to three inches per year, the boundaries, which are rock against rock, can't really slide past each other. They are basically stuck. The boundaries "bend" and stress builds up. Eventually the stress overcomes the resistance to sliding and then there is a release of energy, movement along the fault, and a resulting earthquake.

Besides this dramatic evidence of plate tectonics in action, Point Reyes offers another clue that it is situated on a plate boundary. The rocks on the west side are quite different from those on the east side of the San Andreas Fault. The best match that has been found so far are rocks found in the Tehachapi Mountains 300 miles to the south! The same story has been reconstructed for Bodega Head just to the north of Point Reyes. On one side of the fault the rock type is granitic. On the other, it is the Franciscan complex, consisting of sandstone, greenstone, and serpentine. The differing rock types offer valuable clues to scientists trying to decipher the geologic history.

By matching the rock type here to its southern origin, they are able to deduce the path of the plate movement.

If you stand here and consider that this piece of land was once 300 miles to the south, you get a pretty good mental demonstration of the entire plate tectonic process.

After marveling at the disjointed fence, continue around through a meadow to close the loop and return to the parking area.

Directions: From Highway 1 in Olema, take Bear Valley Road west into the park, and then turn left towards Bear Valley Visitor Center. Access is free. There are restrooms and a picnic area. There are two parking lots. Park in either one, but the upper lot is closest to the trailhead. Make sure you allow time to visit the excellent visitor center before or after your walk.

44. Black Diamond Mines

EFFORT:..Moderate
LENGTH:...5.5 miles
GEOLOGICAL FEATURE(S):..Mining
LOCATION:...............................Black Diamond Mines Regional Preserve

Description: On this trip, we will explore the site of historic coal and sand mining operations, visit a pioneer cemetery, and maybe do a little wildlife watching. In the 1850s, coal was discovered here in the foothills of the Diablo Range and several mines were set into operation. Five separate towns sprung up around the mines, occupied primarily, but not exclusively, by Welsh immigrants. This was the largest coal mining operation ever in California, producing nearly four million tons.

By the turn of the century, coal mining stopped and the people left or turned to cattle ranching. Mining of a different sort began here in the twentieth century. From the 1920s until 1949, underground activity resumed as 1.8 million tons of sand were mined here. The Somersville-area mine produced sand used by the Hazel-Atlas Glass Company in Oakland. The Nortonville-area mine supplied sand to the Columbia Steel Works in nearby Pittsburg. Mine shafts, tailing piles, an old cemetery, and some other remnants of the past are scattered in these now peaceful hills in this 3,700-acre park.

In spring, wildflower displays here are among the best in the East Bay, decorating the open grassy hillsides and cool canyons with swaths of purple, yellow, white, and red. There is an extensive list of wildflowers available in the Visitor Center. Among the many flowers we saw in April were California buttercup, Indian paintbrush, California poppy, blue dick, California mustard, and lupine.

Bird-watching opportunities are also good. On our trip, we did see several birds, including an aggressive turkey vulture which buzzed us, and plenty of slowly circling red-tailed hawks. We did not see any other animals, but there are reportedly raccoons, skunks, opossums, bobcats, foxes, coyotes, deer, and mountain lions in the area.

As is the case in all of the Diablo foothill parks, summer can be brutally hot and dry. The best time to visit is winter or spring.

Get a trail map at the entrance kiosk, as there are many trails crossing each other in the area we are going to explore, and it can be confusing even if you have the trail map. This hike was planned by stringing together several trails to take you to a majority of the mining history sites, including the interesting Rose Hill Cemetery. But there are certainly much shorter routes if you prefer. In fact, on a short loop of the park's heart, you can see most of the sites of interest and take a mine tour. We suggest signing up for a tour as soon as you arrive if you plan on doing it. The tours are popular and often fill up, so you may have to wait a while. It's worth it, though, to see the extensive tunnel system built through the sandstone.

From the parking area, walk uphill on an old road to a fork. The Nortonville Trail goes straight towards the picnic area and the Stewartville Trail goes left. Head straight through the picnic area, past a tailing pile on the left, to the Greathouse Visitor Center. This is a really cool stop, so don't miss it. The Visitor Center and Mining Museum is housed in a large underground chamber at the end of a mining tunnel. Artifacts from the mining operations and towns are on display there, including a couple of Chinese coins and children's toys. The four types of coal (anthracite, bituminous, subbituminous, and lignite) are displayed, with a short description of how coal is formed.

Most of the coal found in the U.S. occurs in the Appalachian Mountains, and is much older than the Eocene-age coal found here. Coal is made by the compression of masses of plant material that once grew in a swampy environment. Over time the plants are buried and, through pressure and heat, the non-carbonaceous material is driven out of the deposit. With increased pressure and time, the coal becomes more and more pure carbon material. Lignite, the least pure type of coal, is made of barely decomposed plant matter, just one stage past peat. Lignite is the type of coal that was mined here. Anthracite, at the other end of the scale, is made of almost pure carbon.

Coal was deposited so abundantly in the Eastern United States that the time of deposition, the Pennsylvanian and Mississippian periods, are often lumped together and referred to as "the Carboniferous." The Carboniferous period occurred between 360 and 286 million years ago. To find coal in Northern California that was deposited 50 million years ago is exciting because it provides evidence that a swamp-like environment existed here at that time.

You will also see a model of a mine, and a description of the method used to get the sand. In "room and pillar" mining the sand-stone is blasted out to form "rooms," and the sandstone left intact between them form natural support pillars.

After leaving the Visitor Center, facing its entrance, climb up the railroad tie staircase to the right. This will lead you up to the Greathouse Portal, the original opening to the sand mine, now barred. Peer inside to see the tunnel disappearing into the distance. Step onto the Lower Chaparral Trail on your left and follow it to another junction. In addition to the mining remains, evidence of the human settlements include the exotic plant species still growing here today, including the

black locust, pepper tree, almond, eucalyptus, and tree of heaven.

Just ahead and to the left is a large pile of sand. Go over and check it out. This is the sand that was mined here to produce glass. You will be struck by how white and pure it is. The rock from which the sand was derived is called "quartz arenite," which is the name given to very pure sandstone where the grains are all the same size. Throughout the park you will find such sandy spots alternating with light-colored sandstone, crumbly shale outcroppings, and very black, loose soils which are decomposed dark shales. Return to the trail and continue south on Chaparral Loop.

To the left of the trail you will see train tracks and a mine opening. Above the tunnel is the date "1930." This is the Hazel-Atlas sand mine that operated from the 1920s until 1949. Samples of the glass made from sand mined here are on display in the museum.

Return to the trail and retrace your steps to the previous junction next to the sand pile. The Lower Chaparral Trail is to the left. Go straight to return to the picnic area on the eastern side of the Chaparral Loop. Return to the Nortonville Trail and go left towards the cemetery, which is visible as the cluster of trees on a hilltop to the west.

At this point, you have probably wandered around for about 0.8 miles.

Go through a gate and pass a muddy pond on the right. Cattle are likely to be lounging around the pond. At a fork, bear right. This wide dirt road is open and hot. It is uphill to the cemetery, so this is one of the least pleasant stretches of our route. Rose Hill sits at 1,506 feet. Puff up to the cemetery gate and go past a huge old willow tree to explore the grave markers. Take time to read some of them. You will notice that a large percentage of the graves here contain very young children and infants. Many more contain people who died as young adults, including women who died in childbirth. When you consider how small these towns were and how short a time this area was occupied, it seems like these Jones and Richards families were trudging up that hill on a far too regular basis to bury a family member.

Exit the cemetery out the back gate and follow a footpath down to the Nortonville Trail. Turn right on it and continue through the green hills to a junction with Black Diamond Trail under high-voltage power lines. This is Nortonville Pass.

A large loop can be made by taking Black Diamond Trail all the way around a rocky ridge and back up to this point. Looking ahead down Nortonville Trail, you will see that we are about to go steeply down for a half mile. On this out-and-back route, that means that coming back is going to be a monstrous endurance test. By taking the big loop route, you can avoid that, but the trail is longer. There is yet a third option, which we will detail shortly.

For now, continue on Nortonville steeply down the open slope for a half mile. At the bottom you will reach a junction with Black Diamond Trail. Turn left on it and go through a gate.

At the next junction with Coal Canyon Trail, bear right to follow Black Diamond Trail. After 0.7 miles on Black Diamond Trail, you will join paved Black Diamond Way. Continue 0.14 miles to a junction with the top end of Coal Canyon Trail on the left.

Continue on pavement for 0.2 miles to a junction with Cumberland Trail on the right. Take it a short distance to visit an adit and an air shaft. Although the adit appears on the trail map, we were unable to locate it after searching alongside the trail for several minutes. If you do find it, you can apparently go 75 feet inside this horizontal mine opening with the help of a flashlight.

We easily found the air shaft, since there was a marker next to the trail and a narrow footpath leading to it. Stooping, you can walk into the opening and look up to see a grate and light above. This shaft was used to vent harmful gases from the mine. Retrace your steps to get back on Black Diamond Way.

This is where you make your decision regarding the way back. If you continue on Black Diamond Way, you will make a wide loop and come back out on Nortonville Trail just above the long downhill slope, avoiding that torturous half-mile climb. So why would we want to hike up that horrible dusty half mile to Nortonville Pass if we don't have to? The answer is Coal Canyon. It is a charming little adventure that we are grateful to have stumbled upon. In a park with so many hot open roads to hike, this hikers-only trail is a completely welcome diversion. And now that you are done with your history lesson, why not treat yourself? Be advised, however, that Coal Canyon Trail is steep and uneven, and may be strenuous for some.

For our chosen route, backtrack on Black Diamond Trail to the junction with Coal Canyon Trail. Turn right onto it and explore Jim's Place, a hollowed out room in the sandstone with a chimney and "shelves" carved into the walls where someone named Jim presumably lived for a while. Duck into the shade of pine trees on this narrow trail. Notice the huge pine cones and scan the trail for pine nuts. They are black or dark brown and oval-shaped, about the size of sunflower seeds, and were an important source of nutrition for the native Bay Miwok tribes.

The trail goes steadily downhill into the narrow canyon. It is a rocky and rough single-track, but all the more fun for that. The trail is 0.88 miles long, and you will be sorry when it is over. It soon joins up with a deep creek bed, usually dry. If you are lucky enough to catch the water running, you will have a perfect adventure in this canyon, walking beside water splashing down the steep grade towards the canyon bottom. When we were here in April, the creek bed was dry, but the flowers were vigorously blooming all around us.

Cross the creek bed a couple of times on the way down, which is no problem when it's dry. We walked through some of the fine white sand along the way, and then walked across one of those black shale slopes, the rock crunching like cinders underfoot. The smooth sandstone was there as well. Look out for loose pieces of coal along the trail. They will be generally rectangular in shape and look sort of like burnt wood. If you find one, notice how easily it falls apart between your fingers. The coal found here is extremely friable and of generally poor quality.

At the bottom of the canyon, the trail spills out into a wide flat area where you walk forward to exit the canyon and join up with Black Diamond Trail. Look back at your little canyon, choked with rocks and shrubbery, and then proceed on Black

Diamond Trail back to the gate and junction with Nortonville.

Turn right and trudge up that punishing half-mile climb. Let's hope you didn't come here on a hot day. At the top, congratulate yourself, catch your breath, and continue past the cemetery and back to the parking lot.

Directions: Take Highway 4 to the Somersville Road exit in Antioch. Go south on Somersville Road to the Preserve entrance. Park in the lot at the end of the road. There are toilets and picnic areas here. On weekends, an entrance fee is charged.

45. Trail Through Time

EFFORT:..Difficult
LENGTH:..8 miles one way
GEOLOGICAL FEATURE(S):...................Erosional Features, Fossils
LOCATION:..Mount Diablo State Park

Description: The geology of Mount Diablo is like an undisciplined work of fiction, jumping back and forth in time and abruptly from place to place. The topography of the mountain is upside down. The highs are low and the lows are high. It's called *topographic inversion.*

The Trail Through Time takes you up the mountain from the Miocene (which spanned a time from 24 to 5 million years ago) to the Jurassic period (208 to 144 million years ago), covering 150 million years. This appears to violate a basic rule of geology, which is that in any given sequence of rocks, the oldest rocks are always located on the bottom. However, in this case, the original rocks were deposited in the right order, with oldest rocks on the bottom, and then

tilted up. After the rocks were tilted, the softer Miocene rocks eroded away, while the harder Jurassic Franciscan Formation rocks resisted erosion and remained topographically high. So the trail proceeds up the mountain and back in time. (An alternate way to complete this hike is to hike downhill one-way and have a second car waiting at the bottom.)

The Trail Through Time is a project being undertaken by the University of California Museum of Paleontology with Mount Diablo State Park, the Mount Diablo Interpretive Association, The Lindsay Museum, and other local groups. The focus of the new interpretive trail is to take visitors to rock outcrops, fossil sites, and areas of botanical and archeological interest. Students from

Monte Vista High School in Danville are developing a field guide for the trail, and creating a virtual field trip so that even non-hikers can experience the mountain's points of interest on the Internet.

The trail will begin on Blackhawk Road at 750 feet in elevation. It takes you past Blackhawk Quarry, a very rich deposit of Miocene mammal fossils. As you go through Sycamore Canyon, you pass through sandstone and mudstone deposits containing numerous marine fossils.

Continuing, the trail reaches Rock City at 1,300 feet, a 50 million year old sandstone outcrop exhibiting interesting erosional features. The path crosses the Mount Diablo Thrust Fault on its travels through the Cretaceous Period. At 2,300 feet, it reaches the Sunset Picnic Area.

On the last climb of the trail, you enter the Jurassic Period characterized by the ancient sea floor deposits of basalt, shale, chert, and graywacke. At 2,900 feet, the trail reaches Juniper Campground and then continues paralleling the Summit Road to the Summit at 3,849 feet.

At the time of this writing, the trail was not yet built, but segments of it are already in place, and most of these locations can be visited today on existing roads or trails. To keep abreast of development, visit the Mount Diablo Interpretive Association's web site at http://www.mdia.org/geotrail.htm.

Directions: From Highway 680 in Danville, take Diablo Road east towards the park. The road will become Blackhawk Road immediately after the southwest entrance to the park.

46. Donner Creek Canyon and Falls Loop

EFFORT:..Difficult
LENGTH:..6.0 miles
GEOLOGICAL FEATURE(S):......................................Erosional Features
LOCATION:...Mount Diablo State Park

Description: This very steep loop takes you up one side of Donner Canyon and back on the other, with a seasonal waterfall at the back of the canyon. For the best waterfall, take the hike in winter, but be aware that the trails can be muddy and even harder to negotiate. We went in mid-April and couldn't imagine a better time. The astounding variety of wildflowers blooming from one end of the hike to the other was more than sufficient reward for the effort. The trails were dry, but the creeks were still flowing, and the waterfall, though modest, was running. Avoid this trail in summer, however, as it will kill you.

Among the flowers you may see blooming in spring are California poppy, lupine, birds eye gilia, blue dick, blue-eyed grass, fiddleneck, globe gilia, California buttercup, goldfield, brodiaea, bush monkeyflower, hound's tongue, Indian paintbrush, Indian warrior, Ithuriel's spear, chinese house, cow parsnip, miner's lettuce, mules ear, and cream cup. Of course, these flowers will be receiving visitations from numerous butterflies and bees.

This is also a trail which can introduce you to the geology of the mountain, from the sedimentary mudstone at the trailhead, through metamorphic serpentine, and then igneous basalt at the falls. Wow, this trail has it all!

From Regency Drive, step past the gate on the left and walk down to the trail. Turn left and go past the gate marking the state park boundary. The park's trails are well signed, so if you pay attention to the signposts, you will easily find your way.

Head south on Donner Canyon Road, walking along Donner Creek, passing through stately blue oaks, California buckeye, and gray pines. Looking back, you have a good view of the large diabase rock quarry nearby.

The road is wide, running across the 140-million year old Knoxville Formation, a Mesozoic clayey mudstone. If it has rained recently, this material creates sticky mud and an uncomfortable hike. You will share the road with equestrians and bicyclists. Various trails take off from this road, but resist them for now. Near the start of the hike, watch for ground squirrels in the grass at the edge of the trail. In some spots along the creek, the calls of cicadas are boisterous. The road will climb gently for the first mile, a deceptive beginning.

After almost a mile, you will reach the Donner Cabin site on your left. It was once a park residence, but burned down several years ago. When you reach a junction with Hetherington Loop Trail, you may choose to take it, as it parallels the road. We recommend it for several reasons. It is cooler and a little less steep than the road, and it is more scenic. It is also a hikers-only path. Otherwise, continue straight on Donner Canyon Road. The rest of us will turn left onto the narrow Hetherington Loop Trail.

As the trail climbs, you will enter a chaparral habitat, characterized by toyon, sage, manzanita, yerba santa, and buckbrush. This section climbs steeply, dipping in and out of dense shrubbery, producing wildflowers in earnest. The trail joins back up with Donner Canyon Road eventually. Turn left onto it. Proceed to the junction with Meridian Ridge Trail, where you turn right. This is the beginning of the loop section of our trip. If you continued on Donner Canyon Road, you would reach Cardinet Oaks Road, which will be our return route. You could go either way at this junction, but we believe that the steep ascent to come is a little easier on the shaded single-track footpath we are approaching than on the open fire road and the sunny east side of the canyon.

It is on the Meridian Ridge Trail that you will first notice some serpentine, California's state rock. Serpentine forms from the reaction of hot seawater with peridotite, a material derived from the upper mantle. The seawater was heated by the extrusion of mantle material (as magma) onto the ocean floor. After millions of years, the serpentinized peridotite creates an unusual soil that hosts a distinctive plant community dominated by manzanita, digger pine, and scrub oak. You can recognize exposed serpentinite by its gray-green color and waxy feel.

You have gained enough elevation by now to see down to the valley below and the town of Clayton. Look back occasionally for these views.

Climb a short distance to the junction with Middle Trail, a tiny opening to your left. This narrow trail switchbacks uphill mercilessly through a jungle of shrubbery and a huge variety of wildflowers. It's a beautiful trail, mostly encased in brush, but sometimes emerging into tiny flower-filled meadows. Watch your step as you go; the fall down into the canyon is a long one. When the view opens up for brief stretches, you will see a fascinating geologic formation across the canyon. Don't worry, you will be over there soon, up close and personal.

At the junction with Falls Trail, turn left. Climb about a quarter mile until you come to a creek where you will find a good spot to sit down and catch your breath. Shortly after this, the trail crosses a shallow creek and heads uphill again. Near the creek is where the ladybugs hang out in winter, covering the rocks and tree branches in semi-hibernation. As warmer weather comes, the beetles will mate and leave for the coastal valleys.

Emerging onto a ledge overlooking the canyon, you will see the waterfall falling down the back of the canyon, to your right. The long stream falls over a mossy backdrop.

The prevailing rock will change again, this time to dark basalt, or greenstone, created from volcanic eruptions on the ancient seafloor at a divergent boundary. These are the same volcanic eruptions that resulted in the serpentinized peridotites described earlier. This rock has been dated at 190 million years old. It was brought here when the Farallon Plate was subducted under the North American Plate.

You come near the falls about a half-mile beyond the creek crossing.

The waterfall flows over and through the basalt. Just a few feet further on the trail is a nice place to stop for a break. When you're ready, continue on the single-track trail as it traverses the back of the canyon and turns to head north on the other side. In some spots, this trail is scary, extremely narrow with steep drops on the left. Finding a place to allow people to pass you can be difficult. But this segment of the hike is one of the best, and is perfectly safe if you watch where you're stepping and keep the children close. The flowers on the slope to your right are gorgeous with the brilliant colors of red Indian paintbrush, golden poppies, purple lupine, and Chinese houses. Poppies grow in the crevices of rocky outcrops that punctuate this canyon wall. Down below you the creek tumbles along.

At last you reach the outcrop that was so tantalizing a sight from across the way. Fractured beds of reddish brown Franciscan chert reveal their structure, alternating with bands of shale between each layer. Chert, which also goes by the common name of flint, is a sedimentary rock from the deep ocean, composed of the recrystallized skeletons of radiolarians, tiny single-celled creatures that lived millions of years ago in the open oceans.

A few steps along, you will come to a wall of rock exhibiting fine chevron folds, contortions created by high pressure and temperature deep underground. Chevron folds are near and dear to geologists and never fail to punch up their pulse rate.

As you continue on this trail, a waterfall will come into view quite some distance below you. Happily, nature has placed a couple of boulders beside the trail here for a strategic perch. Sit here with a view of the canyon and waterfall below and the rocky flower-covered hill above. This spot will also put you eye level with some turkey vultures as they swoop through the canyon.

When you are rested, continue over a bump of a hill and descend steeply to Cardinet Oaks Road about a half mile from the waterfall. Turn left and walk the wide road steeply downhill. Make your way back down the canyon until you reach a junction with Donner Canyon Road in another half mile. Turn right and continue your descent for another 1.5 miles to the trailhead.

Directions: From Concord, drive through Clayton to Regency Woods. From Marsh Creek Road, turn right on Regency Drive and go to the end of the road. Park on the street beyond the last houses. There are no restrooms, water or picnic tables here. Pack up your snacks and take them along to enjoy on the trail. Access is free.

47. Fossil Ridge Trail

EFFORT:	Minimal
LENGTH:	1.5 miles
GEOLOGICAL FEATURE(S):	Fossils, Erosional Features
LOCATION:	Mount Diablo State Park

Description: This is a trek up to the top of Fossil Ridge, a hogback with exposed marine fossils.

The trail leads through grassland and oak woodland. Like most trails on this mountain, the best time to visit is in early spring when the wildflowers are blooming, new green grass covers the hills, and the heat is tolerable. We hiked this trail in early March when a few blooms were already out and the green of the grass and trees was clean and fresh. This is not an exceptionally pretty trail. The main point of it is the geology, which is also not spectacular, but it is interesting. We suggest combining this trail with a trip to Rock City (following hike) just up the road.

Find the trailhead on the south edge of the parking area at a gate. Start climbing steeply uphill on a partially paved service road. As you gain elevation, you will have good views of the surrounding ridges and the mountain summit.

After about five minutes of walking, the trail becomes easier as it levels out. The paved section of the road will end, but the trail will still be a wide, easy road with some up and downhill stretches. The trees thin out on top as you climb gradually into a fully exposed segment of the road. On your left, the hillside drops off steeply. On your right, in the distance, you have views of the Coast Ranges. On a clear day, this will be a little sugarcoating for this walk.

At 0.66 miles, you come to the end of the road and a turnaround. A trail sign reads "End of Trail." This is pretty deceptive because this is really where the real trail begins. Look to the right of the turnaround and locate a single-track trail up to the top of the ridge just ahead of you. Climb up to a wooded area with exposed rocks. Once you reach the top, you have some more good views towards the coast. Turn left to follow the ridgetop.

Examine pieces of the exposed rock periodically to discover the fossils. They are mostly clams, and mostly broken up into a fossil hash, which is indicative of a turbulent depositional environment. Think of the bits and pieces of shell you find on a beach. Because of the turbulent motion of the waves crashing against the shore, it is rare to find a whole, undisturbed shell in the sand. In keeping with the geologic theme of "the present is the key to the past," the broken up fossil hash suggests that the depositional environment of the sandstone ridge was a shoreline environment, such as a beach.

The most interesting offering of this trail is not the fossils, however. Continue across the ridgetop for a short distance until you emerge onto a grassy knoll overlooking a canyon. Look across the canyon to the hillside directly in front of you. You will see the exposed rock running up the hill in two distinct linear outcrops. Notice that the vegetation patterns are different on one side of the outcrop than the other. On one side you have brush and trees. On the other there is mainly just grass.

This is a good place to discuss the structure of a hogback. This ridge and its partner across the way are composed of alternating beds of sandstone and shale, marine layers which were once on the bottom of the sea. During the natural process of orogeny (mountain-building), they were lifted and tilted to a nearly vertical plane. During subsequent periods of erosion, the softer shale layers have weathered more readily than the sandstone, creating gaps between the sandstone layers. The exposed rocks you see are the sandstone. The vegetation differences result from different soil types. Certain plants prefer shale soils, others sandstone.

This is the end of the trail. When you're ready, return the way you came.

Directions: From Interstate 680 in Danville, take the Diablo Road exit. Go east as the road becomes Mount Diablo Scenic Drive and then South Gate Road. Follow South Gate Road to the Uplands Picnic Area which is across from Lower Rock City picnic area and just before you reach Rock City.

48. Rock City

EFFORT:..Minimal
LENGTH:..Varies
GEOLOGICAL FEATURE(S):...................Erosional Features
LOCATION:................................Mount Diablo State Park

Description: The name of this place beckons, doesn't it? Before we visited for the first time, it brought to mind images of the Flintstones' Bedrock. Oddly enough, while we were there, it did the same. And we were not alone. Children clambering through the wind caves spoke of their "bedrooms."

Rock City is a massive playground of boulders, wind sculptures, and depressions created in fine-grained sandstone by wind and water erosion. There are paths leading to and among different groupings of the rocks, but this is not a formal trail or even a hike. It is a meander. Walk among the rocks and crawl into the shallow caves and have fun.

Near the beginning of the trail is a trio of interconnected caves, wildly entertaining to the youngsters as they move freely among the three rooms. Further down the trail is a lovely little cave that has openings on both sides, forming a kind of miniature Utah-style arch which you can pass through.

One of the highlights of this stop is Sentinel Rock. It's a steep climb up 200 feet to the viewing platform, but it is worth the effort because it gives you a good overview of the boulder playground. Take the trail from campsite #20 in Live Oak Campground. The climb is aided by steel cables.

Spend as much or as little time as you want to before taking advantage of a picnic table. If you have time, combine this stop with Fossil Ridge Trail (previous hike). Together, they make for two easy adventures and a very pleasant day trip.

Directions: From Interstate 680 in Danville, take the Diablo Road exit. Go east as the road becomes Mount Diablo Scenic Drive and then South Gate Road. Follow South Gate Road to Rock City. Parking may be difficult to find on weekends, but you can park alongside the road if necessary.

49. Castle Rock Trail

EFFORT:..Minimal
LENGTH:...3.0 miles
GEOLOGICAL FEATURE(S):.........................Fossils, Erosional Features
LOCATION:..................................Diablo Foothills Regional Park

Description: This nearly level, wide road is popular with equestrians and bicyclists, as well as local residents out for a weekend stroll. For us, it is a visit to stunning sandstone outcrops and marine fossils.

From the parking area, you will notice the equestrian and cyclist trailhead across the road. The hikers' route is past the gate on the paved road into Castle Rock Park. You can take either. The trail above skirts around the main park area and also allows you to avoid climbing a gate, but the gate is easy, so don't worry about it.

Walk up the paved road into the park past the picnic area, swimming pool, and park buildings. This is a private park, but hikers are allowed trail access through it. The road turns to gravel past the restrooms. You will be walking through Pine Canyon alongside Pine Creek all the way with moderate shade. The landscape is primarily rolling grass-covered foothills of Mount Diablo with oak trees providing contrast. The trail is an old wagon road called Stage Road.

Leaving Castle Rock Park behind, you will pass a gate and continue to a fork. Bear right to stay on Stage Road. Before long you arrive at a sandstone wall on the right which clearly exhibits bedding. The rock wall is tilted to almost vertical and several distinct layers are revealed.

A short distance further you arrive at a rock on the right with a hole bored through it by water erosion. You won't be the first person to climb up into the round room inside the rock. It's a cozy little den with two windows, big enough to sit in.

The creek is on the left, and beyond that is the beginning of the intriguing series of sandstone crags known as Castle Rock. Notice the many caves and holes in the cliff face. If you have your binoculars, you will be able to see that the holes are used by nesting birds. The white streaks beneath the holes are a giveaway. Hawks, including red-shoulders and Coopers, are often seen in the oak trees near the trail. You may also see golden eagles.

There are seven creek crossings on this trail, and it may not be much fun from December to March, depending on rainfall and horse traffic. In fall, the first several of the crossings will be dry, but during rainy season, you will get wet fording them. There are also a couple of gates which you may have to climb over when locked.

After the first stream crossing, you will spot a narrow footpath leading to the right through the grass. In spring when the grass is growing, this path may not be apparent. If you come to the second creek crossing, you missed it, but by turning right and following the edge of the creek a short distance, you will be there. Take the footpath past a grape arbor of sorts to a slide in a tall cliff above the creekbed. There is a rich layer of marine fossils in this cliff. Some of these wash down to the creekbed each year. If you look carefully for whitish rocks, you will find pieces of this exposure. Thick clusterings of mollusk shell fragments can be seen. This sort of rock, composed mainly of shells with some sandstone, is known as a "hash" for somewhat obvious reasons. Shell hashes in the

Diablo foothills are generally of the Briones Formation. You can see these on Rocky Ridge in Las Trampas Regional Park, Fossil Ridge on Mt. Diablo, and various other locations in the area. If you look closely at the shell pieces, you may find some that are large enough to recognize as a clam, the dominant type of fossil. Pectens, the bivalve mollusk made famous as the symbol for Shell Oil Company, also occur, but are less common.

Why are the shells so completely shattered? Deposited in a shallow marine environment, the shells were slammed about by waves, turbulent storm currents, smashed on rocks, and generally abused until finally coming to rest and being buried.

It was at this detour to the fossil site that we came upon a bobcat, and got within twenty-five feet of it before it sauntered off along the creekbed. It was also very near here that we saw a clutch of about twenty quail in the underbrush. Mountain lions have reportedly been spotted in Pine Canyon over the years, but it will be quite unusual if you see one.

Returning to the main trail, continue to the second creek crossing. Good views on the left of Castle Rock are still with us as we ford the stream for the third and then fourth time, keeping Pine Creek and the Mount Diablo State Park boundary to the left. After the fourth crossing, a couple of picnic tables are available for a rest or snack.

Streams following the fourth crossing contained a small amount of running water, but it was easy to step across on rocks.

Eventually you will come to Pine Pond, a reed-choked body of water frequented by ducks. This is the turn-around point.

On the way back, after passing the picnic tables, you may want to descend to the creek below to the right. There are several footpaths down to the trail there which edges right up to the state park boundary fence. This detour will keep you away from speeding bicycles and horses.

Directions: In Walnut Creek on Interstate 680, take Ygnacio Valley Road east to Oak Grove Road. Turn right (south) and continue as this road becomes Castle Rock Road. Proceed to the end of the road where it is blocked by a gate and there is parking on the left. Access is free. There are no facilities.

50. Round Top Loop

EFFORT:..Minimal
LENGTH:..1.7 miles
GEOLOGICAL FEATURE(S):..Volcanism
LOCATION:...........................Robert Sibley Volcanic Regional Preserve

Description: Round Top is one of the highest peaks in the Oakland Hills, and is what's left of a 10-million year old volcano. The Preserve houses evidence of this past in debris of several types of volcanics, including basaltic breccia, rhyolite tuff, and lapilli agglomerate. There are exposed dikes and ancient mudflows. However, the volcanism on display here is not very dramatic, so we would not recommend it to anyone who has to travel any distance. For locals, though, it is worth a visit.

You'll find the trailhead on the left of the exhibit building, or you can start on a paved fire road on the right side. We prefer the foot trail. There is a map at the exhibit building, behind glass, which you can study before setting out, since we found no brochure to take with us. Also, lots of different trails and fire roads cut through the preserve, so if you get the trail set in your mind, you will be better able to follow it.

Be prepared to share your time here with dogs. This is a very popular dog walking area with the local residents. If you bring your dog, there are plastic bags at the fire road entrance.

During the first leg of the trail, Round Top will be on the right. The road is unshaded and hot in many seasons. At Marker 2, you will see an exposed volcanic conglomerate with paleosol (literally, "ancient soil"), with iron in the soil giving it a reddish color. The road is rocky, cutting through a chaparral-like landscape. We were there in October, yet a few resilient poppies were blooming. Also in color, were some pyracantha bushes with their bright red berries.

When you come to the split between the Volcanic Trail and Round Top Loop, make a choice. We recommend continuing on the Volcanic Trail if you have the time and energy. If you do, you will see some interesting outcrops. We are going to detour as far as a colorful little gorge.

On the Volcanic Trail at Marker 8, you will see a contact place between the Orinda sedimentary deposits and the volcanics, broken by a near vertical chert bed.

At marker 9, there is a massive basaltic outcrop separated from more weathered basal conglomerate by a fault. Even if you are not a geology buff to a great degree, you will still find the little canyon past the gate enjoyable. Suddenly you are facing a wall of multicolored rock, in pinks and reds. The colors came about from hydrothermal alteration associated with steam and gases released from the volcano. Depending on the time of day, there is shade in this curve formed by the walls around you.

Turn around here and head back to the split with Round Top Loop to continue.

If you are watching, and the day is a clear one, you will have occasional views of the San Francisco Bay and Golden Gate Bridge in the distance.

Back on Round Top Loop, after climbing a bit, you will come upon a spot where someone has arranged concentric circles of rock into a sort of labyrinth. If you follow the path around and around, you end up at the center. Look closely and you will see that those visiting before you have left offerings, as though they have made a symbolic journey into themselves. The day we were there, there was an acorn, a bead, and a nickel. If stumbling on this geometric construction surprised you, there is more to come.

Further along the trail you will come to the edge of a cliff. Look down into the canyon. It has a marshy bottom and a large labyrinth like the one you just passed. It also has a smaller rock circle on a ledge,

and a rock outline of a human hand. Use any of the several little spur trails to find a good spot at the top of the canyon to take a picture from on high before following the path around, and eventually down to the canyon bottom.

The rock circles appeared in 1972; their builder is unknown to park officials, who periodically clean out the offerings left at their centers, a teletubby here, a Cheeto there, the trinkets of our culture. Once you emerge from the canyon, the trail changes quite a bit. You'll go over a ridge on a gravel road, between two pine trees, and then descend a narrow, rocky footpath into a burned-out eucalyptus grove. The dead branches clattering in the wind sound like dry bones. This is a somewhat steep downhill walk. After this, you will be walking among trees on the shady last leg of your hike back to the exhibit building and parking lot.

Although there is one picnic table near the front gate, it is not very inviting. You can carry your lunch and spread a blanket at the bottom of the rock circle canyon, or you can take advantage of your location and find another park to picnic in. There are several parks along Skyline Boulevard, including Tilden Regional Park and Redwood Regional Park.

Directions: From Highway 24 just east of the Caldecott Tunnel in Oakland, take the Fish Ranch Road exit west to Grizzly Peak Boulevard. Stop at a turnout for a gorgeous view of the Bay. It will astound you. Turn left and drive to Skyline Boulevard, proceeding on Skyline to the park entrance. While you're driving on Skyline, you can contemplate the fact that the road follows the trace of the Hayward fault. Access is free.

51. San Andreas Fault Trail

EFFORT:...Minimal
LENGTH:...1.5 miles
GEOLOGICAL FEATURE(S):....................................Fault Activity
LOCATION:...Los Trancos Open Space Preserve

Description: The 1.5 mile San Andreas Fault Trail is a self-guiding interpretive loop with nine numbered stops keyed to a brochure. Definitely pick up the brochure at the interpretive panel at the edge of the parking area. The brochure explains fault movement and earthquake mechanics, and it has a map of the trail, which will be useful. The trail was built in 1977 to increase public awareness of our geologic environment. You will learn about sag ponds, benches, and other earthquake phenomena, and recognize evidence of fault activity on the landscape.

You can walk the fault trail loop and leave it at that, or you can make a longer loop to explore the other offerings of this small preserve. The San Andreas Fault cuts this preserve in two, marking the boundary of the American and Pacific Plates. As we have discussed before, the two plates are grinding against one another as the Pacific Plate moves northwestward. Friction prevents the smooth movement of the plates against one another, causing a tremendous build-up of stress. When enough stress builds, the rocks at this boundary will snap into new positions, releasing all of that pent-up energy in the form of an earthquake. In this area, the movement along the fault averages 3/4 inch per year.

From the west side of the parking lot, go through the fence, find the narrow hikers-only path, and climb to a viewpoint and the first stop. From this vantage point, you can see Loma Prieta 23 miles to the southeast on the North American Plate. That mountain gave its name to the disastrous 1989 earthquake along this fault.

You are standing on the eastern edge of the Pacific Plate. The Stevens Creek Canyon marks the boundary between the two plates. Seems a bit eerie to be standing at such a temperamental spot on the Earth's crust.

Continuing on the trail, at the second stop you will see Mount Diablo rising up to the east and San Francisco in the distance to the north, and, of course, Mount Tamalpais just beyond it. Closer, you can see Crystal Springs Reservoir and the San Andreas Lake in the valley defined by the San Andreas Fault.

As you walk this trail, take a moment to examine some of the boulders along the way. Many of these are coarse conglomerates, a sedimentary rock composed of different types of pebbles cemented together. The source of these rocks is Loma Prieta. They were washed down by streams, and those that ended up on the Pacific Plate moved along northward away from the mountain to their eventual present-day positions.

Throughout this hike, you will pass posts with either yellow or white tops. The yellow-topped posts mark the location of the major fault. The white ones indicate minor faults.

After stop #2, turn right and then immediately right again to resume the trail. You will arrive at a junction.

Go straight and then at the next junction, go straight again.

The trail takes you through a meadow where you will find wildflowers blooming in spring. You will be walking among madrone, California bay, oak, coyote brush, poison oak, and ferns. Many of the magnificent old oak trees are covered with moss and various types of lichens, and the bays perfume the air. In the shady, damp areas, watch for mushrooms. When leaf litter is high, the trail may become indistinct in spots.

You will walk generally eastward for 0.3 miles before reaching stop #3. A wooden bench is positioned here, as well as the fault markers. To your right is the grassy slope leading up to Page Mill Road, and to your left is a somewhat flat area, after which the slope continues down to the creek. The flat spot is called a bench. It is created by the continual activity of the fault. As the ground ruptures in an earthquake, the sides of the rupture pull apart. In time, these fill in with dirt. The area where this occurs tends to be flat. The trail goes past the bench to the left here.

At station 4, you will see the reproduction of a fence that moved as much as three feet to the northwest during the great 1906 earthquake. Part of the original fence is still standing, but the section showing the offset is a reproduction. Although this is pretty impressive, it is a fraction of the offset observable at Point

Reyes National Seashore (see Hike #43). If you look down the line of yellow posts, you will see that the fault runs right through the fence offset.

This is sort of a fun place to separate from your hiking partner for a moment, each of you standing beside one of the fence sections. Standing on either side of the fault, wave at each other knowing that if you stood there long enough, you would eventually lose sight of one another. However, we do not have millions of years to fritter away, so continue on, heading west to stop #5. Just after this stop, the trail splits. The trail coming in on the right is the return of the loop. Bear left here to start the 0.7-mile loop portion of the hike.

Stop #6 offers an exciting remnant of the 1906 earthquake, a sag pond. A sag pond is a place where the fault has created a depression, or sag, in the

overlying rock. If you come after rains, as we did, there will be an actual pond here. Otherwise, it will be a dry depression.

After this stop, you will walk parallel to a minor fault marked by white-capped posts, and then loop back to head east again and walk through thick and fragrant vegetation to close the loop. Retrace your steps from here back to the parking area.

Directions: From Interstate 280 in Palo Alto, turn west on Page Mill Road and drive seven miles to the parking area on the right. You can also reach the trailhead by driving one mile east off of Skyline Boulevard. If the lot is full, park across the street in the Monte Bello OSP lot. Access is free. There is an outhouse on the Monte Bello side.

52. Stevens Creek Nature Trail

EFFORT:...Moderate
LENGTH:..3.0 miles
GEOLOGICAL FEATURE(S):...Fault Activity
LOCATION:...Monte Bello Open Space Preserve

Description: Monte Bello, or beautiful mountain, is former ranchland tucked within a huge patchwork of parks and open space preserves, sharing boundaries with

Upper Stevens Creek County Park, Los Trancos OSP, Rancho San Antonio OSP, and Skyline Ridge OSP. This positioning would undoubtedly be an advantage for the long-haul hiker. For us, however, the beautiful mountain is plenty large enough to contain our day-trip.

Today's route will allow you to visit several varied ecosystems of the preserve, from dense forest to open grassland, while traversing the San Andreas Fault Zone. On your drive up Page Mill Road, where the road dipped abruptly, you drove across the fault. Most of this trail is a pretty creekside trek without much geology to recommend it. We are including it here as an extension to the San Andreas Fault Trail (previous hike) across the road at Los Trancos Open Space Preserve. That trail is so short and the preserve so small that it is natural to spill over into Monte Bello. With its fault zone features, it is a natural second course for the day.

From the parking area, climb on a partially-paved trail to the viewpoint above the canyon to get yourself oriented. Sit on the stone bench here to take in the view of Stevens Creek Canyon and the grass-covered ridges across the way. Following the canyon down, you can see Loma Prieta in the distance, the epicenter of the big 1989 earthquake. Stevens Creek, which starts on the slopes of Black Mountain, follows the San Andreas Fault for the length of this preserve and empties into Stevens Creek Reservoir. It then continues through the Silicon Valley to eventually reach San Francisco Bay.

From the viewpoint, you can also see a striking feature of the fault zone—the dramatic shift in plant communities from one side to the other. Where you sit, looking directly out and down, bare, grassy hills dominate. Just to the right where Stevens Creek runs, dense forest prevails. We have noted this phenomenon before and by now you are aware that the type of plants growing in a particular area are a direct indicator of the type of soils found there. The soils on the Pacific Plate differ from those on the American Plate because they originated far to the south, yet one more piece of evidence that things on the surface of the planet do not stay put.

The geological features of this trail can be taken in from this viewpoint without any hiking, but hiking is what we're here for, right?

The nature trail actually begins about a third of a mile to the left. Since we will be making a loop, starting here is just the same. Time to get up and go for a walk. Turn to the right and descend on the dirt path.

The trail leads across flower-studded hills and then descends through the rich riparian habitat of Stevens Creek Canyon. Along the way is the occasional sign telling us about the flora and fauna. As you leave the open sun and approach the creek, thick woods of oak, California bay, and Douglas fir envelope you. In summer, this trail is a cool respite. In winter, the trail is likely to be muddy and punctuated by several running rivulets.

Look out for poison oak, as it grows vigorously near the creek. Also growing here are ferns, gooseberry, currant, blackberry, thimbleberry, elderberry, big leaf maple, California bay, Douglas fir, live oak, and tan oak. Depending on the time of year, the creek will either be gushing by or dancing lightly. The trail follows alongside the creek for less than a mile before intersecting a multi-use trail. Turn left and start heading away from the creek and out of the canyon. After just over a half mile on this trail, you will reach a junction with Canyon Trail. Turn left onto it, descend and cross a creek on a log, and then climb out the other side. Continue climbing up into open grassland.

Watch for black-tailed deer in the oak woodland and flowering meadows. You may also be lucky enough to see a coyote or bobcat hunting for rodents. We saw plenty of hawks and some deer tracks, but no other animals on a winter outing.

There are some steep uphill climbs as you make your way back up to the viewpoint area. Along Canyon Trail, the distinctive conglomerate boulders we saw in the previous hike reappear.

You will pass a spur trail on the right as you near the end of the journey. That path leads to a small parking lot on Page Mill Road, another starting point for this hike. After this junction, you are back on Stevens Creek Nature Trail.Continue 0.3 miles up to the viewpoint to close the loop and return to the trailhead.

Directions: From Interstate 280 in Palo Alto, turn west on Page Mill Road and drive seven miles to about a mile before you reach Skyline Boulevard, to the signed parking area on the left. There is a pit toilet. Access is free. Take a map from the display stand with you, as there are many unsigned trail junctions along the way.

53. Mine Hill Trail

EFFORT:...Moderate
LENGTH:..6.0 miles
GEOLOGICAL FEATURE(S):..Mining
LOCATION:....................................Almaden Quicksilver County Park

Description: Almaden Quicksilver County Park preserves the remains of historic and prehistoric mining activity. Native Californians mined cinnabar, a beautiful red mineral composed of mercury and sulfur, at this site. They dug a tunnel and removed the mineral using stone tools. The cinnabar was valuable for use as a pigment and widely traded.

Later, the cinnabar was mined for the mercury it contains, commonly referred to as quicksilver. Mercury mining began in the 1840s and was used as an amalgamating material for gold. The mercury was of paramount importance to the gold rush, for without mercury the gold could not be refined.

Cinnabar continued to be mined until 1972 when the Environmental Protection Agency banned the use of mercury to refine gold. By then, it was seldom used any more, having largely been replaced by safer cyanide techniques. Mercury is still used in developing countries, however, despite the danger.

In addition to gold refining, mercury was heavily used in the 19th century in the hat-making industry, particularly in making beaver pelt hats. The mercury caused the hats to be stiff enough to stand straight up. Mercury is very damaging to the central nervous system, and is thought to be the chemical responsible for the term "mad as a hatter."

The New Almaden Mine was the most productive mercury mine in North America, spawning a busy town where, by 1865, 1,800 people resided. Large-scale mining ceased by 1927, and the population eventually dispersed, as is typical of mining communities.

The southeast section of Almaden Quicksilver Park has a wide variety of terrain and a large number of mining remains. The Mine Hill Trail, an old mining road, starts at the Hacienda entrance and runs the entire length of the park for 7 miles to the park's northwest entrance at McAbee Road. Many trails branch off from Mine Hill Trail leading to old mines, camps, and a cemetery. The landscape is primarily grass-covered hills with some oak woodland. The park is well used by local residents on foot, horseback, and bicycles.

At the Hacienda Entrance, check out the mining museum before hitting the trail. Also, consult a trail map. There are lots of route options here, and you may want to string together your own combination of trails to best meet your interests. We have put together a rough figure-eight style route designed to hit as many of the historical sites as possible without covering too many miles. There is one major mine on the other side of the park, which you can walk to on the Mine Hill Trail, but we have listed that site as a separate hike starting from the McAbee Road entrance (see following hike).

Walk around the gate at the trailhead and start on wide Mine Hill Trail through an oak woodland environment. To the west you will see the Hacienda Reduction Works site with its fenced in collection of old mining machinery. Also note the Almaden Quicksilver Chimney on a hill. Built in the 1870s, the chimney vented sulfur fumes from the reduction works.

At 0.4 miles, you will reach a junction with Hacienda Trail to the right and English Camp Trail to the left. Continue straight on Mine Hill Trail.

Climb steadily, but gradually, up switchbacks to 1,000 feet at Capehorn Pass, reached after a little over a mile. You will climb through grassy slopes, gaining altitude. As you go higher, the landscape will be dominated with a chaparral environment of manzanita, madrone, and broom. In season, wildflowers include blue dicks, buttercups, saxifrage, Indian warrior, padre's shooting star, Johnny jump-ups, baby blue eyes, lupine, and poppies. At the pass, you will be rewarded with a great view of San Francisco Bay.

The Hacienda Trail heads off to the right here at the pass, leading to the Mockingbird Hill park entrance. Ahead, the trail forks. The right fork is the Randol Trail. Go left to stay on Mine Hill. If you are hiking in morning or evening, keep a lookout for deer. They are often seen along the trail. Also be aware of the serpentine outcrops as you go. The same hydrothermal fluids that resulted in the deposition of the cinnabar vein altered the surrounding country rock to serpentine.

Continue another 0.65 miles to a junction with Day Tunnel Trail, right. The mine entrance is sealed, so there is not much to see, but it is a good spot for a picnic, with a table and a view, if you are ready for that. Otherwise, continue on Mine Hill Trail another quarter mile to English Camp, an old mining encampment.

From here follow Mine Hill Trail for 0.3 miles. You will come to April Trail which goes right for 0.2 miles to the April Tunnel. Continue on the Mine Hill Trail past the old Powder House for another 0.4 miles. A short (0.1 miles) spur trail goes left here to visit the San Cristobal Mine site on 1,740 foot high Mine Hill. Go ahead and take this little detour where you can walk into the mine tunnel up to the point where you encounter a locked gate.

Return to the Mine Hill Trail and continue 0.3 miles to the trail's high point at Bull Run. A side trail goes a short distance to the Catherine Tunnel on the right. Mine Hill continues ahead along the open ridge on its way to the far side of the park, but it will continue without us.

After your long climb, take advantage of the picnic area here before turning left onto the Castillero Trail and passing through a gate. Now we will be heading back west, rounding the south side of Mine Hill. After 0.6 miles, you will encounter Hidalgo Cemetery Trail. If you want to visit the cemetery, it is a half mile from this junction. This side trip will add a mile to the length of our route.

The Castillero Trail continues 0.4 miles to a complex junction where the Yellow Kid Tunnel Trail and the English Camp Trail come in from behind and right, and Church Hill is ahead and right. English Camp is on our left, and directly ahead, the Castillero Trail crosses through another gate and then joins up with Mine Hill

Trail. For a change of pace and a slightly shorter route than Mine Hill, let's take English Camp Trail back. It will head generally west. If you find yourself heading southeast, you are probably on the Yellow Kid Tunnel Trail instead.

Shortly, you come to the Main Tunnel site. From here, it is almost a mile to the junction with Mine Hill Trail, downhill. When you reach it, turn right, go around the trailhead gate, and back to the parking area.

Directions: From Highway 101 in San Jose, exit on Highway 85 east. Exit on the Almaden Expressway heading south. Proceed 4.2 miles to Almaden Road. Pass through New Almaden on Almaden Road to the Almaden Quicksilver County Park Staging Area on the right, next to the Ranger Station and museum. Access is free.

54. Senador Mine Loop

EFFORT:	Minimal
LENGTH:	2.0 miles
GEOLOGICAL FEATURE(S):	Mining
LOCATION:	Almaden Quicksilver County Park

Description: There is one major mine located near the McAbee entrance to this park, the Senador

(Senador). See the previous hike for a more intensive exploration of the mercury mining history to be found here.

Walk past the gate and the restrooms at the end of the road and begin hiking on the Senador Mine Trail. It heads through grass-covered hills, passing a junction with the New Almaden Trail on the left. That will be our return route. Continue to the mine site on a fairly level course.

Three huge concrete structures are the remains of the mine's 40-ton Herreschoff Furnace, built in 1915. The Senador Mine opened in 1863 and was worked until 1926. The reduction plant was built in 1915. Its multi-hearth furnace and electric dust precipitator were the first ever used in the quicksilver industry. The mine produced 20,000 flasks of mercury. Large piles of mine tailings can be seen nearby. There's a picnic table and horse trough here.

From the mine site, the trail climbs up to a high point and then curves around to the south with views of the Almaden Valley and Santa Teresa Hills. To the south, Guadalupe Creek runs below Guadalupe Reservoir and its dam. The fish in the reservoir are unsafe to eat due to mercury poisoning as a result of the mining operations. Mercury runoff from these mines continues to contaminate San Francisco Bay to this day. Mount Umunhum (Ohlone for "hummingbird") is the highest peak at 3,486 feet.

At the end of the Senador Mine Trail, you come to the Guadalupe Trail. Hop onto it and go left. To the right, Guadalupe Trail goes down to the creek to run parallel to it and on past the dam and reservoir. There is a picnic table down by the creek about a half-mile from here if you want to extend your hike a little by going down to the shade of the oak trees by the creek. You will need to come back up to this junction to continue, adding a mile to the route.

From here, the Guadalupe Trail will continue for 0.6 miles to a junction with Mine Hill Trail and New Almaden Trail. You can take either one back to the trailhead. The New Almaden route is slightly shorter. Turn left on New Almaden Trail and proceed 0.3 miles to the junction with Senador Mine Trail. Turn right and continue a short distance to the trailhead.

Directions: From Highway 101 in San Jose, exit on Highway 85 heading east. Exit south on the Almaden Expressway and then turn right on Camden Avenue. Turn left on Leyland Park Drive, and then right on McAbee Road. Proceed to the end of the road and park along the street. Access is free.

55. Tafoni Trail

EFFORT:..Minimal
LENGTH:...2.6 miles
GEOLOGICAL FEATURE(S):.....................................Erosional Features
LOCATION:........................... El Corte de Madera Open Space Preserve

Description: The reward of this hike is the intriguing weathered sandstone formations at trail's end. They appear out of place and oddly fascinating, sculpted by water over time. You and the kids will not be able to resist climbing on and in them.

After walking through a shady forest on a wide, level road, you reach a junction. Follow the sign to the right, and shortly you are there. This section of the trail is open to hikers only, but the rest of the trail is popular with mountain bikers, so expect them. We saw several on a Saturday trip.

The sandstone sculptures are tucked in among the trees, undulating tawny boulders with smooth surfaces. Cast off your daypack and scramble among them to find a good spot to relax. Although there were plenty of people out on the trails, we had these rocks to ourselves.

Tafoni is a term that is applied to any rock that has weathered so that it has a honeycomb structure. Although there are various hypotheses regarding the formation of theses types of structures, we think the explanation provided for Mount Diablo's Rock City applies best here. At Rock City, it has been suggested that percolating groundwater dissolved the cementing minerals in the sandstone and then deposited the material on the outer layers, creating a sort of shell. When water penetrates through the shell, it encounters the easily eroded sandstone and carves out a smooth, circular cavity, leading to these interesting formations. This process is sometimes referred to as cavernous weathering. Tafoni is usually found near the sea coast. The name comes from Sicily where impressive honeycomb structures have formed in the coastal granite.

After exploring the tafoni formations and their many pockets and crevices, head back to the junction. At this point, you can return the way you came, or you can proceed ahead on a quarter mile spur trail to a perfect picnic spot with a view of the Pacific Ocean.

Directions: Head west on Highway 92 towards Half Moon Bay. Turn south on Highway 35/Skyline Boulevard and proceed 8.5 miles to Skeggs Vista Point parking area on the east side of the highway. This parking lot must be entered from the other direction, so drive further along and turn around. Once you've parked, cross the highway on foot and walk north a few feet to the trailhead, which is a fire road. Access is free. There are no facilities.

Tafoni Trail

56. Castle Rock and Goat Rock Loop

EFFORT:	Moderate
LENGTH:	3.4 miles
GEOLOGICAL FEATURE(S):	Erosional Features
LOCATION:	Castle Rock State Park

Description: This loop will take you to three of the main attractions of the park, two weathered sandstone outcrops and a waterfall, and will route you along Ridge Trail for spectacular views. Note that you can shorten the trip by turning around at either Castle Rock or Castle Rock Falls.

Take the shady Castle Rock Trail among madrone, Douglas fir, black oak, coast live oak, and tan oak trees. After 0.2 miles, take a right onto a dirt road. At 0.3 miles, you will reach 40-foot Castle Rock, a huge sandstone formation, and namesake of the park. You may see rock climbers training here. Explore the sandstone caves at your leisure on the 0.6 mile loop around the sandstone formation.

Descend to join Saratoga Gap Trail and walk along the creek through a second-growth redwood, Douglas fir, and madrone forest. Enjoy the stumbling creek and the mossy rocks and branches, as well as several types of ferns thriving here. Depending on the season, look for mushrooms or wildflowers in the lush landscape. Wildflowers you may see include coral-bells, Ithuriel's spear, miner's lettuce, and woodland madia. Cross the creek over a bridge and continue on the other side.

Notice that the creek will pick up some speed as you approach the waterfall. At just over one mile, you reach an observation deck framed by madrone providing views of Castle Rock Falls and the surrounding area. The waterfall tumbles over a cliff face into the canyon below. On the opposite cliff, look for rock climbers inching their way up.

Leaving the creek and the forest canopy, the path continues along a steep hillside through chaparral, ascending with some rough spots, but generally easily. It will be hotter here among the manzanita and toyon, as well as more rocky. Look for blooming bush monkey-flower, Indian paintbrush, lupine, winecup clarkia, madia, Chinese houses, sun rose, mariposa lilies, and chamise.

At 1.8 miles, cross a bridge and come to a signed junction 0.2 miles further. Turn right and cross on the east side of Varian Peak. Wildflowers on the hills may include California buttercups, red maids, and Indian paintbrush.

Your views across ridges and deep valleys out to Monterey Bay and beyond will be wonderful as you climb this steep, narrow trail. In places, you will scramble over rocks. In one place, you will cling to a handhold to help you negotiate some narrow steps carved into the cliff. Don't worry, the trail will get easier soon. At the Ridge Trail junction, turn right.

At the next junction, go left and soon arrive at the interpretive exhibit and some benches. Find Goat Rock Trail and follow it to Goat Rock, another sandstone formation with interesting weathering patterns. Chances are good that someone will be climbing here. Take the trail around to explore the other side of the formation.

Return to the Ridge Trail, turn right, and head back to the Saratoga Gap Trail, where you will turn left to hike the final 0.4 miles to the trailhead.

Directions: From Highway 92, take Highway 35 south. Pass the junction with Highway 9, heading south on Highway 35 for 2.6 miles further to the Castle Rock State Park parking lot on the right. There is an entrance fee.

57. Moses Spring Trail

EFFORT:...Minimal
LENGTH:..1.8 or 2.0 miles
GEOLOGICAL FEATURE(S):.................Fault Activity, Erosional Features
LOCATION:...Pinnacles National Monument

Description: Pinnacles National Monument is a little different from most parks. The park road does not go through from one side to the other, so you have to choose which entrance you want for the day. If you have the inclination, you can walk about four miles between the Bear Gulch Visitor Center on the east side and the Chaparral Entrance on the west side.

The two sides are like twin parks or parallel universes. They both have lots of amusing boulders and a set of caves. They both have a peaks trail, a wilderness trail, and a canyon trail. They both have visitor centers and approximately the same flora, fauna, and geology. But they also have differences. There is more surface water on the east side where our trail will turn up a natural spring and a reservoir. On the west side, there are more dramatic cliffs. We are going to hike the two cave trails in the park, and have some fun climbing through the rocks.

Because the geologic history of the park is the same for both of the trails, we will describe it only once, here.

The "pinnacles" are the weathered remnants of an ancient volcano that used to be located in the Mojave Desert about 200 miles away. Over the last 23 million years, the pinnacles have been traveling north from southern California to their current position, as the Pacific Plate moved along the San Andreas Fault. A similar phenomenon has been described at Bodega Bay, where the granite rocks of Bodega Head are in no way related to the Franciscan Complex on the east side of the San Andreas Fault. These granites are similar in composition to rocks found far to the south in the Tehachapi Mountains or even Baja California. Anomalies like the Pinnacles and Bodega Head are some of the most observable evidence we have for the speed and direction of plate movement along this dynamic boundary. Today, the monument is moving an average of one inch per year northward.

The result of this extraordinary activity is an area of intriguing rock formations for all levels of hikers to marvel at. Geologists theorize that this mountain once stood nearly a mile higher than 3,304-foot high North Chalone Peak, the highest point in the park today. Long-term erosion has broken it down to the craggy surface features which remain. Some day, even less of the old volcano will have moved further north.

The original bedrock here was granite. Look closely and you may see pieces of the granite caught up in the overlying rhyolite, as xenoliths. Also look for a light green pumice tuff, formed from volcanic ash, separating the granite from the rhyolite and occurring sporadically elsewhere. In the park are examples of several volcanic rock types, including perlite (a rhyolitic volcanic glass), rhyolite, dacite, and andesite. About 60 percent of the rocks in the monument are breccia, a conglomerate of chunks of rhyolite which can be clearly seen embedded in the mass.

Even on this easy hike, make sure you bring water, especially in summer, and be prepared for cave temperatures between 50 to 60 degrees, regardless of the outside temperature. Bring flashlights to explore the water-sculpted caves, the most visited attraction at Pinnacles. This area floods during heavy rains, so the trail is not always open.

From the parking area, find the trailhead for Moses Spring Trail to the south. You will reach a fork at 0.2 miles, the High Peaks Trail heads off to the right. We will be going left and looping back around to this junction.

You will walk along a creek and on some moss-covered stones, which can be slippery. The most likely wildlife you will see will be lizards scampering over the rocks, but there are rattlesnakes, bobcats, and even mountain lions in the park. We saw none of these predators. Trees near the water sources include live oak, buckeye, and sycamore. Blue oaks grow on hillsides, and in the drier areas, you will find chaparral plants like chamise, buckbrush, and manzanita.

After passing into the Little Pinnacles area, you will go through the caves on Bear Gulch Cave Trail, leaving Moses Spring Trail, which runs alongside the caves. The Bear Gulch Cave is 0.4 miles long, and not technically a cave, but rather a pocket created in a canyon where rocks have fallen and enclosed spaces beneath them. There is a bit of rock climbing required, but it is easily accomplished by most folks. If it's early spring, water will be dripping down the walls along this trail. Look for frogs and bats in the caves. The bats will begin to stir at dusk.

After exploring the cave, emerge on a path to Bear Gulch Reservoir, which is the far point of the trail and a spot to consider having lunch. You can choose to return the same way you came out for a 1.8-mile hike, or catch the Chalone Peak Trail on its way north from here to make a 2-mile loop. You can also stay on Moses Spring Trail on the return, avoiding the caves, and passing beside Moses Spring.

If you take Chalone Peak Trail back, head north on it to a junction with High Peaks Trail and turn right. Make your way 0.3 miles further to the previously encountered junction, and turn left to reach the trailhead.

Directions: For this hike, you will want to enter the park at the east entrance. There is no road linking the east and west entrances of the park. From King City on U.S. 101, take the First Street exit, heading east. Turn onto Highway G13/Bitterwater Road, and go 15 miles to Highway 25. Go 14 miles to Highway 146 West, and proceed 5 miles to the Bear Gulch Visitor Center, and then to the end of the road to the trailhead. An entrance fee is charged. There are restrooms, picnic tables, and water at the parking area.

Pinnacles National Monument *(Courtesy National Park Service)*

58. Balconies Cliffs and Caves

EFFORT:..Minimal
LENGTH:...2.4 miles
GEOLOGICAL FEATURE(S):......Fault Activity, Erosional Features, Caves
LOCATION:...Pinnacles National Monument

Description: For a description of Pinnacles fascinating geologic history, please see the previous hike, Moses Spring Trail.

This trail will take you past imposing boulders with close-up views of the dramatic Balconies Cliffs, and then will take you through some tight, dark places in Balconies Caves. Bring a flashlight to explore the caves, which include some completely dark chambers. There is water flowing through at certain times of the year, and if the water level is high, the caves may be closed. With its many tall cliffs, like the 700-foot high

Machete Ridge, this side of the park is popular with rock climbers, and you are likely to see them on your hike.

Although the trail is an easy hike, the cave portion of this route requires rock scrambling and may pose a challenge to some people.

Find the trailhead on the east side of the parking lot. Walk on the obvious path bounded by a split-rail fence to a fork and a map. Right is the Juniper Canyon Trail. Go left on the Balconies Trail.

Proceed on a wide, level gravel and dirt path, passing numbered posts.

The numbers correspond to a trail brochure that was being rewritten during our visit in May, 2002. Since the numbers and their descriptions will probably have changed somewhat with the revision, we will not reference the old brochure.

The fence ends shortly after the trail begins and your views of the pinnacles get better as you approach Balconies Cliffs. After post #3, you'll cross a wooden footbridge, the first of several, passing over the west fork of Chalone Creek, which was dry during our mid-May visit.

After the second bridge, you will reach the impressive boulders that will accompany you all along this trail. Stop and look at the rock closely and you will see immediately that it is composed of lots of different smaller rocks cemented together. This is pyroclastic breccia. The "cement" holding all these bits of rock together is the hardened volcanic ash from an ancient mud-flow, and the primary rock is rhyolite (which you can recognize because of its distinctive pinkish color). The size of the individual boulders is impressive. Imagine the force and energy involved in moving rocks that size. The sound alone would have been deafening as the massive boulders churned together in a river of mud. As the energy eventually dissipated from the moving river of rock, the mudflow slowed to a standstill, hardened, and was finally buried by more sediment and more mudflows, eventually becoming the rock you see before you today.

The trail becomes shaded as you are regaled by the chirping of cicadas and you get your first glimpse of the sheer wall of the Balconies Cliffs. If there are climbers on the face of the cliff, you should be able to spot them fairly easily, even without binoculars.

Start downhill under two large boulders creating an archway, and cross a couple more bridges and a climbers access trail going right. After 0.6 miles, you come to a junction just across one of the bridges. You can go either way at this point, as this is the beginning of a loop, but we recommend going left. There seem to be fewer uphill stretches in that direction, or at least no long uphill climbs. Also, if you are following the interpretive brochure, the numbers go clockwise.

Go left on Balconies Cliffs Trail and begin climbing up towards the Cliffs. The climb is not strenuous, but there are sections of open sun, so a hat would be helpful. Balconies Cliffs are a sheer wall of pinkish rock (the breccia) with black stripes of manganese oxide fairly regularly spaced along the face. You can see why this location is popular with rock climbers given the vertical pitch of the wall.

Make a hairpin turn and head away from the cliff as you continue climbing. It was on this stretch of the trail that we saw our first butterfly Mariposa lilies in bloom. There were just a handful of these delicate beauties at first, but we saw a few dozen on the upper portions of the Balconies Cliffs Trail. There were, in fact, many kinds of wildflowers blooming along our trail. We saw California goosefoot, suncups, wind poppies, clarkia, the brilliant red cobweb thistles, Chinese houses, Douglas wallflowers, gray mule ears, bush poppies, and shooting stars.

While we are talking about non-geology attractions, we may as well mention the fauna we glimpsed on our walk. Most happily, we saw a family of California quail with five newly hatched chicks, tumbling through the grass trying to keep up with their parents. We saw hawks in the sky above and lizards in the rocks below, and a plenitude of butterflies, including several swallowtails. Both scrub jays and Steller's jays made appearances in this somewhat mixed ecosystem that includes coast live oak, California buckeye, chamise, buckbrush, manzanita, and gray pine. We also saw a rattlesnake, so be on the lookout.

The trail is routed roughly along the base of Balconies Cliffs where it begins to descend to a 3-way trail junction, reached after 1.4 miles. The Old Pinnacles Trail comes in from the left. Continue straight onto the Balconies Caves Trail.

Although the geology doesn't change along this section, the trail

One-Eye Charley

Born Charlotte Parkhurst in 1812, Charley disguised herself as a boy when she ran away from an orphanage. Life as a man had its appeal for Charley. She kept up the disguise for the rest of her life. At first she worked as a stable boy and then came out west in 1851 and became a stagecoach driver on a route from San Jose to Santa Cruz. Highwaymen and narrow mountain roads were among the hazards that had to be dealt with by drivers (whips). Charley lost an eye during an incident with a horse and wore a patch from then on. She drank, smoked cigars, chewed tobacco, and became the first woman to vote in a presidential election in 1868, an event commemorated by a plaque in Soquel.

At one point, Charley got pregnant and lost the baby in childbirth, so apparently not everybody thought she was a man. Charley retired in the 1860s, ran a saloon for a while, then raised chickens. She died of mouth cancer in 1879, and it was revealed to the world in the Watsonville Pajaronian that one of the toughest and best whips of the day had been a female.

experience certainly does. Pass beside a breccia wall on your right side to the entrance to the caves, marked with a heavy metal gate. This is a good time to locate your flashlight. You'll need it because shortly after you pass into the cave, daylight disappears entirely.

Like the Bear Gulch Cave on the east side of the monument, this is not actually a cave, in the true sense of the term. It is instead a rock-choked canyon, or talus passage, where pockets have been created between and under fallen rocks. In this case, the rocks have been packed in so tightly that the light is completely blocked out. You will be surprised at how completely dark it is. Be very careful in the chambers, as they are sometimes low and tight. Move slowly and watch where you are going. The path through the cave is easy to spot, but requires some scrambling and rock climbing towards the end where you climb up and out. Since the rock climbing portion is near the exit where some light enters, you can put your flashlight away to free up your hands for climbing. The dark portion of this stretch of trail is quite short, just long enough to give you a sense of adventure without a fright.

After climbing out of the cave, proceed through a two-foot wide slot between rock walls. Within this narrow chasm, several boulders are caught where they fell. You will be ducking beneath them. One enormous boulder was too large to fall between the walls, so it forms a sort of roof across them. Exit through another metal gate and squeeze between the boulders on the left. This completes the cave experience and you will emerge back on the flat Balconies Trail.

Soon you will arrive at the loop junction. Continue straight to finish out the 0.6-mile return to the parking area on the Balconies Trail.

Directions: This trail is in the west section of the monument, and there is no road between the east and west, so you will need to enter via Highway 146. From Salinas on Highway 101, go 22 miles south to Soledad, and take the Highway 146 (Front Street) exit. Drive through town, turning right on East Street to stay on Highway 146. Turn right again on Metz Road and follow it out of town. Where Metz Road continues on to King City, turn left to stay on Highway 146. Drive east 11 more miles on Highway 146 to enter the monument. The road becomes one-lane with a lot of ups and downs, but is paved all the way. It is also an extremely beautiful drive in the spring past hillside vineyards and through vigorous chaparral.

Stop at the ranger station to pay the entrance fee, and then pull ahead to the parking lot. There are picnic tables, restrooms, and water. The ranger station is also a small visitor center with information about the flora, fauna, and geology of the park.

59. Old Cove Landing Trail

EFFORT:	...........................Minimal
LENGTH:	.........................3.0 miles
GEOLOGICAL FEATURE(S):	.............Erosional Features
LOCATION:	......Wilder Ranch State Historic Park

Description: This former dairy land became a state park in 1974, and is now 6,000 acres, 900 of which are under cultivation. It contains a historic site where ships came in during the last half of the nineteenth century to load lumber. Another curiosity of this park is that it is a Brussels sprouts farm, producing 12 percent of the U.S. crop. Wilder Beach is a preserve for nesting snowy plovers, so the park serves a variety of purposes.

Our trail is an excellent coastal walk with views of a seal rookery, interesting pocket beaches, and the historic cove. We found ourselves stopping often to admire our surroundings, so allow more time than you might usually for a 3-mile walk. Even if you aren't interested in the geology (nah!), you will find plenty to recommend this trail.

Begin on an old ranch road at the edge of the parking lot. It is signed "Nature Trail" in some places. Be advised that this is a popular bicycle trail, so be aware of oncoming two-wheelers. Cross over some railroad tracks and head towards the ocean on a wide, easy trail. On your left is a marsh area that is off limits to visiting humans. On the right is a field sometimes planted with brussels sprouts.

At 0.6 miles you will be next to Wilder Beach to the left where there are numerous wading birds poking about for a meal. There is a viewing deck here and a bench. This will be your first good view of the ocean. It was here that we encountered a bobcat on the trail. It did not seem afraid of us, and let us take its picture. Seeing wild animals is always one of the highlights of a hike, so we were satisfied with our choice of trail on this sunny January day.

In addition to the bobcat, we saw several squirrels, brown pelicans, seagulls, and red-winged blackbirds.

At 0.7 miles out, you come to a spur trail to the left that leads out onto a narrow stretch of land that drops off steeply on either side. Unless you suffer from vertigo, take this path and stand at the end looking back at the eroded cliff faces of the coast. This vantage point offers a good view of the vertical mudstone and sandstone beds and their blocky joint patterns. This also gives us a good stopping point to discuss the composition of the local bedrock.

142

Old Cove Landing Trail

particles of the stone together. This makes a fairly strong and hard sedimentary rock, but the formation is highly fractured and faulted. The various layers were deposited at different times and differ in composition, which also affects the erosion process. Some layers are more resistant than others.

Return to the trail and continue until you get to another footpath leading beachward. If you want to get away momentarily from the bicycles and get closer to the beach, you can take this trail and make your way parallel to the main trail closer to the edge of the cliff.

You are standing on a formation known as the Santa Cruz Mudstone, a Miocene sedimentary deposit. It is composed of fine-grained silts and clays, washed to the sea by streams, and the shells (frustules) of diatoms, common one-celled marine plants. You're familiar with diatoms in the form of diatomaceous earth, but the tiny organisms are also used for make-up (blusher) and in some tooth-whitening products. The shells are made of silica, which forms a sort of glass when subjected to heat and pressure during the rock-forming process. This "melted" silica becomes the cement that binds the

Among the interesting sights along this trail are the numerous rocky shelves, or shore platforms, which jut out into the waves. They are nearly flat on top, so that when the waves crash over them, they leave a foamy runoff that looks like a carpet of snow at first, and then like a lovely waterfall as the water runs off the flat surface back to the ocean. One of the best places to view these platforms is at the end of our trail between Fern Grotto Beach and Sand Plant Beach. These black fingers are the more resistant layers of chert, above which the softer siltstone layers have been eroded away by wave action.

As you follow the main path again, you will have produce growing on your right. When we were there, red and green Swiss chard were flourishing. At 1.2 miles, you will come to Fern Grotto Beach. A steep dirt trail leads down to it beside a small rivulet running in a rocky channel. At the bottom, duck under or climb over the fallen tree and you are on the beach. To your right is the fern grotto, a sea cave where ferns grow from the ceiling and sides, and water drips through the joints in the sandstone.

Notice that you are standing in a deep recess in the sea cliff. One of the things that creates such interest along a coastline is the lack of homogenous erosion. Wherever the waves hit the land, erosion occurs. But it occurs at varying rates. Right here, the land has eroded further in than the cliffs on either side of us. Where there are faults and fractures in the bedrock, areas of weakness may occur. A surge channel then forms where the waves attack that area, and eventually, the channels deepen and widen, carving out a little inlet or fern grotto.

The beach here is perfect for a picnic. And if you want to make this the end of your hike, the total trip is 2.5 miles. We suggest pushing on just a short distance, however, for some gorgeous views of the surf. Climb back up to the main trail and continue just up and around the next bend. There you will come upon Sand Plant Beach, which you can recognize by the marshy looking area at its back. Just admire the view here. Descend to the beach if you wish. The trail has now become the Ohlone Bluff Trail as it continues north.

The trail back is the same trail you came in by. If you want to go further, you can continue on the Ohlone Bluff Trail for as long as you like before turning back.

Directions: Heading north on Highway 1 from Santa Cruz, go four miles to the Wilder Ranch State Park turnoff on the ocean side of the highway. Go to the end of the road and park in the lot. You will see the trailhead with a sign reading "Nature Trail" on the southwest side of the lot. To avoid the day-use fee, you can park along Highway 1 just before the park entrance. Restrooms are available.

60. Point Lobos Trails

EFFORT:	Minimal
LENGTH:	4.0 miles
GEOLOGICAL FEATURE(S):	Erosional Features
LOCATION:	Point Lobos State Reserve

Description: Point Lobos is well known as one of the most beautiful spots on the Pacific coastline, and it is a well-deserved reputation. In addition to gorgeous scenery, it is also replete with interesting geology characteristic of the continental edge. Its human history includes Ohlone Indians, whalers, and Chinese fishermen. Some evidence of these occupations can be seen on the trails and in the park museum. One of the biggest draws in the park is its grove of Monterey cypress. This is one of only two places in the world that these interesting trees grow naturally. Give yourself several hours to explore this park. It is quite small, but you will want to take your time to enjoy all it has to offer.

You can start this trail at any of the parking areas from Cypress Grove to Bird Island. We will describe it starting at Bird Island, the south end of the road. Wherever you begin, the trail simply hugs the coastline going north or south.

Pick up the Bird Island Trail and go south through sparse tree cover along the bluff overlooking the ocean. As you round a bend and head east, you will suddenly come upon your first view of China Cove, perhaps the most beautiful little beach you will ever see. The water is an incredible shade of azure blue and the sand on the idyllic beach is a creamy white. On the far side of the cove, you can see an archway punched into the rock wall. Framed between branches of cypress along the trail, you could not dream up a more attractive scene. If you are here when wildflowers are in bloom, so much the better, but this spot is beautiful all year round.

The trail loops around the cliff edge above this beach leading to a long wooden staircase, which will take you down if you want to detour. Otherwise, continue on the trail around the cove and out towards a trail junction. The left arm goes around to a staircase down to Gibson Beach, another lovely white sand beach, and another possible detour. For our route, go right towards Bird Island through a channel with poison oak on either side. Stay to the center of the trail to avoid the poison oak.

As you head west with Gibson Beach on your left, you will come upon several more natural arches in the surf at the edges of China Cove and the rocky outcrops on the near side of Bird Island. This cluster of arches punched out of the granite is our first significant geology stop on this trail. Arches like these occur when a place of weakness, such as a fault or crack, meets a powerful erosive force. The wave action gradually breaks the rock down, carving out a hole. As the erosion continues, the hole widens into a larger and larger arch, thinning the top span until one day it collapses under its own weight. The pillars remaining are called sea stacks. On this section of trail, looking back towards shore, you will see a sea cave. The same process is at work creating that feature. Some sea caves will eventually become arches.

At a trail fork, go either direction to begin a short loop between Bird Island and China Cove.

The large, light brown colored island directly offshore is Bird Island. In spring, flocks of Brandt's cormorants gather there to nest. In winter, you will probably see just a few seagulls occupying the island. Look for lounging harbor seals on the rocks, and throughout your stay in this park, watch for sea otters floating on their backs near shore. We saw three on our visit. Binoculars will come in handy here. Quite a few visitors claimed to see great congregations of sea otters bobbing in the surf, but a look through the lenses correctly identified the debris as logs

and kelp. Binoculars will also come in handy to scour the ocean for signs of passing gray whales between December and May.

In one particular spot, close to the loop beginning, with a good view of several arches, if you look at the exposed cliff face nearby, facing seaward, you will see abalone shells protruding from the top soil layer. This is nothing to do with geology, but it is interesting. The Ohlone Indians camped here and fished for plentiful abalone, tossing the shells into mounds. As you walk this and the next section of trail, you will no doubt notice the numerous shell fragments at your feet. These are the remains of some tasty prehistoric barbecues.

After closing the loop, return past China Cove back to the parking area, completing the first mile of the trip. Continue straight through the parking lot and rejoin the trail on the north side. Now you are on the South Shore Trail, which hugs the coastline going north around some treacherously eroded inlets to Hidden Beach and Weston Beach. In one spot, the trail is an exposure of sandstone sandwiching a rough conglomerate, the three beds distinctly visible. This conglomerate, formed of rounded stones, is known as the Carmelo Formation and originated in an underwater canyon about 39 million years ago. It is the dominate rock type at Hidden Beach.

Even more fascinating bedding is coming up. At Weston Beach, the sedimentary rock has weathered into some intriguingly colorful banded surfaces. The layers of rock are highly differentiated. Each layer represents a particular type of depositional environment. The fine-grained sandstone and shale are made of material deposited under fairly gentle conditions, while the coarser gravels represent a more violent episode of nature, such as a storm event.

There are many geologically interesting spots along this trail, indicative of the rather complicated history of the Pacific coastline. The next important stop is at Sand Hill Cove. Here you will see a yellowish sandstone full of potholes and deeply eroded into smooth bowls and ridges, providing natural settings for tidepools. Be careful as you walk on this rock; it is very slippery close to the surf, and there are many small creatures living on the surface of potential stepping stones. Potholes like those found here are formed by the circular motion of water, carrying stones which grind into the rock, swirling around as they go.

Continuing north on the trail, you will climb up to finish the South Shore Trail at its junction with Sand Hill Trail. Turn left here and head towards Sea Lion Cove. On windy days, the brown pelicans will float by

like hang gliders in their mysteriously graceful fashion. Soon you will hear the barking of California sea lions as you approach a junction with Sea Lion Point Trail. You can detour to the left to follow it out to a view of Sea Lion Rocks, or continue inland to the right to the Cypress Grove parking area.

Cross through the parking area to find the Cypress Grove Trail, which is a 0.8 mile loop of the magnificent Monterey cypress trees, and the last trail on our tour. Head out a short distance to a fork. Bear left and enter the cypress grove. Flowers to watch for include the sticky monkey-flower, blue blossom, lizard tail, and star zigadene. We spotted a single purple iris blooming in the grove in January. You will walk among the trees for a short distance before emerging again at the rugged coastline. Walk around Pinnacle Cove where you will notice the coarse granite that is the other dominant rock type in the park. This is the Santa Lucia Formation and may surprise you, looking more like something you would find in the Sierra Nevadas than the California coast.

Continue around the headlands over a rocky trail and back into the cypress grove. Soon you reach a short spur trail leading left. Go ahead and take that out to North Point for a nice view of Cypress Cove and the bay. Return to the main trail and go straight to close out the loop.

Continue straight to the Cypress Grove parking lot.

From here, retrace your steps on the Sea Lion Point Trail, Sand Hill Trail, and South Shore Trail to return to the Bird Island parking area and the end of a roughly four-mile hike, depending on your side trips. No doubt you will have taken a few.

Directions: From Monterey, go south on Highway 1 for six miles. Turn into the park on the right side of the highway.

Proceed through the entrance kiosk and park where you can. Parking is difficult to find in this park, especially on weekends. Most of the time, you will see cars lined up along Highway 1 outside the entrance due to lack of parking inside. If necessary, you can park outside and walk in. Parking is easiest to find the further into the park you go. There is a fee. Restrooms, picnic tables, and water are available at several locations.

61. Limekiln Trail

EFFORT:..Minimal
LENGTH:...1.8 miles
GEOLOGICAL   FEATURE(S):..Mining
LOCATION:..Limekiln Creek State Park

Description: Named for the late nineteenth-century limekiln operation, this park offers beachfront, redwoods, deep canyons, and a bit of California history. There is only one trail in the park—this short trek to the kilns, which starts at the campground and takes you through Limekiln Canyon.

You will follow the West Fork Creek and cross three bridges, passing a small waterfall along the way. The first bridge takes you over Hare Creek. The second is over Limekiln Creek. The trail bears left from here. But wait, there's a bonus for insiders. Just after the second bridge, you will find an unmarked spur trail to the right along Limekiln Creek. This path will take you to the 100-foot tall Limekiln Falls in less than half a mile with a little boulder hopping along the way. The waterfall is split by a knob at the top and drops like Rapunzel's tresses over a sheer limestone cliff to the rocky gorge below. The side trip is well worth it.

When you are ready, return to the main trail and continue.

At the end of the trail stand four large kilns at the base of a limestone deposit. The lime produced here was used to make cement and limestone bricks in the 1880s. The lime was put in wooden barrels and taken by wagon to the harbor at Rockland Landing to be transported to San Francisco and Monterey by ship. There is very little limestone in California, so this deposit was a rare and valuable commodity.

The kilns stand tall and dark amid the redwoods and encroaching underbrush. They are made of pieces of now-rusted steel riveted together to form the round ovens. One of them has a large stone base. They are hollow and each has an opening near the base which is lined on the inside with brick. The lime was removed from this opening.

The limestone, calcium carbonate, was placed into the ovens, along with wood for fuel, and the lime "cooked" out of them. Redwood provides excellent fuel for this purpose, since it burns long and steady. The heat from the fire burns carbon out of the rock, leaving lime powder (calcium oxide) behind.

These kilns were built and operated by the Rockland Lime and Lumber company. It was not unusual for a lumber company to make lime as well, or for the two industries to coexist. The by-product wood from the lumbering business was used to fuel the kilns.

Return the way you came and lunch at the picnic area near the park entrance.

Directions: From Carmel, travel south on Highway 1 about 55 miles to the signed park entrance. Park in the day-use lot just past the entrance kiosk. There is a fee.

62. Nipomo Dunes

EFFORT:..Minimal
LENGTH:...2.2 miles
GEOLOGICAL FEATURE(S):..............................Dunes
LOCATION:.......................Guadalupe-Nipomo Dunes Preserve

Description: The Nipomo Dunes cover a vast 18 miles of coast in Central California. The complex contains the largest single dune in the western U.S., Mussel Rock Dune, 500 feet high. Some of this accumulated sand is very old, going back 18,000 years to the Pleistocene ice age. Huge amounts of sediment eroded off of the Santa Lucia Mountains and were deposited along this coast, eventually being blown, grain by grain, inland. Over time, vegetation took hold and created a somewhat more stable environment, though it is still fragile. Many of the plants living on the dunes are rare or endangered. The Nipomo Mesa lupine, in particular, grows nowhere else, and only a few are found here.

Because of the mix of saltwater, freshwater lakes, and brackish waters between, this is a good place to do some bird watching. Some of the birds are passing through on their annual migration routes, and some live here year-round.

This trail takes you over wooden boardwalks across Oso Flaco Lake to the beach. The walkways are here to allow visitors access to the dunes without harming them. Do not venture off the trail. Not only is the plant life tenuous here, but many birds lay eggs in the dunes. Start off through tree cover from the parking lot towards the lake, which you will reach in 0.2 miles. Head left across a bridge to the west side of the lake.

On the other side of the bridge, the trail becomes a boardwalk through the dunes, where lupine may be blooming among the coastal scrub. At a junction with a trail going left, continue on the board-walk, right. The boardwalk deposits

you at the beach after a tad over one mile.

From here, you can find your own entertainment in the sand and surf until you are ready to return.

Directions: From Highway 1 in Guadalupe, go north to Oso Flaco Lake Road and turn west. Proceed 3 miles to the parking lot. There is a fee.

The Great Valley is a vast alluvial plain making up the fertile interior of California. It is 400 miles long and up to 50 miles wide, flanked on the west by the Coast Ranges and on the east by the Sierra Nevadas, both of which offer up their rainfall and snow melt to the valley. Most of that water eventually converges into the San Joaquin Delta system and flows out to the Pacific Ocean through the San Francisco Bay. These complex water systems create many tule-lined sloughs and marshes that teem with wildlife. Once, vast herds of elk and antelope ranged in the valley. These are now gone, except for a few protected enclaves, but the waterways still provide essential habitats for huge numbers of migratory birds.

Topographically, the valley is basically flat, ranging in elevation from below sea level to 400 feet high, with a couple of tall exceptions—the Sutter Buttes north of Sacramento, and the Kettleman, Elk, and Buena Vista Hills in the southern region of the valley.

Geologically, the story of the valley is a story of sediment, thousands of feet of it. During glaciation in the nearby Sierra Nevadas, huge amounts of sediment accumulated at the base of the glaciers. As the glaciers melted, rivers flowed through them, carrying the sediment as glacial out-wash into the trough of the Great Valley.

Beneath the Cenozoic alluvium there is even more sediment and sedimentary rock, deposited from seas and lakes that covered the Great Valley in the geologic past. It is easy to imagine how sediment filled the trough that was the Great Valley. But how did it become a trough in the first place? The answer, of course, lies in plate tectonics.

Beginning in the Cretaceous, when the Pacific Plate began to subduct under the North American Plate, the Great Valley basin began to form landward of the subduction zone. Between the basin and the subduction zone was a topographically high area, the crumpled rocks of the leading edge of the continental margin. Sediment from this highland was carried into the basin by turbid currents and landslides. The basin subsided slowly under the weight of more and more sediment filling the great trough. The depth of these Great Valley sediments is unknown but estimated to be as much as 40,000 feet.

During the Eocene, immense lakes covered the valley, the largest of which was Lake Corcoran in the western valley. This lake left a formation called the Corcoran Clay, consisting of fine clays, volcanic ash, and diatomite, which covers 5,000 square miles of the San Joaquin Valley today. The seas withdrew by the end of the Pliocene. Those of us who live in the valley are frequently reminded of the watery history of the area by the many mollusk shells found in our gardens.

All of this sediment has provided one of the most fertile agricultural areas in the world, and much of the valley is devoted to farming. Possibly the most geoeconomically significant fact about the valley is that it contains rich oil and gas fields formed from ancient marine deposits at its southern extremities. Significant petroleum deposits are located in the Kettleman Hills, Elk Hills, Wheeler Ridge, Lost Hills, and Buena Vista Hills.

Because of the flat, featureless landscape, there are not a lot of hiking opportunities in the valley catering to our theme. After all, we are not going to take you walking through an asparagus field to look at the peat dirt. There are very good wildlife trails, especially birding, but the geology trails are anomalies. One of the few places here that meets the criteria, in fact, is the Sutter Buttes, the most pronounced anomaly in the Valley. However, there is one place in this province of supreme geologic importance, the Carrizo Plain, which offers two fascinating trails.

Trails of the Great Valley:

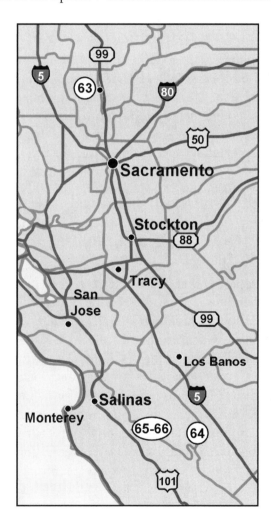

63. Sutter Buttes

EFFORT:	Varies
LENGTH:	Varies
GEOLOGICAL FEATURE(S):	Volcanism
LOCATION:	Sutter Buttes

Description: You can't help but notice them, whether you're driving along Interstate 5 north of Sacramento or looking at a topographical map of California. Rising up from the flat valley floor is a small group of curious mountain peaks, looking mysterious and misplaced. The Sutter Buttes, which show up as a prominent bump on the smooth valley floor, have been nicknamed "the smallest mountain range in the world." They are unquestionably of volcanic origin, but their genealogy has not been firmly established. Some scientists have proposed that this volcano is the southernmost feature of the Cascade Range. Others consider it an isolated, anomalous event, primarily because it does not much resemble the larger and younger Cascade stratovolcanoes, and also because there was no continuing volcanic activity after its eruptions in the Pleistocene, about 1.5 million years ago. Several peaks, North Butte, West Butte, South Butte, and Twin Peaks, to name a few, rise to a maximum height of 2,117 feet (South Butte). The buttes cover an area of 75 square miles, 10 miles across, and are composed of andesite, dacite, and rhyolite.

The native Maidu Indians appropriately named this unusual and sacred place "Histum Yani," or Middle Mountains of the Valley. Their grinding holes can be found here in the andesite. Their legends identify this place as the origin of the first man and woman, and as the resting place for their spirits after death. The buttes have had various names since the Maidu. The first European to name them, Luis Arguello of Spain, called them "Los Picachos," the peaks. They have also been known as the Marysville Buttes, Sacramento Buttes, and Los Tres Picos. In 1849, they became Sutter Buttes, renamed after John Sutter in the year after gold was discovered at his sawmill.

Almost all of the land is privately owned, and permission must be obtained for hiking there. Because of this, most people gaze over at the oddity while driving through the valley, never getting a closer look. Also because of this, the early European history of the place has been preserved, and the wild character of the land has been maintained. It is primarily grassland and oak woodland, similar to the Diablo Range in surface character, hot and dry in summer, and green, blooming, and inviting in spring. Wild animals that live on the hills include several species of bats, lizards, ringtails, feral pigs, rattlesnakes, turkey vultures, and golden eagles.

There are historic homesteads in the canyons, valleys, and on the peaks—corrals, barns, schools, pioneer cemeteries, and other remnants of early settlers. The land is used for cattle and sheep ranching these days, as it has been since the first European settlers came. Because of the unusual circumstances of hiking this land, we are departing somewhat from our customary trail description. To experience the buttes, you will probably do so as part of a guided tour, so we are providing tour information instead. Other groups, such as student researchers, are accommodated by some of the landowners as the need arises.

Tours are led in spring and fall by the non-profit Middle Mountain Foundation, which gives a share of the hiking fees to the landowners. Only 15 people are allowed on each guided hike, and they are popular and must be reserved. Several of the hikes are day-long events and somewhat strenuous. A "Geology Trek" is one of the conducted hikes, focusing on the natural history of the buttes, but most of the other tours will touch on geology to some extent. The Foundation offers a variety of hiking experiences, including a full-moon evening stroll, a bat research trip, and others.

Directions: Call the Middle Mountain Foundation at (530) 671-6116 to make reservations for guided hikes. Visit their web site at http://www.middlemountain.org for a description of the hikes offered.

64. Joaquin Rocks Trail

EFFORT:..Moderate
LENGTH:..9.0 miles
GEOLOGICAL FEATURE(S):.....................Erosional Features
LOCATION:.............................Clear Creek Management Area

Description: The Joaquin Rocks are intriguing 300-foot high sandstone monoliths in a remote area on the west side of the San Joaquin Valley, visible from Interstate 5. This trail takes you to the base of those rocks and through a very special environment. A huge expanse of public land administered by the Bureau of Land Management comprises a rugged and wild recreation area in the middle of California. The Tumey Hills (23,000

Robin Hood of the El Dorado

Although he did not give his spoils to the poor, one of the more magnanimous nicknames for the outlaw Joaquin Murieta was "the Robin Hood of the El Dorado." The name emerged because of rumors that Mexicans throughout California gave him shelter as he fled the many lawmen and posses scouring the land for him. He was a ruthless bandit who often targeted Chinese miners, robbing and killing them. He was so feared throughout 1850s California that a special force was commissioned in 1853 to go after him, the California State Rangers.

Murieta apparently started out in California as a miner on the Stanislaus River. By some accounts, he was dispossessed of his claim by white men who beat him and raped and killed his wife. However, there is also a story about his widow holding a religious revival at the base of the Joaquin Rocks some time later. Murieta's identity has always been questionable, as there were apparently several Mexican Joaquins in those days with bad reputations.

The Rangers caught up to Murieta on July 25, 1853 just southwest of present-day Fresno and killed him. To prove that they had accomplished their mission, they cut off his head, preserved it in a jar of alcohol, and displayed it in Stockton, San Francisco, and Mariposa County, asking people who could confirm Murieta's identity to sign affidavits.

Some people still doubted that the right Joaquin was caught, and rumors continued to circulate that he was on the loose. Other stories reported that he had escaped to his native Sonora, Mexico. Whether or not Murieta was actually captured, the reign of terror of California's most nefarious bandito came to an end.

acres), Panoche Hills (35,000 acres), and the Clear Creek Management Area (50,000 acres) make up this playground which attracts hikers, bikers, OHV enthusiasts, hunters, astronomers, rock collectors, and bird watchers. Between the Clear Creek Management Area and I-5 lie the Joaquin Rocks, named for the notorious bandito, Joaquin Murieta, who frequented the area (see inset).

To begin our hike, from the parking area, walk past the gate on the road along the Joaquin Ridge. The landscape is typical oak woodland and bare, rolling hills. In summer, this trail can be unpleasantly hot.

There are numerous old mines in the area remaining from nineteenth century chromium, mercury, and asbestos mining, including the largest mercury mine, New Idria Mine, which operated until the 1970s. Some areas are closed due to mercury and heavy metal contamination. Another hazard to be found here is naturally occurring asbestos. This is probably more of a concern for off-road enthusiasts than those of us on foot, but BLM advises visitors to avoid the area during dry or dusty conditions. Previous asbestos mining has dispersed asbestos fibers into the local environment. Do not drink any of the stream water, as it may contain fibers. Avoid digging or kicking up dust.

The underlying bedrock of these bare hills is the New Idria Formation, a serpentine uplift about 65 million

Clear Creek Management Area *(Courtesy Bureau of Land Management, James Pickering)*

years old. This large, friable mass is the source of the asbestos. As we have seen in other serpentine environments, the unique soils create a distinct ecosystem which harbors specialized and rare plants. The threatened San Benito evening primrose is found here, and Brewer's clarkia, coast morning glory, and the talus fritillaria. The nearby San Benito Mountain Research Natural Area protects the unusual plant community, and is the only place in the world where the Jeffrey pine, foothill pine, coulter pine, and incense cedar grow together. Rare animals can be found around Clear Creek also, including the southwestern pond turtle, the two-striped garter snake, the foothill yellow-legged frog, the big-eared kangaroo rat, and the prairie falcon. You might also see more common animals, such as deer, bobcats, and raccoons.

In addition, this area is quite a draw for rockhounds. Over 150 different semi-precious minerals occur here, including the California state gemstone, the rare benitoite, a phosphorescent blue crystal. The only known commercial deposit of benitoite is mined in the Clear Creek area. Other minerals collected here include serpentine, jadeite, cinnabar, tremolite, topazolite, and neptunite. Because this is BLM land, collecting is allowed. Geology, biology, and botany field trips are regularly conducted throughout the area because of its many and varied characteristics. It is also extremely popular with wild pig hunters.

Walking along the ridge road, if you have a clear day, you will have fantastic views to the east, across the valley to the Sierras beyond.

After walking for four miles, you will reach the Joaquin Rocks Trail. Take it and arrive at the base of the sandstone formations in less than a mile. Watch out for poison oak here. If you climb up into the rocks, you may find teeming vernal pools cradled among them, depending on the time of year of your visit. The pools harbor fairy shrimp, algae, and other small organisms.

When you are finished exploring the rocks, return by the same trail.

Directions: Access is through the BLM Clear Creek Management Area, overseen by the Hollister Field Office. From Interstate 5 south of Los Banos, take Panoche Road west to Panoche, about 15 miles, then turn south on New Idria Road for 21 miles to Idria. About four miles further south, you will come to a parking area at Wright Mountain. There are no facilities. Access is free.

65. Painted Rock Trail

EFFORT:..Minimal
LENGTH:...1.3 miles
GEOLOGICAL FEATURE(S):...................................Erosional Features
LOCATION:...Carrizo Plain National Monument

Description: The Carrizo Plain has been regarded as a special place by native peoples for thousands of years, and the Painted Rock outcrop was even more special. As a rocky spot on an arid, flat plain, and as a place directly on the San Andreas Rift Zone, it is not hard to imagine why these rocks are lavishly decorated with pictographs and were considered a place of power to the native Chumash and Yokut people. Today, this land has regained some of its former sacred status.

The 250,000-acre Carrizo Plain Natural Area was established in 1988 to protect habitat and restore the native environment. It is the largest contiguous remnant of the ecosystem that covered most of the Great Valley before it was settled, grazed, and converted to farmland. In January 2001, President Clinton upgraded the Carrizo Plain to a National Monument because of its biological, geological, and cultural importance. California's newest federal parkland is jointly managed by the Bureau of

Land Management, the California Department of Fish and Game, and the Nature Conservancy. The ongoing restoration efforts are designed to protect and reestablish native flora and fauna. Farming and ranching in the 1880s took its toll here, as it did in the rest of the Central Valley. Today, cattle are used to graze on non-native grasses, then removed when the native varieties begin to emerge. It is expected that this practice will encourage the native grasses to eventually dominate.

The Carrizo Plain was formed long ago as the bordering Temblor and Caliente mountains were rising. Fault movement on the San Andreas and San Juan faults caused the land between to sink, forming a closed basin. Runoff from the mountains created a huge lake and filled the basin with rich sediments. Soda Lake, a 3,000-acre playa lake, is what remains of that vast prehistoric sea. It is the centerpiece of a large alkali wetlands environment. In winter, water accumulates in the lake bed. In summer, the water evaporates, leaving behind sulfate and carbonate salts. This process is repeated every year. Birders can take advantage of a boardwalk around the lake to observe the huge flocks of migratory birds stopping here in winter. Thousands of sandhill cranes can be seen, as well as many other types of waterfowl, along the marshy shores of the lake.

Animals that live here year-round include the ground squirrel, rabbit, giant kangaroo rat, San Joaquin kit fox, blunt-nosed leopard lizard, antelope squirrel, burrowing owl, tarantula, California condor, tule elk, pronghorn antelope, and coyote. The elk and antelope living here now were reintroduced. They were hunted to extinction in the area in the late 1800s and early 1900s.

You may spot golden eagles and many other types of raptors, including rough-legged hawks, red-tailed hawks, kestrels, harriers, and ravens. Songbirds are also abundant, including mountain bluebirds, western meadowlarks, and yellow-billed magpies. From March through mid-July, this trail is closed to protect nesting peregrine falcons.

In spring, wildflowers are prolific on the plain, including blankets of baby blue eyes and yellow blooms of locoweed amid fields of native bunchgrass, saltbush, and desert needle grass. The endangered California jewelflower, Hoover's woolly-star, San Joaquin woolly-threads, forked fiddleneck, Carrizo peppergrass, Lost Hills saltbush, and Temblor buckwheat are native to the plain. Many of the plants here, however, are exotic species brought in by settlers from Europe and Asia.

The Carrizo Plain is renowned for its topographical expression of the San Andreas Fault. The fault runs along the eastern side of the plain where you

Painted Rock, (*Courtesy Bureau of Land Management, James Pickering)*

can drive beside it on Elkhorn Road. At Wallace Creek, an exemplary version of a fault offset stream drainage can be observed on the Wallace Creek Interpretive Trail (next hike).

The rugged Caliente Range to the southwest has yielded Miocene fossils of camels, horses, rhinos, and crocodiles, testifying to a very different prehistorical environment. The area is also noted for its oil fields. One of the largest is just east of the Temblor Range near Taft.

The Carrizo Plain is indeed a geologically interesting landmark. Keeping in mind a little about its biological and historical significance will enhance your walk out to the rock formation.

The sandstone Painted Rock outcrop sitting conspicuously on this plain contains 45 distinct paintings.

The paintings were created by different peoples over the last few thousand years, but were done primarily by the Chumash, who are known for their elaborate, multi-colored pictographs. This is one of the most impressive Chumash sites, containing human figures, geometric designs, snakes, seals, turtles, and other animals drawn in black, white, and red lines. Unfortunately, the rock art was badly vandalized in the 1920s, when it was shot up and covered by graffiti. What is still visible, however, is enough to let us appreciate the great cultural heritage of this site.

The rocks form a semicircle and house many nooks for animals. In some places, you will observe rocks blackened by the soot of campfires. A lot of people have probably stopped here over the ages to make camp.

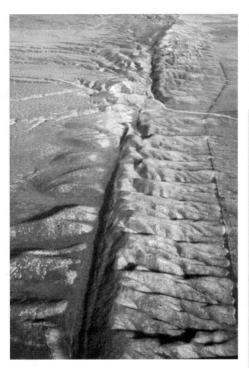

San Andreas Fault on the Carrizo Plain
(Courtesy U.S. Geological Survey)

it approached the ocean, about 20 million years ago. After exploring the rocks and their ancient artwork, return by the same path.

Directions: From Highway 101 in San Luis Obispo, proceed north 8 miles to Highway 58. Go east 52 miles to Soda Lake Road. Turn right and proceed 8 miles to the monument boundary. Drive 7 miles further to reach the Guy L. Goodwin Education Center, where tours to the rocks and the fault can be arranged on weekends in April and May. Proceed another 2.7 miles to the trailhead. Note: The pictograph site is closed during raptor nesting season, March through July 15. There is a restroom at the visitor center. Access is free.

The coarse sandstone originated as sediment deposited in a river delta as

66. Wallace Creek Interpretive Trail

EFFORT:..Minimal
LENGTH:...0.7 miles
GEOLOGICAL FEATURE(S):...............................Fault Activity
LOCATION:.........................Carrizo Plain National Monument

Description: On January 9, 1857, an earthquake with an estimated magnitude of 8.0 occurred just north of the Carrizo Plain. This event, known as the Fort Tejon quake, caused about 30 feet of lateral offset within the Carrizo Plain, and ruptured the surface along the trace of the fault for about 220 miles. It was one of the greatest earthquakes ever recorded in the United States. When people talk about "the big one" in California, this is the type of earthquake they have in mind.

The fault also runs along the base of the Elkhorn Hills, which exhibit many large alluvial fans emerging from the stream mouths. The fault, of course, is the San Andreas.

Wallace Creek offers us the opportunity to observe many typical features of a fault zone laid out by nature in a fashion that could not be improved upon by artifice. This site has been called the best example of fault offset stream drainage in the world.

The trail has numbered posts to correspond to the trail guide. You start out along Wallace Creek, which is dry most of the year. It drains the nearby Temblor Range into the plain. Between posts 1 and 2, the creek bends distinctly, creating an *offset channel*. That is where the fault cuts across it, marking the meeting of the North American and Pacific Plates. The southwest side of the fault is sliding slowly northwest. The northeast side is moving the opposite direction, as we have previously seen. Eventually, this movement drives the two sides of the creek apart, creating the offset, which is currently about 420 feet.

Continue along the fault. You will see evidence of other offset channels as you go, but they are not as obvious as the one on Wallace Creek. At post 5, you come to what geologists call a *beheaded channel*. This is a stream that has been separated from its original source by movement along the fault. There are several such channels along the fault. In some cases, the new channel cuts straight across the fault, telling you that it is younger because it has not been offset.

Scientists have determined that the age of Wallace Creek is 3800 years. By measuring the offset (420 feet), they are able to determine the rate of movement along the fault. Those figures result in an average of 1.3 inches per year. It is important to remember that the movement occurs in sudden jolts, or earthquakes, in response to building pressure, and is not ongoing or even regular. The Fort Tejon earthquake, for instance, created a 30-foot offset at Wallace Creek. This event was witnessed by Spanish travelers.

The nearby Temblor Range with its white cliffs is composed of marine sediments and is less than 2 million years old. You can locate whitish Monterey shale fragments in Wallace Creek that have washed down from that range. The San Andreas fault scarp runs along the base of those mountains.

Directions: From Highway 58 heading east from San Luis Obispo or west from McKittrick and Highway 33, go southwest on 7 Mile Road for 0.2 miles to a junction with an unpaved road. Turn left (south) on this road and drive along the fault to Wallace Creek. On the left side of the road, turn into a small parking area, signed for Wallace Creek. The road is not passable after a storm, but otherwise can be driven by passenger cars.

CHAPTER 6
THE SIERRA NEVADAS

This huge mountain range is the defining feature of eastern California, extending 400 miles north to south, and ranging from 40 to 100 miles wide. It tilts westward and rises to a height of 14,495 feet (Mt. Whitney), the highest point in the continental United States. The mountains are composed primarily of granite, supporting vast forests, hundreds of beautiful lakes, deep canyons, remnants of glaciers, and supreme opportunities for hiking and many other types of recreation.

The eastern side of the range drops off steeply, reflecting the structural tilt of the granite block that forms these mountains. This side is more barren, drier, and harsher than the west because it is in the rain shadow of the Sierra Nevada. Pleistocene ice age glaciers are responsible for many of the features in the range, including Yosemite Valley. There is also visible evidence of volcanism, such as the warm waters of Hot Creek and the basalt columns at Devils Postpile. We will visit both.

On the western side of the range, the mountains descend more gradually, forming an expanse of foothills leading down into the Great Valley. Most of this foothill region is known as the Mother Lode, the mining district that spawned the 1949 Gold Rush. Technically, the Mother Lode is a 120-mile long belt of gold-bearing quartz veins beginning in Mariposa at the southern end and ending at Georgetown in El Dorado County in the north. Many of the gold-bearing veins are found along the major fracture known as the Melones Fault Zone.

As you traverse gold country, you will visit many historic sites, and cross paths with such colorful historical figures as Black Bart, Lola Montez, Lotta Crabtree, Mark Twain, Bret Harte, Kit Carson, and John C. Fremont. In addition to these notables, many ordinary folks made their way to California to find gold or take part in the boom in some other way. Busy towns sprang up all along the hills, including one named after two of the aforementioned figures, Twain Harte. People from around the world settled near the mines, and, in many cases, left abandoned communities when the gold ran out.

Highway 49, a 300-mile long channel through the heart of gold country, was given its number in 1933 in recognition of its location through Gold Rush territory. If you travel this route, you will visit many of the towns established during the Gold Rush. Some, such as tiny Chinese Camp, provide a glimpse into the multicultural composition of 1850s California.

The Sierra Nevada mountains are the result of the same tectonic forces we introduced earlier. The impact of the Pacific Plate slamming into the North American Plate was enormous. The resulting compressive stresses reached deep within the earth from Mexico to Alaska. The stresses began in the Pacific Coast area of California in the Jurassic and culminated in the Rocky Mountains towards the end of the Cretaceous, in a mountain-building event known as the Rocky Mountain Orogeny. Almost all of the geology of California can be related back to this event, and the Sierra Nevada batholith is no exception. Some areas of the western United States were intensely folded. Some areas were faulted with older rocks thrust over and on top of younger rocks. Other areas, such as the Sierra Nevadas, experienced a huge outpouring of magma.

Several episodes of magma intrusion took place over millions of years to form this mountain range. The molten rock cooled extremely slowly underground, miles below the surface. Each of these masses is called a pluton after the Roman god of fire, Pluto. Together, all of these plutons form a batholith (from the Greek for deep, *bathos*, and rock, *lithos*), a huge expanse of volcanic rock which extends far into the earth.

This is where the story of gold begins. As the magma cooled, it formed a thin, hard crust on the outside of the magma chamber, deep within the earth. As the crust formed, it shrank and cracked as it cooled. The cracks reached down into the still molten magma within the magma chamber, allowing mineral-laden steam to escape out through the fissures in the barely-solid rock material. As the steam hit the open-air cracks, the minerals carried in the steam began to precipitate out onto the sides of the cracks as a result of the change in pressure. Minerals precipitate out at their own unique temperature, a useful tool for geologists in reconstructing earth's history. The first minerals to precipitate include precious minerals made of silver, tungsten, molybdenum, and gold. Later minerals include those made of zinc, tungsten, and lead. When the magmatic system is cool and close to surface temperature and pressure, quartz precipitates out, filling in all the space that is left. That is why gold is found in association with quartz veins, because at one point all the minerals existed together in the hot magma below.

A period of relative quiescence followed the outpouring of magma in the Jurassic. The mountain peaks were steadily eroded through much of the Tertiary. During the Pliocene, the entire area underwent faulting, and resulted in the Sierra Nevada block being upthrust and tilted westward. In the Pleistocene, the temperatures dropped and the mountains were subjected to the erosive power of water and ice, as valley glaciers carved out domes, arêtes and U-shaped valleys.

Glaciers are classified into two broad categories—valley glaciers and continental glaciers. Valley glaciers are the familiar striped ribbons of ice and debris that begin in cirques and flow down the mountainside. Valley glaciers can be seen in California at Mt. Shasta, Yosemite, and Mt. Whitney. Elsewhere in the United States, valley glaciers are abundant in Glacier National Park in Montana, and in Alaska. Continental glaciers, on the other hand, are thick sheets of glacial ice that covered much of Europe and North America during the Pleistocene, such as the well-known mile-thick sheet of glacial ice that covered New York. Continental glaciers still visible today include the glaciers that cover Greenland and Antarctica. Continental glaciation never made it to California, because the Sierra Nevada mountains served as a barrier to the thick sheets of ice. The glaciers that carved the magnificent scenery at Yosemite were valley glaciers.

Because of the vastness of the Sierras and its geological richness, we will present this chapter in three sections: the foothills, or Mother Lode, the High Sierras, and the Eastern Sierras. Topographically, they are quite distinctively different, of course, and the types of geological attractions are dissimilar as well. Put succinctly, the Mother Lode is about gold mining, the High Sierras are about glaciation, and the Eastern Sierras are about volcanism.

With all of that ground to cover, let's get started.

Trails of the Sierra Nevadas

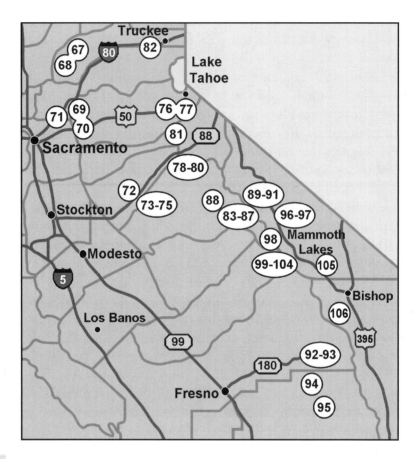

THE MOTHER LODE

You will not be surprised that the majority of geology hikes in this section are centered around old mining sites. But the foothills of the Sierras are also noteworthy for their splendid show caves, four of which are included here, all within a 15-mile radius of one another. The mines are located in the granite bedrock, but the caves are in limestone.

67. Diggins Loop

EFFORT:	Moderate
LENGTH:	1.0+ miles
GEOLOGICAL FEATURE(S):	Mining
LOCATION:	Malakoff Diggins State Historic Park

Description: The site of the world's largest hydraulic gold mine, Malakoff Diggins is a pit more than a mile long, a half-mile wide, and nearly 600 feet deep. The North Bloomfield Gravel Mining Company operated the mine between 1866 and 1884, and yielded millions of dollars worth of gold, as well as the gravel by-product. At the park museum, you can learn about the environmentally devastating practice of hydraulic mining. From this operation alone, 50 million tons of tailings were washed down the Yuba River.

Hydraulic mining is accomplished by blasting away hillsides with huge water monitors and routing the debris through sluice boxes. During full operation, eight of these devices were employed around the clock. A couple of the monitors are displayed on Main Street. The debris and the enormous amount of water used to sluice the gold rushed downhill, causing flooding in Marysville and Yuba City. In 1884, in one of the first environmental rulings ever passed, a judge ruled that the mining company must stop flushing sediment downstream. At its height, North Bloomfield had 800 residents, including a Chinese quarter, but after hydraulic mining was banned, the town was all but abandoned.

Before setting out on the trail, you might want to sign up for the North Bloomfield town tour. Several old buildings are still intact and others have been reconstructed, including the drugstore, saloon, and barbershop. If you don't take a ranger-led tour,

Malakoff Diggins *(Courtesy California Department of Conservation)*

you can walk around on your own and look in windows.

For the quickest access to Diggins Loop, we suggest starting at the cemetery. Drive a short distance southwest on North Bloomfield Road. A sign for the cemetery will show you where to turn in on the right. A Catholic church stands here at the road's edge. Also located here is the old schoolhouse, which is worth a look. Platforms have been set up to allow you to peer in the windows of the two classrooms with their rows of antique desks. There are also two outhouses flanking the school, each with a four-holer plank inside. The outhouses are not original, but the planks look to be the real thing.

After a detour through the fence-enclosed cemetery, walk along its left side on Slaughterhouse Trail. Just past the cemetery you will come to a trail junction. Turn left towards The Diggins. Now you are on the Diggins Loop. Enclosed in a pine woodland, you will begin to descend steeply for a stretch, entering an area dominated by manzanita. Notice that the ground is covered with boulders. In other places along the trail you will encounter piles of gravel. These are the remnants of the mining operation.

When the trail levels out again, it will cross over a dirt road and then come to a T-junction. A trail sign points you to either the "South Side" or the "North Side" Diggins Loop Trail. For quick access to the bottom of the giant pit, go right. The trail becomes the bottom of a gully and is filled with loose gravel as it takes you downhill through the bleached cliffs of the mining pit. The unnaturally exposed white and reddish sediments create an attractive setting not unlike badlands topography.

Once you bottom out, the trail disappears and you are walking on a sandy, marshy plain with a small rivulet of cool water running through it. Willows grow near the water and an abundance of song-birds occupy this spot. We saw deer tracks near the stream as well.

When you are ready, go back up the trail to the junction with South Side. To continue on the loop, go straight. If you want a short hike of about a mile, you can turn left here and return to the cemetery and trailhead.

The Diggins Trail continues around the giant pit. Another trail option is the Rim Trail, which traces the pit's rim. This trail is 3 miles long and offers a different perspective. Despite the devastation that took place here in the nineteenth century, this is now an attractive and enjoy-able trail, especially if you are not here at the height of summer. Up at the high points, you get a good view across the pit to the sharply eroded, sparkling white spires of the cliff face. The trail rolls up and down among manzanita bushes and pine trees along the edge of the pit.

You will come to an intersection with the Hiller Trail, which goes left past the Hiller Tunnel on its way to North Bloomfield Road. Turn around and return to the trailhead whenever you are ready, or complete the loop.

Directions: From Nevada City on Highway 49, proceed north to North Bloomfield Road and turn right onto it. It is 16 miles to the park. Although the road starts out smooth and civilized, it becomes a very different route further on. This is quite a scenic, but rough route. If you are prepared for it, the way is pass-able by most vehicles in good weather. The road becomes dirt and drops down into the South Fork of the Yuba River canyon at Edwards Crossing, and then crosses a wooden plank bridge over the river, climbing back up a steep and winding pitted, dirt road on the other side. Enter the park and take advantage of the viewpoints to stop and get an overview of the mining pit. There is also a stop at Hiller Tunnel, an engineering marvel. You can walk 100 yards from the pullout along a creek to a drainage tunnel dug out of the rock. If you brought your flashlight, you can explore inside the tunnel a bit. Shortly after this stop, the road becomes paved and takes you into the main area of the park.

An alternate route is a good, paved road with expansive

views, also about 16 miles from Nevada City. From Nevada City at the spot where Highway 49 and Highway 20 diverge, proceed north on Highway 49 for 10 miles. Turn right on Tyler-Foote Crossing Road and drive about 8.5 miles to North Columbia where the road becomes Curzon Grade Road.

Continue on this road for about 4 more miles, and you will then be on BackBone Road. Turn right on Derbec Road and then bear right onto North Bloomfield Road. Proceed into town. There is a day-use fee, payable at the museum. There are restrooms across the street.

68. Hardrock Trail

EFFORT:..Minimal
LENGTH:...2.5 miles
GEOLOGICAL FEATURE(S):...Mining
LOCATION:.............................Empire Mine State Historic Park

Description: This park houses the remains of one of the most successful hardrock gold mining operations in the U.S., and the most profitable one in California. Hardrock mining is a method that involves digging or blasting the ore out of the earth and then crushing it into powder with huge machines called stamps. The gold is then leached out of the crushed ore using mercury or cyanide.

During the 1849 Gold Rush, miners flocked here to strike it rich, but the gold in this area was not easily reached. Gold was discovered on this site in 1850 by George Roberts. In 1879, San Francisco businessman William Bourn took over the Empire Mine, dug deep and finally made the

mine pay off. The Bourn influence in the San Francisco area was widespread, ranging from financing the Panama-Pacific International Exposition, constructing the Opera House, and building the luxurious family estate, Filoli House, in Woodside. The Bourn Cottage near the Empire Mine is not nearly so grand as that home, but it is quite lovely and open for tours.

The hugely successful gold mine was a combined effort of Bourn vision and hard-working Englishmen. Miners experienced in hardrock mining of tin and copper came from Cornwall, England in the 1880s. One of their important contributions was the pumping technology that kept water out of the tunnels. The water table today lies at about 150 feet and the mine is flooded, but during its operation, the mine's tunnels reached a depth of 11,000 feet. A whopping 5.8 million ounces of gold was extracted from the mine between 1850 to 1956.

The Cornish miners seemed to have been a sour lot, as you will note when you see their pictures in the Visitor Center. While you are in Grass Valley, perhaps you will sample a Cornish pasty, a staple in the miners' lunchboxes. These savory meat pies are still sold around here.

Because the mine was operated for over one-hundred years, many of the buildings and much of the machinery are preserved on site. Our adventure here is a mixed bag. Only a small part of the walk is an actual hiking trail. The Hardrock Trail takes you to the mine shaft, old buildings, the Bourn Cottage, grounds, and outlying ruins. We will present a route that we think will be the most rewarding way to experience the park, though the official trail brochure routes you a somewhat different way.

Start at the Visitor Center. In the former carriage house, you can read about the history of the mine and see photographs of the Bourn family, the miners, etc. But the most interesting thing to see here is the scale model of the Empire Mine. It is housed in a separate room inside a glass cube. The incredible detail of the model will serve as a vivid

Cornish Miners *(Courtesy California Department of Conservation)*

introduction to the vast network of tunnels that made up the mine. Tunnels were blasted out with dynamite each day in a continual effort to expose and remove the gold-bearing quartz. By the time the mine was closed, there were over 360 miles of tunnels.

Exit at the back of the Visitor Center building and turn right at the junction, towards the cottage. Most of year the landscaped grounds leading up to the cottage are replete with blooming flowers. In the middle of summer, cascades of blue hydrangeas dominate. You will pass by the ruins of the Ophir Cottage, the home of the mine superintendent, which was burned down in 1935. Ophir is a biblical place name meaning "land rich in gold," and it was from Ophir

WHATEVER LOLA WANTS

Eliza Gilbert, an Irish girl raised in India, defied her mother and convention when she set out for a career as a dancer. She learned flamenco, changed her name to Lola Montez, invented her bizarre "Tarantula Dance," and burst forth on the stages of the world. She married twice, and among her many lovers were the composer Franz Liszt and King Ludwig of Bavaria. Hobnobbing with the world's elite, Lola wielded her whip across the globe, landing eventually in the U.S.

So how did she end up in Grass Valley? Well, in those days, the Mother Lode was not the sleepy B&B retreat it is today. Also, by this time, Lola had worn out her welcome in quite a few places, and needed a town small enough so that she could be the undisputed center of attention.

She chose Grass Valley because it was close to the Eureka Gold Mine, in which she had $9,000 worth of stock. She threw big parties and kept a monkey and grizzly bear as pets. She mentored her neighbor, Lotta Crabtree, and helped the child develop into a successful performer.

Lola's house still stands at 248 Mill Street in Grass Valley. Down the street at 238 is Lotta Crabtree's house.

that King Solomon reportedly got the gold with which to build his temple. The clubhouse appears on the left. Residents and visitors enjoyed a variety of recreational activities here, and it is still used today.

After the clubhouse, the path veers right through a gauntlet of pink rose bushes towards Bourn Cottage, an 1897 English manor, where the Bourn family lived. We recommend taking the half-hour tour of the inside of the cottage. On your own, you can explore the formal rose gardens behind the house and the reflecting pool in front on a lower level.

Leave the cottage area and walk back towards the Visitor Center, then continue straight towards the mine yard. On your right you will see a metal grate over a stone-lined tunnel entrance. Apparently, this was built to show potential investors the "mine entrance," but really goes nowhere. In the mine yard, start with the bank of wooden buildings on your left. Explore the offices where antique phones, typewriters, and bathroom fixtures spark your imagination. You will see the furnace where the gold and mercury amalgam was heated to separate the gold. The mercury was then collected and reused. The gold was melted and molded into ingots to send to the U.S. Mint in San Francisco.

After wandering through these buildings, cross the yard to the machine shop. The mine operation is like a small village, nearly self-contained. Unlike some mines, however, the miners did not live on site. They lived in town and walked to work each day.

Next, go down into the mine shaft itself. You will encounter a metal gate across the shaft inside. On the right sits the man-skip, the rail-riding sled that whisked the miners down the shaft for 4,650 feet. The day we visited the park, a "miner" was in the shaft to answer questions. A smithy was working in the black-smith shop next door, and various other costumed folk were on hand to lend some historic color to the place. Check with the park ahead of time if you want to visit on one of the living history days.

Make your way past the many old rail cars, generators, and other machinery to the hoist house where the constant movement of men, supplies, ore, and waste rock was controlled.

Next you come to the stamp mill building which once housed eighty 1,750-pound stamps to crush the ore. Today these hills are peaceful, but during the mine's operation, these huge stamps ran continuously, pounding the ore with booming thunderclaps which rang out for three miles around.

Exiting the mine yard, turn right and hop on the Hardrock Trail. You will soon pass the auxiliary generator site on the left. The trail heads into oak, Ponderosa pine and Douglas fir woods. On the right is a clear meadow surrounded by an airy woodland. You will soon come to the site of the Orleans Mine. Poke around here for a few minutes and then continue on the trail. You will come to a junction. To complete the short loop, go right. If you want more of a hike, there are several trails to choose from by turning left here and crossing Little Wolf Creek. You can continue on the main trail for just over a mile to reach the back door of the park, Pennsylvania Gate, which is a staging area for equestri-ans and dog walkers.

For the short loop, continue right on the Hard Rock Trail. The next stop is the cyanide pond on the left. This was installed in 1910 to refine the ore even more efficiently than the mercury process (and is considerably safer to use than mercury). The pulverized rock from the stamp mills was taken to a cyanide-laced pond. The cyanide causes the gold to leach out of solution, and an electroplating step completes the process.

Continue back towards the mine yard, passing the final stop, one of the old stamps set up alongside the trail. Continue straight to return to the Visitor Center and the end of the tour.

Directions: From Highway 49 in Grass Valley, proceed east on East Empire Street to the park visitor center. On the way, you will pass the Pennsylvania Gate staging area. If you want to avoid an entrance fee, you can park here and walk in, but the fee was only a dollar a person when we visited. There are picnic tables and restrooms. To begin, you go through the Visitor Center where the entrance fee is collected.

69. Monument Trail

EFFORT:..Minimal
LENGTH:..0.75 miles
GEOLOGICAL FEATURE(S):...................................Mining
LOCATION:.........................Marshall Gold Discovery State Historic Park

Description: This is where it all began. On this stroll about town you will visit the site of the gold discovery that kicked off the California Gold Rush of 1849. It happened here in 1848 when James Marshall found gold on the South Fork of the American River while building a sawmill for John Sutter.

There are a few sites you'll want to hit on this visit. One is the Sawmill Site Monument near the river's edge. Afterwards go down to the river to the actual site of the gold discovery, and a replica of the sawmill. The gold turned up in the mill's tailrace.

In summer, you will no doubt see people rafting, a popular recreation on the American River.

Next, go to Main Street and walk down it. This is part of the history tour. When you reach Sacramento Street, turn right and walk up to Church Street. Cross it and continue along Sacramento Street to the Vineyard House. Here you will find a trail on the right. This trail will take you into the park and uphill to the James W. Marshall Monument and Marshall's cabin. James Marshall is buried under the monument. From the monument, you have a good view of the valley and river. Returning to the main trail, go right to continue the loop and head downhill back to town.

Directions: From Sacramento, head east on Highway 50 towards Placerville. Turn north on Highway 49 and proceed to Coloma. Park on Main Street or in the lot at the Interpretive Center (there is a parking fee).

70. Gold Bug Mine

EFFORT:	Minimal
LENGTH:	1.2 miles
GEOLOGICAL FEATURE(S):	Mining
LOCATION:	Gold Bug Park

Description: The Gold Bug Mine is listed on the National Register of Historic Places, and is one of Placerville's most visited relics from its Gold Rush origins. Placerville was first named Dry Diggins, later Hangtown, and then was renamed to put the focus back on mining and away from the spurt of hangings that took place here. As you might imagine, Gold Bug Park is a popular field trip destination for elementary school students, so you may prefer to visit on a weekend.

Pick up a hard hat and cassette player in the gift shop and enter the hard rock mine's drift on your self-guided tour. A drift is a horizontal tunnel into a mine. Inside the mine, the temperature remains steadily between 52 and 57 degrees, just as it might in a natural cave. The recording guides you step by step onto the wooden walkway in the lighted mine. A flashlight will be of use to illuminate details on the ceiling and walls. The trail is short and flat and easily navigated. During our tour on a weekend, we were alone in the mine, which made it easier to imagine what it would be like to be inside with a pick, digging out the ore.

The cassette tape is informative as well as a lot of fun. The narrator tells the story of the mine as you walk along, including old mining legends with colorful characters. The tape also tells you when to stop, where to look, and describes what you are looking at. You will see quartz veins, dynamite holes, and learn the meaning of various mining terms such as "shaft" and "adit" while looking at examples.

Gold Bug Mine was opened in 1888 by William Craddock and John Dench and was originally named Hattie Mine after Craddock's daughter. In 1926, it was sold to John McKay and renamed.

You will walk 352 feet through the main tunnel. At the back, an airshaft provides cool fresh air flowing in at around 55 degrees. Walk back out the same way.

After you emerge from the mine, take the Priest Trail up the hill to the Priest Mine with its dirt floor and no lighting. This mine dates from 1849 and is available for touring by special arrangement. There are many other mines in the park, more than 250, but they are closed to the public. You will see an airshaft and tailing piles on your walk, which brings you back after a half mile to Big Canyon Creek and Gold Bug Lane.

Turn left and walk on Gold Bug Lane to Hendy Drive. Turn right and walk a few steps to a trail which parallels Hendy Drive going north. This is Stampmill Trail. Walk on it for a short distance to the Joshua Hendy Stamp Mill, housed inside a large barn. A volunteer will be available inside to answer questions. There are eight huge stamps on the mill, once used to crush the ore taken from surrounding mines. Also in the building are various displays and artifacts from the Gold Rush era, including a working scale model of the stamp mill. The stamp mill is fascinating and not to be missed.

After touring the building, exit and return to the trail, continuing

north on Silver Pine Trail. The Silver Pine Mine was one of the largest operated at this site. Follow this trail for 0.30 miles, looping back south to join the Springhill Trail, which will return you to Gold Bug Lane. Consider visiting the Hattie Museum before or after your walk.

We were torn in deciding which was our favorite, the mine itself or the stamp mill. Even if you don't have time to hike the trails, visit both of these attractions.

Directions: From Highway 50 in Placerville, take Bedford Avenue north and turn right into the park on Gold Bug Lane. There are picnic tables and restrooms.

71. Griffith Quarry Trails

EFFORT:..Minimal
LENGTH:..3.0 miles
GEOLOGICAL FEATURE(S):...............................Mining
LOCATION:................................Griffith Quarry County Park

Description: This park marks the site of a historically significant granite quarry. From 1864 to 1918, a Welsh immigrant with the improbable name of Griffith Griffith operated the quarry to supply building material for the emerging cities of California. You will find the quarry site much as it was left by Griffith when the company closed

its doors. This is also a pristine natural area where native animals and plants flourish, including rattlesnakes, so be on the lookout. You can explore all the trails in this small park by hiking three miles.

The museum in the parking lot used to be the office of the Penryn Granite Works. In the town of Penryn, you can see the Masonic Hall that was built from granite quarried here. Much of the granite ended up in buildings in Sacramento and San Francisco.

Start at the interpretive sign near the parking lot. Beside the sign, on your right, are the remains of the old polishing mill, the first one built in California. There is nothing left except some foundation stones and part of a rock wall. To the left is an old granite-lined well. Walk past that to the gated road. The trail is the road behind the gate.

This road leads out through oak woodland and chaparral, taking in the perimeter of the park, circling around the center where side trails lead to the quarry holes. You can take any of the spur trails for overlooks to the larger holes. Keep clear of poison oak in the dense brush alongside the trail.

You will come to your first overview of the quarry in just a minute or so, on the right. Before you is an immense pit littered with large chunks of granite. At the bottom is a scummy pond. If you make your way to the right around the pit, you will get a view of a tunnel opening down below on the left.

On the left side of the road, you will see a trail marker #5 and some stone steps leading down. That footpath is an alternate route if you prefer it to the road, but it is a bit longer. Continuing on the road, you will curve to the right.

If you stay on the Tailings Trail, you will make the rounds in 1.5 miles. You can then explore the central section at will, hiking the Quarry Trails, which wind around the various quarry holes. The smaller holes are fenced off to keep people from falling in. The trail is flanked by the occasional digger pine and lots of California buckeye trees. In fall, the toyon will be hung with bright red berries.

Directions: From Interstate 80 take the Penryn exit and proceed on Penryn Road to Taylor Road. Turn right and continue to the park on the right, on the corner of Taylor and English Colony Road. Access is free. There is a portable toilet and drinking fountains.

72. Black Chasm Cavern

EFFORT:	Minimal
LENGTH:	N/A
GEOLOGICAL FEATURE(S):	Caves
LOCATION:	15701 Pioneer-Volcano Road, Volcano, CA

Description: Calaveras County's newest nugget is an amazingly beautiful and fragile living limestone and marble cave that was opened to the public in September, 2000. It was something of a secret prior to development. The cave was declared a National Natural Landmark in 1976, but available to only a few individuals and groups for study. Its landmark status was granted primarily due to its substantial colony of rare helictite crystals. These are unusual looping and twisting white fingers of calcite that are hollow like soda straws, but growing at every possible angle.

As recently as February 2001, a spectacular new chamber was discovered, and there may be more to come. Exploration of the cave continues, although some passages are so choked with delicate crystals that spelunkers avoid passing through in order not to damage them. So far, the public tour is limited to a few rooms, estimated to be about one-sixth of the tourable cave, but the trail system will continue to expand. Great care is being taken to preserve the cave's natural state, including the construction of expensive elevated trails designed to keep visitors off of the floor. The stairs, railings, and viewing platforms are made from recycled soda bottles instead of traditional materials such as wood to avoid leaching chemicals into the environment.

Fortunately for us, visitors of earlier generations were able to enter only the first few feet of the cave, so damage characteristic of that time is limited to the area just inside the entrance. Otherwise, the preservation is exemplary.

The cave is managed by Sierra Nevada Recreation Corporation, which also manages other area caves open to the public. When we visited, tickets were sold out of a trailer, and signs of construction were everywhere, both aboveground and in the cave. There is now a 3,000 square foot Visitors Center with restrooms and exhibits. A cave-cam to allow visitors to see into the chambers which are too fragile to tour, is being planned.

The Landmark Tour includes the Colossal Room, 100 feet across and 150 feet deep, and the Landmark Room, famous for its massive arrays of helictites. Be prepared for stairs, lots of them, as the tour is essentially a trip downstairs and then back up. It begins by passing through a narrow opening and descending down the first flight of stairs to a platform suspended between the walls of the fissure. You can see well-lit stalactites, stalagmites, helictites, draperies, flowstone, columns, and other familiar cave formations. Looking down, you will see a small portion of the deep turquoise lake seventy feet below, colored by naturally-occurring calcium bicarbonate. A Rapunzel Tour is planned to take visitors down to the lakes for a close-up view, but for now, this is all you will see of the mysterious water below.

This is the best spot on the tour to recognize that the cave was formed along a joint, and the basic shape of the area is a narrow chasm that you will traverse almost vertically from top to bottom. Because of the sheer vertical drop almost immediately within the entrance, this cave would not have been a viable human habitat. No archeological artifacts have been found here.

The walkway continues through the Landmark Portal and down into the Landmark Room, which contains impressive displays of spectacular helictites in the walls and ceiling. Helictites are formed under unusual conditions, which include water under pressure and the presence of certain trace minerals. As water droplets emerge through the rock to an exposed, vertical wall, they cling to it by surface tension. Rings of calcite are formed where the droplets make contact, and build up into hollow tubes. These tubes begin in a more or less horizontal manner and then twist and turn in bizarre shapes as random crystals grow. Since helictites must battle gravity, they do not usually grow much larger than a few inches, but at Black Chasm Cavern there are many long helictites, including one near the entrance to the cave that measures twelve inches long.

The Landmark Room also contains one of the most beautiful flowstone formations you will come across. Your guide will point out some of the small passageways that may eventually host cave-cams. You can easily see that these crystal-choked passages will not allow for visitors, walkways, ladders, etc., without significant destruction.

This is the end of the tour, from which you retrace your steps up to the entrance, squeezing past the next tour group along the way.

Not yet on the tour is the colossal Hall of Arches, a complex maze of marble arches that span wall to wall over and under each other. We will return in a couple of years to see some more of this amazing underground fantasy as it is further revealed to the public.

Directions: From Stockton, take Highway 88 east to Pinegrove. Turn left at Volcano-Pinegrove Road and continue three miles to the bottom of a big hill, make a steep right turn onto Pioneer-

Volcano Road and continue about 1500 feet. Turn right at the Black Chasm National Natural Landmark entrance. You will come to a parking area alongside the road. This is overflow parking. Continue past it to the main parking area and visitor center. The cave is open daily for public tours. Expect a reasonable wait of about an hour for your tour time, the perfect opportunity to sit down to a picnic lunch. gemstone mining and nature hikes are other activities to enjoy while waiting. There is a fee for the tour.

73. Mercer Caverns

EFFORT:..Minimal
LENGTH:...N/A
GEOLOGICAL FEATURE(S):......................................Caves
LOCATION:..............................Sheep Ranch Rd, Murphys, CA

Description: Tours of lovely Mercer Caverns are 45 minutes long, descending to a depth of a 16-story building into the limestone. On view are typical cavern formations—stalactites, stalagmites, flowstone, soda straws, etc. A guide leads you through the chambers. Some of the passages are narrow, and some of the stairway climbs are steep. After climbing all the way down, you will have to climb back up again.

This cave system is noted for its collection of rare aragonite flos ferri, a type of aragonite that grows in a dendritic, or treelike pattern. Your guide will point these out to you.

The first people to use Mercer Caverns were the native Yokuts, for whom it was a mortuary. They brought their dead here and rolled them through the opening. The Yokuts abandoned the cave when they moved along on their seasonal migration following the animals and plants they depended on for survival.

The cave was rediscovered in 1885, which is when tours began, so it is the longest continually operated commercial show cave in California. In the earliest days, the first paying visitors descended into the cave with ropes. You, however, will walk on stairs with the aid of electric lighting.

While you are in Murphys, you may as well stop in for another geologic wonder. In the last decade, the Mother Lode has emerged as a second California wine country, replacing gold mines with wineries. The beautiful Kautz Ironstone Vineyards is one of the finest. The winery is modeled after a 19th-century gold stamp mill. In the jewelry store, you can walk into a bank-style vault which houses an astounding 44-pound gold nugget — unearthed by the Sonora Mining Company in nearby Jamestown in 1992. It is valued at 3.5 million dollars, and is quite an amazing thing to behold. It is sights like this one, which is a vivid reminder that there is still gold to be found, that rekindle gold fever in the minds of visitors.

Directions: From Highway 49 in Angels Camp, turn left on Murphys Grade Road. If you reach the junction with Highway 4, you have missed it. Continue towards Murphys. As soon as you enter town, and just before you get to the historic Murphys Hotel, turn left on Sheep Ranch Road and proceed to the Mercer Caverns parking area. There are restrooms and a gift shop. There is a tour fee. The cave is open daily for tours.

74. Moaning Cavern Walking Tour

EFFORT:..Minimal
LENGTH:...N/A
GEOLOGICAL FEATURE(S):..Caves
LOCATION:............................5350 Moaning Cave Road, Vallecito, CA

Description: Discovered in 1851 by gold miners, the main chamber of Moaning Cavern is large enough to hold the Statue of Liberty. Its "moaning" is created by water drops falling into holes in a bottle-shaped flowstone formation and echoing through the cave.

There are three tour options available for this cave. The easiest is the 45-minute walking tour. The guided tour descends through marble passageways into the main chamber, taking you down 235 stairs to a depth of 165 feet. At the bottom of the chamber, excava-tions have uncovered the remains of prehistoric people who fell into the cave thousands of years ago. As you descend, your guide will discuss the geology and history of the cave. The way out is back up the stairs.

Another option for the slightly more intrepid is The Rappel, in which you descend 165 feet by rope into the main chamber. No experience is necessary, but children under 12 are not allowed to rappel. All equipment is provided, and the adventure takes about 45 minutes.

And for the even more daring, there is the Wild Cavern Adventure Trip, which begins with the rappel and then takes you through some of the other deep chambers and passages in the cave. Wearing lighted helmets, you will climb and crawl your way through undeveloped sections with an experienced guide. All clothing and equipment is provided. This is a 3-hour tour (reminds me of another 3-hour tour that went horribly wrong), and can be reserved by calling (209) 736-2708.

Directions: From Stockton, take Highway 4 east to Angels Camp and stay on Highway 4 until you see the sign to turn onto Parrotts Ferry Road. Turn right on Parrotts Ferry Road and go one mile. Turn right on Moaning Cave Road at the Moaning Cavern Park sign. The cavern is open every day, year round. There is a fee for the tour.

75. California Cavern Trail of Lights

EFFORT:..Minimal
LENGTH:...N/A
GEOLOGICAL FEATURE(S):...Caves
LOCATION:.........................9565 Cave City Road, Mountain Ranch, CA

Description: Opening to the public in 1850, California Cavern was the state's first show cave and is State Historic Landmark #956. It contains many striking crystalline formations, which can be observed on the 60 to 80 minute Trail of Lights Family Walking Tour. Two other tours are offered, which are described below.

The walking tour trail is nearly level and well lighted as it takes you through the cave, visiting several rooms, including the recently discovered Jungle Room, named for the crystalline "vines" covering the ceiling.

Another tour offered is the two to three-hour Mammoth Cave Expedition, which involves crawling and squeezing through passageways connecting 13 chambers. Reservations are required, and participants must be at least 8 years old.

A more rigorous tour option is the three to four-hour Middle Earth Expedition, where groups are led through about 80 percent of the cavern system from the east entrance to the west exit. The trail is a mile long and consists of crawling and squeezing through narrow passageways in the Mammoth Cave area. Next you will go through the Middle Earth area, discovered in 1980, in which you will walk through deep, sticky clay. You will then examine horizontal fissures in the

Cave of the Quills, and pass by raft across Tom's Lake. After exploring more chambers with beautiful crystalline formations, you will climb ladders to the world above. Participants must be at least 16 for this trip. Reservations are required.

For the last two tours, call (209) 736-2708 for reservations. The Trail of Lights tour does not require advance reservations.

Directions: From Stockton, take Highway 99 north to Lodi, then Highway 12 east to San Andreas. Turn left on Mountain Ranch Road and go approximately 8 miles. Turn right on Michel Road at the California Historical Landmark sign that says "California Caverns." Follow the signs for approximately 2 miles to the driveway on the left. There are restrooms, picnic tables, a nature trail and a Visitor Center on site. The cave is operated spring through fall, every day. There is a tour fee.

THE HIGH SIERRAS

Making your way east from the golden, oak-studded hillsides of the foothills, you leave the valley haze and heat behind and enter the blissful mountains. The High Sierras are characterized by thick conifer forests, glacial tarns, smooth granite, alpine wildflowers, cool, clear streams, and plenty of solitude. The two men we most associate with this section of the state are naturalist John Muir and artist Ansel Adams. Both have wilderness areas named after them. There are several other wilderness areas in the Sierras, as well as three national parks and plenty of national forest for public recreation. There are numerous trails and a whole lot of hiking going on. The Pacific Crest Trail makes it way steadily along the top of the range, across its entire length. Our paths will cross the PCT on occasion as we peer at rocks on our exploration of High Sierra geology.

76. Pyramid Creek Trail

EFFORT:...Minimal
LENGTH:...2.6 miles
GEOLOGICAL FEATURE(S):...Glaciation
LOCATION:..El Dorado National Forest

Description: For low-effort day-hikers like ourselves, this trail offers something not easily found, a fairly painless access route into beguiling Desolation Wilderness. Horsetail Falls is the destination, a tall 300 feet of whitewater plunging over the cliff in a dramatic series of cascades and cataracts. Come in the late spring or early summer to see the waterfall at its most robust, but autumn is also an excellent time to visit, when the worst of the heat is past and the trees near the creek are turning yellow. Whenever you visit, bring a picnic to enjoy in this charming forest setting.

The bare granite cliffs surrounding Pyramid Creek are considered to be one of the best examples of Pleistocene glaciation in the Sierra Nevada range. In recognition of the creek's value as a recreational, scenic, and natural waterway, the Forest Service has requested National Wild & Scenic River status for it.

Before you begin, sign in at the trailhead. Wilderness visitors must register, even for a day hike. You will start at 6,100 feet in elevation. Head out in an easterly direction, roughly parallel to the highway, which is within earshot.

You will travel through sparse tree cover, ducking in and out of shade. Throughout the entire route, Pyramid Creek will remain on your right.

The trail climbs up into a spacious, circular canyon with high walls on three sides. Shortly after starting out, the trail makes an abrupt turn left, leading you up a stone staircase to a trail sign. Turn right to proceed across granite slabs near the creek. The trail will become indistinct here, but just continue along the creek to a serious swath of whitewater. It's around this point that the roar of the creek begins to drown out the roar of Highway 50 below. Looking towards the back of the canyon, you will get your first view of Horsetail Falls as it wends its way over and down the granite cliff face. On the east side of the canyon, the high, stark cliff offers an excellent view of the bedrock material.

A glacier moved through here about 12,000 years ago, scooping out the valley and leaving behind the long fall of Pyramid Creek, a "hanging" valley. Besides the waterfall and the canyon itself, other features of geologic interest can be found here. While you are enjoying the trail, pause to examine them. Look for ample evidence of frost wedging where hefty boulders have been split apart by the continual freezing and thawing of water within their joints. There are many good examples of differential weathering on the slabs of granite: resistant xenoliths protrude from the bedrock which has eroded around them. Many aplite dikes cut across the rock. You will see these as whitish stringers of quartz and feldspar running through the granite. These, too, are often protruding somewhat, indicating that they are more resistant to weathering than the surrounding ground mass. The occasional glacial erratic can be seen along the trail. They are not as obvious here though as in some other places since there are so many boulders lying about.

Pyramid Creek falls over the cliff at the back of the canyon and then winds around the east side of it to meet up with Highway 50 on the south. Our trail climbs gently beside it for the first 1.3 miles over rocky, uneven ground.

If you lose the trail on bare granite, you will probably pick it up again when it turns back into dirt. Sometimes there are signs, reading "trail," to put you back on course. Sometimes there are cairns. More often, there are little hiker symbols nailed to tree trunks, so look up to find these. But if you can't locate the trail, just head on your own route towards

the back of the canyon and the waterfall, which frequently comes into view.

Along the way, take the time to veer off the trail to explore the creek. There are some idyllic spots along its banks to enjoy a picnic lunch. As the trail routes you north, you will enter a section which is mostly dirt, mostly shady, and mostly level. A few ferns can be found growing here.

After a half-mile you will reach the boundary of Desolation Wilderness. At an unmarked trail junction, paths fork left and right. To the left the trail will soon reach a signed junction with Twin Bridges Trail. You can make a loop out of this hike by taking that narrow path back, but it is somewhat overgrown with manzanita and not nearly as pleasant as Pyramid Creek Trail, so we recommend making this an out and back trip. Turn right at the unmarked junction to continue climbing towards the waterfall. It will be another half-mile to Lower Falls.

As you climb, you get better views of the surrounding terrain. Looking back towards Highway 50, to the southwest, you can see Lover's Leap, a popular rock climbing location.

Once you reach the waterfall, you can cool off in its spray. This is the end of the trail for us, but many people find the idea of climbing to the top irresistible. It is a steep climb with some rock scrambling. Give it a try if you feel like it, since the view from above is heady. Follow a route marked by spray-painted green arrows over granite slabs. Once you reach the top, you come out onto a flat area with incredible views to the valley below. There are many small streams up there heading for the falls, and several pools suitable for swimming. However, you should exercise extreme caution at the top of the falls. Several people have died here. At the time of this writing, the waterfall had just claimed another victim, a woman who slipped and was carried over the cliff.

Return via the same route, or just head back over the bare granite slabs in the center of the canyon. The geological features we came to see are quite abundant there.

Directions: On Highway 50, 18 miles southwest of Lake Tahoe and 80 miles east of Sacramento, park in the lot north of the highway near Twin Bridges. The lot is signed, "Pyramid Creek Trailhead." This lot fills up quickly on weekends, so you may have difficulty finding a parking spot. There is limited parking along the highway, but be careful to heed No Parking and Tow Away signs. There is a fee to park in the lot, and there are restrooms at the trailhead.

77. Big Meadow Trail

EFFORT:..Moderate
LENGTH:..5.2 miles
GEOLOGICAL FEATURE(S):................................Volcanism
LOCATION:................................El Dorado National Forest

Description: It's not all about geology on this trail. Wildflowers are excellent here as well, so time your hike to make the most of that bonus.

Start out going south on a portion of the Tahoe Rim Trail through pine and fir forest, and shortly enter Big Meadow after a half-mile. Cross a wooden bridge and walk through the meadow, then begin a gentle climb through a sparse forest. Keep an eye out for wildflowers along the way, including blue lupine, Indian paintbrush, brown pinedrops, pink monkeyflowers, purple columbine, and aster, which grow in open places within the forest.

After about 1.5 miles, you come to a creek and a meadow rich in blooms. Continuing, you climb up and over a ridge and on through a volcanic environment where ancient mudflows are on view.

After two miles, you descend to reach a junction. The trail to the right leads to Dardanelles Lake. You will bear left instead and negotiate some ups and downs through conglomerate outcrops. Notice that the rocks look like chunky cement, and in a way, that's what they are. During the mudflows created by volcanic eruptions, the ash and mud mixture caught up to existing rocks of varying sizes and "cemented" them together as it cooled. A volcanic mudflow is known as a "lahar," and these secondary effects of volcanoes can be far more devastating than the lava flow itself. Lahars can also be caused by intense rain falling on newly deposited ash after the eruptive activity has ceased. A disastrous lahar occurred in the Philippines after the eruption of Mt. Pinatubo in 1991, burying entire villages and destroying everything in its path. The word "lahar" is now commonplace among the Filipinos; it's a geologic term they know all too well.

Continue along a level stretch of trail through a fir forest until reaching the north shore of rock-rimmed Round Lake. Look to the east side of the lake to see another of those mud flow formations. Walk around the shore until you find the perfect spot for a picnic. After enjoying the lake, head back the way you came.

Directions: From Highway 50 at Highway 89, proceed south on Highway 89 for 5.2 miles to Big Meadow trailhead. Park in the lot on the left just past the trailhead. Access is free.

78. Trail of the Gargoyles

EFFORT:..Minimal
LENGTH:...3.0 miles
GEOLOGICAL FEATURE(S):..................Volcanism, Erosional Features
LOCATION:...Stanislaus National Forest

Description: This hidden gem of an interpretive trail is worth driving a mile on a bumpy dirt road. It's a beautiful and amazing spot which dramatically displays the process of erosion upon soft volcanic deposits. Somebody in the Forest Service seems to have taken some delight in trail naming. In this area, other intriguingly named interpretive trails include Columns of the Giants, Trail of the Survivors, and Trail of the Ancient Dwarfs.

From the parking area, walk up the dirt road to the trail register and a startling overlook of a deep, forested canyon with the mountains beyond them in the distance. Even if you didn't come to hike the trail, this view alone would be worth the stop. To the north and south, tall cliffs circle around the canyon. There is not much tree cover on this trail, so wear a hat and carry water. What trees you'll find are Jeffrey pine, white fir, lodgepole pine, and western juniper. Manzanita bushes are also growing among the sparse ground vegetation.

There is evidence here of several volcanic events—lava flows, lahars (mudflows – see previous hike), and ash deposits. You can immediately see that the cliff edges are fragile and highly eroded. Stay away from the edge. The South Rim Trail follows the south canyon wall, and the North Rim Trail follows the north canyon wall. This is not a loop. You walk to the end of one trail, come back, and walk the other direction. The two trails are similar, but they do have different formations, and it is worthwhile hiking both.

Someone has gone to some trouble to give the formations colorful names, but the trail is not in the best condition. We could not find all the numbered posts described in our trail brochure. Nevertheless, we did not have much trouble identifying the important features. You can start with either the north or south rim. For this description, we are heading south (left facing the canyon).

You are walking on the remnants of a lahar, rock formed by a mixture of volcanic ash and snow or water which flowed as hot mud, collecting smaller rocks and debris along the way. Once the mudflows cooled, the resulting material resembled concrete. You can see the rocks embedded in the ash where they were gathered up.

The dark band of rock around the canyon, below the rim, called the River of Stone by the brochure, is an ancient lava flow that filled a river channel. Above and below the lava are lahar deposits. As you approach the south canyon wall, you get a good view of the "Wall of Noses." Stop and enjoy the metaphor. It is easy to see that the noses were formed by water erosion on the ash flow deposits.

Continuing on the footpath, you head downhill and swing around a tall block of stone which you can see very well once the trail takes you back to the canyon rim. Look back at the eroded stone wall you just detoured around. It looks a bit like a castle. The trail continues only a little further, ending at an overlook of the canyon.

Return the way you came to the trailhead, then continue on the North Rim Trail. At stop #2, you can see the tops of a series of basalt columns fifty or sixty feet tall. Such columns are a natural result of lava cooling at a uniform rate. Cracking patterns form similar to those in a mud flat baking in the sun. If you are interested in such columnar formations, you can drive further up Highway 108 to the Columns of the

Wall of Noses

Giants Trail (Hike #80) where a much more impressive example can be seen. And an even better example, not far away, is at Devils Postpile (Hike #102).

On either leg of this trail, you will notice many granite boulders, or erratics, transported to their current location by glaciers. These big rocks, caught in the ice sheets, acted like grinding stones, polishing and gouging the landscape as the glacier moved through. After the ice retreated, the boulders were left behind.

At stop #7, you will see evidence of how frozen water in the crevices of the lava enlarge the cracks over time and create a fragmented surface. This process is called frost wedging.

The Gargoyles at stop #9 are the interesting columns that have been carved by erosion of the mud flow deposits. Such natural sculptures are formed fairly rapidly in the soft lahar material by wind, rain, and snow.

The trail ends at stop #11. Turn back and return to the trailhead.

Directions: From Highway 108 in Sonora, travel east to Strawberry, continuing a couple of miles before turning right on Herring Creek Road. Proceed 6 miles to the trailhead. This paved two-lane road will narrow after a couple of miles to become a paved one-lane road, after which it becomes a rough dirt road for the last mile. When we visited, the only marker for the trail was a piece of paper stapled to a tree. The paper may not be there when you visit. If you reach a signed fork in the road, you have just passed the pullout for this trail. It is on the left side of the road, an open dirt area with a sign reading, "No Camping Beyond This Point." Stop at the Summit Ranger Station just before you get to Strawberry and ask for a trail pamphlet. This is also a good place for a restroom stop, as there are no facilities at the trailhead. Access is free.

79. Donnell Vista Trail

EFFORT:	Minimal
LENGTH:	0.5 miles
GEOLOGICAL FEATURE(S):	Volcanism, Glaciation
LOCATION:	Stanislaus National Forest

Description: Take fifteen minutes out of your drive across the Sierras to walk this short trail to a grand overlook with superb views of the Dardanelles and the Stanislaus River canyon. At the trailhead, glance through the trail register and sign it if you like.

Located at 6,240-feet high, this paved trail winds past huge granite boulders and low-growing manzanita. A bench has been placed along the way, looking out towards the lava flow called The Dardanelles. It is a nine million-year-old eruption that covers a huge area up to 1,000 feet thick, flowing out seventy miles as far as Knight's Ferry in the foothills to the west.

Continue on the easy trail to the overlook, where a railing separates you from a lengthy drop north into the Stanislaus River canyon. Peer down at the river far below and to the left to Donnell Reservoir, its curving dam, and east to the Dardanelles. You can easily see the profile of the ancient lava flow from this angle, including the Dardanelles Cone. It's a breathtaking vista, and you will want to gaze at it for a while.

When you can tear yourself away from the view, take a moment to walk over the smooth granite nearby and peer at it more carefully. You will see a few incipient potholes left by the rocks swirling in flowing water under the glaciers. There are also many huge xenoliths incorporated into the granite.

Take the same trail back to the parking area.

Directions: From Sonora, take Highway 108 east to the Pinecrest exit, and then go about 18 miles further east on Highway 108 to the Donnell Vista Point on the left. There are restrooms and picnic tables here. Access is free.

80. Columns of the Giants

EFFORT:..Minimal
LENGTH:...0.5 miles
GEOLOGICAL FEATURE(S):..Volcanism
LOCATION:...Stanislaus National Forest

Description: This is an easy walk on a well-worn trail to a cliff of 150,000-year old Pleistocene basalt formations known as the Columns of the Giants. These columns are similar to those found at Devils Postpile National Monument (Hike #102) near Mammoth Lakes, but are more weathered and a little less distinct. The basalt is about 400 feet thick and located in the Middle Fork of the Stanislaus River canyon.

You can see the column formation from the parking area. It's the black wall of rock across the river. Walk south on the trail signed "Trail" and cross the river over a sturdy wooden bridge. When we were here in October, aspens provided bright yellow strokes of color near the water's edge and a couple of amusing water ouzels dove into the frigid water looking for aquatic insects.

Water ouzels, or dippers, are joyful and unusual birds. What they lack in striking physical characteristics, they make up for in behavior. They sit on rocks in streams, bobbing their heads. Then, suddenly, they dive into the current and walk along the streambed underwater. Look for them in fast-moving mountain streams, brownish-black birds a bit smaller than a robin with short tails. You can't mistake them, as they are the only songbird disappearing under whitewater.

We were alone on the trail, except for a squirrel dashing ahead of us and a few Steller's jays hopping on nearby branches.

The landscape is fairly open with well-spaced pine trees as you walk beside the river for a short distance and then turn right away from it.

Head gently uphill and you will soon come upon the huge talus slope of broken columns, with intact columns standing above it. Some of the columns are standing vertically, which is how they form. Some are tilted to a nearly horizontal position by the shifting of the earth's crust.

This lava flow originally covered five square miles. The passage of glacial ice carved it down to two. If you could look down on top of the columns you would be able to see the polished tops, indicating the passage of glaciers. There is explanatory information about how these columns form at the end of the trail. The geometric shapes are created naturally by slow, uniform cooling and cracking of the basalt. Given enough time and enough mass, basalt flows always shrink and crack into a hexagonal pattern. This is because the hexagon represents the most energy-efficient geometric shape in nature.

Walk to the right along the base of the wide slope. The trail will turn away from the columns and loop back to the river, but this return leg of the trail is more challenging, especially near the end when you have a steep descent to the bridge. You will lose nothing by returning along the same path you originally traveled instead.

Although there is a picnic table here, a more inviting lunch spot is just west at the Donnell Vista Point (see previous hike). It is well worth the visit.

Directions: On Highway 108 heading east from Pinecrest, note when you reach Clark Fork Road. Drive 5 miles further to the signed Columns of the Giants trail. Turn right into the parking area. There are toilets and one picnic table here. Access is free.

81. Glacier Meadow Loop

EFFORT:..Minimal
LENGTH:..0.5 miles
GEOLOGICAL FEATURE(S):..Glaciation
LOCATION:...Tahoe National Forest

Description: This is an easy walk on an interpretive trail showcasing the glaciation and succession of the area. It is also extremely easy to get to, beginning at the Donner Summit rest stop off Interstate 80. This is the perfect diversion on your way over the hill, to get out of the car, stretch your legs, and use the facilities. Although you can hear the traffic from the freeway throughout most of the walk, it is only mildly distracting.

As we write this, the trail is unsigned. The Forest Service is working on new signs to replace those badly vandalized and removed some years ago.

Start the trail from behind the building at the rest stop, on the right side just past the picnic tables, or on the northeast side of the Sno-Park parking lot from the Pacific Crest Trail access trail.

You will walk through an alpine forest decorated with huge granite boulders. The trail is fairly easy, but can be wet in spring, and will be buried in snow throughout the winter and into May. In autumn, you will enjoy the colors of the changing season in the surrounding aspens.

On your right, you will encounter a huge sloping slab of granite, well fractured and open like a beckoning ballroom dance floor. Go ahead and frolic on it. While you are dancing, look at the many xenoliths caught up in the granite. There are also potholes here, made by the swirling of stones in streams under the glacier. Look for striations and scratches made from the scraping of rocks along the surface of the slab as the glacier moved above it.

When you are finished at this playground, return to the trail and cross a seasonal creek. There is a large roundish boulder beside the trail that shows a good example of frost wedging. The boulder has been split into four pieces by the continuous freezing and thawing within its fractures. You can tell by the clean surface of the break

that this occurred in the relatively recent geologic past.

Heading south, you will come to the edge of a pond which, when rimmed with snow, is an enchanting little stop in the woods. A sign here marks the trail junction where the south path follows alongside the pond and leads to the Pacific Crest Trail. You can explore it a bit if you like. This is a pretty little pocket of solitude.

Our loop trail continues to the left (north), heading up through more granite boulders on its return to the rest stop. The trail takes you up one section of stone steps, and then down another, where you emerge behind and just east of the rest stop building, completing the loop.

Directions: From Interstate 80 immediately west of Donner Summit, take the Castle Peak Area/Boreal Ridge Road exit. Look for a sign reading Tahoe National Forest Trailhead/Donner Summit/Pacific Crest Trail. After exiting the freeway (and going under it if you were traveling west), turn left and proceed to the Sno-Park. Park near the trailhead at the northeast edge of the lot. The trail actually starts and ends at the eastbound Donner Summit Rest Area, but unattended parking is not allowed there. Access is free.

Yosemite National Park

What can we say about Yosemite, except that we are grateful to have it practically in our backyard. Spectacular waterfalls and gorgeous granite amid evergreen forests are the main attractions here. Some people consider many spots in this park sacred. For rock climbers all over the world it is a shrine, home to magnificent landmarks like Half Dome and El Capitan. The spectacular granite domes and monoliths will imbue the most jaded travelers with awe. We do not believe that anyone is immune to the majesty of Yosemite—from Ansel Adams to John Muir to Teddy Roosevelt, to you and me.

For us, the granite would be enough to justify the national park classification. But Yosemite has more superlatives to offer. It has the deep, glacier-carved Yosemite Valley with its lovely meadows and long-distance vertical views. It has numerous dramatic waterfalls as part of its glacial legacy. And it has three groves of giant sequoias which are the main reason for another national park a little south—Sequoia National Park. It's a crowded park, especially in summer, but as in most national parks, the crowds tend to cluster together on the main road and not venture out on the longer trails. As soon as you walk more than a mile, you will leave most of the people behind. A free shuttle takes visitors through Yosemite Valley year-round. In summer, free shuttle buses run from Wawona to the Mariposa Grove, and from Tioga Pass to Tenaya Lake. Hikers buses run daily to Glacier Point from late spring through autumn and between Tuolumne Meadows and Yosemite Valley from late June through Labor Day.

If you want to see the water shows, come in spring or early summer when the snowmelt is at its height. If you want to avoid the crowds, come in autumn before the snows arrive. If you ski, winter is the season to take in the wonders of cross-country trails. Tioga Road, which passes through the park west to east, is closed in winter, but the heart of Yosemite is open all year.

There are over 800 miles of trails in this park. You could spend several months exploring its vastness. We have chosen just a few, those which we believe most accurately highlight the geology of the park, a story which centers around glaciation.

Directions: These directions to the park will not be repeated in the details for each hike. There are several routes to Yosemite: Highway 120, heading east from Central California, leaves Highway 99 in

Manteca, south of Stockton. Coming from further south on Highway 99, take Highway 140 northeast from Merced. From the eastern side off of Highway 395 in Lee Vining, take Highway 120 west through Tioga Pass. The south entrance is on Highway 41 from Fresno. There is a hefty fee for entering Yosemite ($20 per car last time we went), but it is good for seven days. You will get your money's worth if you are staying a few days. If you live close by, a year's pass is a bargain at $40.00.

82. Lembert Dome Trail

EFFORT:..Minimal
LENGTH:...2.0 miles
GEOLOGICAL FEATURE(S):...................Glaciation, Erosional Features
LOCATION:...Yosemite National Park

Description: Climb up 800-foot high Lembert Dome for great views of Tuolumne Meadows from a height of 9,450 feet. You will have noticed early on in your acquaintance with Yosemite that large granite domes figure prominently in its geology. The entire Sierra Nevada Range is a massive granite batholith. The domes are a result of the natural weathering exhibited by granite. Exposed to rain, wind and cold, they shed layers in a process called exfoliation, or sheeting. The result, after several layers are shed, is a round boulder. This can be observed throughout the Sierras and anywhere that granite is present. But you don't often see boulders as immense as those found in Yosemite. El Capitan, for instance, is believed to be the single biggest granite rock in the world. Other prominent domes include Half Dome, North Dome, Pothole Dome, and Sentinel Dome.

Before heading out on the trail, take a moment to look around and imagine the geologic history of the area. During the glacial epoch, this valley was inundated by a giant river of ice up to 2,200 feet thick. The thickness of a glacier can be determined in part by observing where it did not leave its mark. In this case, the top 200 feet of Cathedral Peak to the southwest was left untouched by the ice. Below that height, the mountain shows evidence of glaciation.

The trail is short but steep, with an average grade of twelve percent, and climbs relentlessly. If you are prone to altitude sickness, don't make this climb. In any case, make it slow and stop to catch your breath often. Having said that, the sheer face of the dome where experienced climbers may be clinging is deceptive. You will be climbing up the other side, which is much easier and requires no climbing equipment.

This dome is name for Jean Baptiste Lembert, a sheepherder and resident who was murdered here in the 1890s. His body was found in a cabin in Yosemite Valley, but his murderer was never found. Start out on the trail by the restrooms, the trail for both Dog Lake and Lembert Dome. Climb around the dome and to the back side through lodgepole pine. The dirt path will give way to bare rock after 0.8 miles. From here, choose your route and climb up onto the granite. There is no trail onto the dome. Make your way up the safest way you can, being careful to get good footholds. Although the coarseness of granite makes it relatively easy to climb, loose material can prove treacherous. If you look for them on your way up, you will see the striations (scratches) left by the passing glaciers. Also notice the conspicuous glacial erratics left on top of the dome.

Your reward for the climb is the stunning, panoramic view. Look out from your high perch over Tuolumne Meadows with its meandering streams and the surrounding mountains named for notable scientists (Lyell, Dana, Gibbs). Sir Charles Lyell was an extremely important early geologist who wrote the first geology textbook, *Principles of Geology*. James Dwight Dana was professor of geology at Yale when the peak was named and wrote the first book on mineralogy. Oliver Wolcott Gibbs was a chemist at Harvard, and the founder of the National Academy of Sciences.

The return trip is on the same path.

Directions: Find the Lembert Dome parking lot at the east end of Tuolumne Meadows off of Tioga Road. This trailhead is shared and signed for Lembert Dome, Dog Lake, Soda Springs, and Glen Aulin Trails. The trail starts near the restrooms.

83. Pothole Dome Trail

EFFORT:...Minimal
LENGTH:...2.0 miles
GEOLOGICAL FEATURE(S):...................Glaciation, Erosional Features
LOCATION:...Yosemite National Park

Description: This is a short hike to an easily reached granite dome which formed about 85 million years ago during the Cretaceous when the magma cooled from the Cathedral Peak pluton. There are several domes you can climb in Yosemite (see previous hike), and all of them are fun, but this one provides an especially good lesson in geology.

From the parking area, look directly across the meadow to the granite dome you are about to climb. In summer, the meadow will be green and blooming red with Lemmon's paintbrush. In autumn, it is dry and golden. Don't stray into the meadows at any time of year, as these meadows are extremely fragile and easily damaged. Although it is tempting to cut across the meadow to the dome, don't do it. This trail is short enough as it is.

Take the trail to the left of the parking area along the edge of the meadow, west and then north. The trail turns east and becomes a narrow track between the base of the dome on your left and the meadow on your right. A few young conifers grow here along the trail.

At 0.3 miles, the trail turns northeast. You will see where hikers before you have left the trail to walk up the gentle east side of the dome. You will do the same. There is a pronounced joint running all the way to the top, making a sort of trail if you want something to follow.

Once upon the smooth granite, the geologist in our party was wriggling with glee. A number of interesting features leap out at you right away. First, the differential weathering is highly pronounced, where little knobs of perfect pink potassium feldspar crystals stick stubbornly out of the bedrock granite. The protuberances are harder than the granite matrix, which erodes away around them.

Even when the feldspar crystals aren't sticking out of the granite, they are remarkable for their incredible size, which plunged our geologist into ecstatic burbles. Feldspar is a ubiquitous component of granite, but we have never seen it so large. These rectangular crystals were two to three inches in length, and are typical in the Cathedral Peak granite porphyry. A porphyritic rock is one that has pronounced phenocrysts set

Pothole Dome

in a groundmass of smaller crystals, which means the original melt cooled in two distinct stages. If you are lucky enough to have a sunny day, the crystal faces and cleavage planes will be sparkling all over the dome, dazzling you. The size of the euhedral crystals indicates that the original pluton cooled very slowly, allowing enough time and space in the magmatic chamber for the true shape of the crystal to form.

Continue upslope. As you approach the high point, the climb gets a little steeper, but continues to be easy. As you gain elevation, you will have better and better views of your surroundings. The next part of this geology lesson comes about two-thirds of the way up where the polished surfaces of the granite are more and more evident. The rock is as smooth as a Corian countertop, polished by rocks carried within the glacier grinding against bedrock as the ice sheet moved. You will no doubt catch the glint of these surfaces if the sun is shining. You may think of glaciers as pure ice, but in fact the bottom of a glacier is mainly rocks and soil held by the ice. Be sure to run your hand over the smooth surfaces to feel just how effectively glaciers can grind.

Nothing grows on this bare granite except in the occasional cleft where the rock has fractured and a bit of soil has accumulated. One such crack can be seen near the summit, and a few small trees have rooted themselves there. The trees help to create the soil that sustains them, breaking down the rock with their root systems.

The top of the dome contains boulders called erratics which were brought here by glacier movement. They are easily identified because they stand out clearly against the symmetry and smoothness of the dome. Roundish boulders sitting on the dome like goose eggs on a platter were carried within the ice sheets and then left here when the ice melted. You can look westward from the summit to see several erratics on the smooth dome across the way. They stand out in profile on the horizon.

Pothole Dome is named for the many potholes on it, mainly on the south slope. Most potholes are found in streambeds, created by boulders jostling around in a depression. These potholes, in contrast, were probably created by rocks swirling in waterways flowing under the glacial ice.

Once you attain the dome's high point, you will have sweeping views in all directions, including the Cathedral Range. To the east is Tuolumne Meadows spread out with its narrow waterways in clear relief.

When you are done exploring the dome (and you can drag your geologist away from it), head back down to its base however you wish and take the same trail back to the parking area.

Directions: From Tuolumne Meadows Information Center, proceed 1.5 miles west on Tioga Road to a signed turnout at the west end of Tuolumne Meadows. The parking area is on the north side of the road.

84. Taft Point Trail

EFFORT:...Minimal
LENGTH:...2.4 miles
GEOLOGICAL FEATURE(S):......................................Erosional Features
LOCATION:...Yosemite National Park

Description: Fantastic views can be had from Taft Point, and the fissures are a geologic marvel.

Descend from the parking area to the trailhead shared with Sentinel Dome and turn left. As you continue downhill, notice a sparkling outcrop of quartz protruding from the ground on the right side of the trail. Stop for a moment to admire the crystals. This distinctive vein of quartz passes under the trail as well, some of it peeking up underfoot.

Fissure at Taft Point

Walk into a sparse, mixed conifer forest. Soon you will reach Sentinel Creek, which you cross by boulder hopping. In autumn, the creek will be dry. The trail continues to a junction at 0.5 miles. The trail to your right heads back towards Sentinel Dome. Continue going straight. After the junction, you will descend into a moister area where water seepage provides habitat for bracken fern and wildflowers. The trees become more dense as well along this section, and their limbs are trimmed with bright green lichen. Trees that have fallen across the trail have been cut to allow passage. You won't see much in the way of views through this section, but this is a good place for wildlife spotting. Steller's jays dart through the trees, and deer may wander along for the green grass growing here. We were lucky enough to spot three grouse scratching among the ferns directly beside the trail. They were wary, but did not bolt. We watched them for quite a while, snapped some pictures, then moved on.

As you approach your destination, the trail becomes somewhat rockier, and you can see that the trees open up ahead. Climb down some natural rock stairs beside friendly granite boulders, then walk out of the forest and across bare granite. A short distance ahead the ground drops away quite suddenly and radically.

Soon you arrive at the edge of a chasm above the first of the Fissures, five vertical fractures in Profile Cliff, extending 3,000 feet straight down to the valley below. The Fissures were created by successive freezing and thawing of the rock, which wedged it apart. Stay a safe distance back, and make sure you have firm footing. Standing on the edge of this cliff, looking so far straight down is a perfect way to make yourself teeter. However, we couldn't resist lying on our stomachs and looking over the edge a couple of times.

One of the narrower fissures has two boulders wedged in it, caught where they fell from above.

Just beyond the Fissures, as you walk near the edge of the cliff, Taft Point has a railing that will provide a safer opportunity for looking over from your 7,500-foot height. El Capitan stands looming before you, a 4,000-foot tall granite monolith, and Yosemite Valley is spread out far below.

This is probably a good spot to stop and reflect on why El Capitan is here, or why any of the features of Yosemite turned out as they did after the patient forces of ice, wind, and water whittled away at them over time. Although we have been talking about the granite as though it is just a single type of material, it actually comes in many different compositions. In 1930, after an exhaustive and still definitive geologic mapping project, F.C. Calkins of the USGS published a paper describing the Yosemite bedrock in which he named the different rock types, such as the El Capitan Granite, the Sentinel Granodiorite, Taft Granite, etc. The differences are mainly in crystal size and the ratios of quartz, feldspar, hornblende, and biotite. These small differences in composition can lead to dramatic differences in the rate and pattern of erosion. El Capitan is composed of Taft and El Capitan Granites, both rich in quartz and resistant to weathering. So there it stands where the less resistant types of rock which used to stand around it have given way. El Capitan, Half Dome, and other big hunks of stubborn rock are largely unjointed. Without joints for erosional forces to gain a foothold, these rocks present a formidable defense against the elements.

You can continue walking west near the edge of the gorge to a dramatic ledge with a single small tree growing on it, and then a little further along to a view facing westward, giving you another perspective. Any of the granite slabs up here make a great picnic table. You will feel like you're on top of the world and will want to stay a while to enjoy the majesty.

When you're ready, take the same route back.

Directions: From Wawona Road/Highway 41, turn onto Glacier Point Road. Proceed 13.2 miles to the Sentinel Dome/Taft Point parking area, two miles before the end of the road. This road is closed in winter. There is a single pit toilet. Parking spaces here are hard to find on weekends and in summer. Consider taking the hikers bus. And definitely visit Glacier Point at the end of the road while you are here for an even better view (yes, it's possible) of Yosemite's most famous landmarks.

85. Glacier Point Trail

EFFORT:..Minimal
LENGTH:..0.5 miles
GEOLOGICAL FEATURE(S):....................Glaciation, Erosional Features
LOCATION:...Yosemite National Park

Description: This short, paved trail offers about the biggest payoff for the smallest effort you will ever find, anywhere. From the gift shop, walk out on Glacier Point Trail to an overlook where a small stone building sits. From the balcony of this building or the viewing deck below it, you get the view of a lifetime. There is no way to oversell this one. This view can bring you to your knees, and, in the process, it will reveal to you all that the word "Yosemite" can evoke.

You stand on the edge of the south cliff above Yosemite Valley where tiny cars are parked in lots dotting the flat valley floor. Instead of looking up at Half Dome, you are looking across at it, and this is probably as close as you will ever get to it, unless you climb it. Bring your binoculars and try to spot climbers on the side of Half Dome. We saw a string of five of them on a trip in October, tiny black specks on that massive rock, not visible without magnification.

You will also want to train those binoculars on the waterfalls on view—Upper and Lower Yosemite, Vernal, and Nevada Falls. Don't forget to feast your eyes on other landmarks—Basket Dome, North Dome, and Clouds Rest.

When you can tear your gaze away from this view, the little hut behind you has information explaining the geology of the glacially-carved valley, and the source of the impressive granite formations.

Continue to the end of the trail and another such view, this time angled a bit differently. It will be hard to leave this spot, so perhaps you should plan your picnic here. When you are ready, return the same way.

Directions: From Wawona Road/Highway 41, turn onto Glacier Point Road. This road is closed in winter. Proceed to the end of the road, past Washburn Point (stop here too), to the Glacier Point parking lot. There are restrooms and a snack and gift shop located here.

86. Porcupine Creek Trail

EFFORT:...Difficult
LENGTH:...6.0 miles
GEOLOGICAL FEATURE(S):.....................................Erosional Features
LOCATION:...Yosemite National Park

Description: This trail eventually leads to North Dome after 8 miles, but since exfoliated domes are certainly not rare in Yosemite, and since we have included others which are easier to get to, this trip will focus on something much harder to find in the Sierras, a natural stone arch called Indian Rock. If you want to, you can push on to the summit of North Dome for its breathtaking views. From the top of North Dome, you get the best possible look at Half Dome.

Head south through a red fir forest to drop down to a paved road. Follow it downhill for about a half mile until you cross a tributary of Porcupine Creek and leave the road. Cross Porcupine Creek itself, and continue uphill for a short distance before descending again. Enjoy wildflower blooms in season as you walk through forest and then meadow.

After the first mile you cross another creek, then walk a flat trail through tree cover. Climb up to a saddle and a trail junction. The left arm goes to Yosemite Valley. The right goes to North Dome. Go right and immediately meet up with another trail junction. Right is for Yosemite Falls. Bear left towards North Dome.

Begin climbing up Indian Ridge. Ford a stream after two miles, then climb through thinning tree cover on a fairly steep route up to a trail junction at 8,140 feet. Right, the trail continues to North Dome. Take the left trail towards Indian Rock. The trail is steep and open over a sandy path up to the arch, reached in another 0.7 miles and 400 feet in elevation. The arch is a bit rough-hewn, as though chiseled by a blind giant.

After checking out the arch, the only such feature in Yosemite, return to the main trail and decide if you want to continue out to North Dome. The views from that vantage point are spectacular. If you don't want to go that far, turn right at the junction and return the way you came.

Directions: On Highway 120, 22 miles west of Tioga Pass, locate the Porcupine Creek Trailhead parking area on the south side of the road.

87. Hetch Hetchy Trail

EFFORT:..Moderate
LENGTH:..5.0 miles
GEOLOGICAL FEATURE(S):................................Glaciation
LOCATION:................................Yosemite National Park

Description: Hike this beautiful and special part of Yosemite and know that you have had a rare experience. Very few of Yosemite's many visitors ever see or even know about Hetch Hetchy. That's mainly because there are no roads within the park connecting it with Yosemite Valley or Tuolumne Meadows. Many visitors to Hetch Hetchy come just for the view from the top of the dam, from which you look out over the reservoir to the wispy Tueeulala waterfall and the raging Wapama Falls, your destination for this hike. If you come on a spring or summer weekend, you will probably see other hikers here, but no crowds.

Hetch Hetchy Valley, now flooded by the damming of the Tuolumne River, was named from the Native American word "Hatchhatchie," a species of grass with edible seeds that once grew there. The history and character of this valley are similar to that of its more famous neighbor, Yosemite Valley. Before the dam, the valley was a plunging, U-shaped gorge carved out by a glacier about 10,000 years ago. Evidence of the polishing action of the glacier is abundant along the trail. Before the glacier, the valley was V-shaped, created by the erosional force of the river. The narrow, steep canyon walls made this spot perfect for building a dam, a project fiercely opposed by John Muir and others and approved by Woodrow Wilson in 1913. The movement to remove the dam is still extant, led by the Sierra Club.

O'Shaughnessy Dam, named for Michael O'Shaughnessy, San Francisco's city engineer at the time, was built between 1915 and 1923. At 312 feet tall, it was the largest structure on the West Coast at that time. Between 1935 and 1938, it was raised another 80 feet. The reservoir supplies San Francisco with drinking water. For that reason, swimming and boating are not allowed. Fishing is allowed, but live bait cannot be used.

Start out walking on top of O'Shaughnessy Dam. From atop the dam, look out over the reservoir and see the two striking waterfalls on the north cliff faces. In the accompanying photograph, the falls are visible coursing down to the valley floor before the dam was built. The wider waterfall is Wapama Falls, which you may have seen while driving in. Even from this vantage point, you can see its abundant spray. The slimmer, more delicate Tueeulala Falls can be seen as well. It too has a drop of more than a thousand feet. Tueeulala dries up in summer, so come in late spring for the best show. Look for

Hetch Hetchy Dome on the north side of the reservoir, and Kolana Rock, Hetch Hetchy's El Capitan, on the south side. Although the view from the dam is impressive, it is nothing like walking across the granite or standing in the spray of the waterfall.

After crossing the dam, you enter a tunnel through the rock. A flashlight would be helpful in the tunnel, but if you don't have one, you can allow your eyes to acclimate and walk carefully towards the light at the other end. There may be some puddles of water on the floor of the tunnel. Upon exiting the tunnel, you will reach the trailhead where there are some informational panels and a trail map.

The trail begins as a wide, sandy path along the northern edge of the reservoir with Wapama Falls visible in the distance. Vegetation along this trail includes big leaf maple, Ponderosa pine, incense cedar, black oak, and poison oak. Wildflowers blooming in spring, include shooting stars, Sierra leisiga, lupine, buttercups, and California fuchsia. Among the wildlife you may see are mule deer, black bear, squirrels, rattlesnakes, and kingsnakes. When we were here, we saw squirrels, a handsome lizard, and several types of butterflies, including Monarchs and Swallowtails.

B 553 Looking up Hetch-Hetchy Valley from Surprise Point.   Photo., San Francisco.

Hetch Hetchy Valley, 1908 *(Courtesy Sierra Club Bulletin, Vol. VI. No. 4, January, 1908)*

At the edge of the trail, notice the piles of grüs, the name given to small bits of disintegrated granite. The trail travels through patches of shade and open sunshine. About the time you lose sight of Wapama Falls, you begin to climb up a gentle grade. Soon you cross a seasonal stream through a fern-lined gully. Much of the charm of this trail comes from its continuously changing character. It will alternate between bare granite to shady oak woodland, to moist meadow grasses. The lovely reservoir will be on your right all the way, and the steep north cliff on your left. As you look up the side of the cliff, notice the dark vertical stripes. These are manganese oxide deposits marking the path of groundwater seeping out of the cliff face. They are most pronounced along the uppermost portion of Tueeulala Falls.

After 0.7 miles, you reach a T-junction. Turn right onto a narrow rocky trail. From here, the path gets more difficult, rising and falling, studded with rocks. Hiking boots are definitely an asset along this trail, and watching your step is critical. You will cross a couple of sections of bare granite. These are excellent spots to observe the glacial polishing and striations.

A bridge crosses over a boulder-filled ravine where Tueeulala Falls flows into the reservoir. By June, you may not see any water flowing here. It will be seeping through the lower rocks or be gone altogether. Looking up, you will see the long, wispy spray drifting leisurely down.

In 2.4 miles, you reach the first of four bridges spanning the gush of water at the base of Wapama Falls, a huge and impressive 1,200-foot torrent. The waterfall is on Falls Creek, a tributary of the Tuolumne River. From your perch on a footbridge across the base of the falls, feel the spray from the powerful white water leaping off the granite cliff. You will want to spend some time here, cooling off in the spray. The time of year of your visit will determine how wet you get.

When you have had enough of this impressive natural spectacle, return via the same route.

Directions: The road is open in May until the first snows in November. On Highway 120, just before the Big Oak Flat Entrance Station of Yosemite National Park, take Evergreen Road north 7.4 miles to Camp Mather. Turn right on Hetch Hetchy Road and drive into the park. Proceed 6.5 more miles to the end of the road at O'Shaughnessy Dam. Stop at Inspiration Point along the way for great views and to get your bearings. Just before you reach the dam, you will pass a comfort station on your right. There are restrooms and a picnic area there. Parking is available at the dam, but no other facilities are located there.

88. Mono Pass Trail

EFFORT:..Moderate
LENGTH:..7.0 miles
GEOLOGICAL FEATURE(S):..Mining
LOCATION:..Yosemite National Park

Description: Beginning at Dana Meadow, take this trail up to Mono Pass straddling the crest of the Sierras at 10,600 feet. The total elevation gain along the way is about 1,000 feet. There is sparse vegetation and lovely bare granite. The historic Prescott Mining District is located at Mono Pass. It contains three 1880s mines: Ella Bloss, Ella Bloss No. 2, and the Golden Crown. They are well-preserved, and miners' cabins still stand here. This pass was the main trans-Sierra route for the Mono Basin Paiute who traded salt and obsidian with the Yosemite Miwok for acorns and berries.

The trail starts by routing you through a lodgepole pine forest. About a quarter mile along, you break out of the tree cover to enter a small meadow. After a half mile, cross Dana Meadows Creek. You will then begin to climb a moraine, and cross a couple of small streams feeding Parker Pass Creek before reaching an old cabin.

At two miles, you come to a junction. Stay on the Mono Pass Trail. From here, the trail climbs more steeply, passing another old cabin, then levels out somewhat and brings you to a small lake. A spur trail heading south from here takes you to a group of five cabins. These whitebark pine structures housed the miners of the Golden Crown and Ella Bloss mines. From here, take a look at Mt. Gibbs to the north. The upper reaches of that peak are composed of unstable metamorphic rock, and are prone to movement. The lower slopes are more stable granite. The movement is caused by ice wedging, that is, the perpetual freezing and thawing of water in cracks in the rocks, forcing the cracks to widen and the rocks to break apart.

The trail climbs the last 1.5 miles, with some steep stretches. It breaks out of the mature lodgepole pine forest onto a broad, westward dipping plain, mantled by a green meadow with lots of wild onions. Flowers along this trail include lupine, Indian paintbrush, phlox, and mountain mint. To the east of the cabins lies Summit Lake with willows growing at its west end. At the pass, scattered, windswept whitebark pines dot the ground where meadow recedes to bare rock.

From these heights, you get a great view of Mono Lake to the east.

The mine followed a skarn deposit with silver mineralization. Skarn is a general term for pre-existing metamorphosed rocks that are adjacent to plutons. It was the heat from the pluton that metamorphosed whatever type of rock was originally there. Mono Pass is atop a thin roof pendant overlying granitic rocks, hence the skarns. The ancient seafloor that once covered the granite batholith has been largely stripped away over time. The remains of the sediments, which have been twisted and crushed, are the "roof pendants," remnants of the ancient "roof" which covered the granite. Pockets of these roof pendants can be found throughout the Sierra Nevadas, and are often the site of mining operations. Their metamorphic composition allows for the crystallization of precious minerals, such as gold, in the formation.

Angular granitic peaks of the Kuna Crest rise to the west. The trail leads down the east side of the range through Bloody Canyon. Its name was earned for the many horses that were injured or killed going through it. The canyon is lined with sharp rocks which cut the flanks of horses and pack animals, and leads steeply down to the Mono Lake plain.

Return on the same path.

Directions: From Tioga Road, locate the trailhead at Dana Meadow. An alternate route is from the Walker Lake trailhead off of Highway 158. This trail is a difficult 5 miles to Mono Pass up Bloody Canyon.

89. Gaylor Lakes Trail

EFFORT:..Difficult
LENGTH:..4.0 miles
GEOLOGICAL FEATURE(S):..Mining
LOCATION:...Yosemite National Park

Description: Take this popular trail a mile to reach Middle Gaylor Lake, then Upper Gaylor Lake, and on to the ruins of an unsuccessful silver mine at 2.0 miles. At these high elevations and with a steep pitch, the climb will be difficult for most people.

Start out at over 9,000 feet on a rocky trail through forest and meadow, switchbacking up a roof pendant of metamorphic rock to a ridge-top at about 0.75 miles. Views all around are spectacular here in the high country of Yosemite with Gaylor Peak to the north, the Cathedral Range and Mammoth Peak to the south. You can also see Granite Basin and its two sparkling tarns ahead in the distance. Below you is Middle Gaylor Lake.

Descend on a treacherous rocky trail to its shore after a mile of hiking. Middle Gaylor Lake is at 10,334 feet high. Continue around Middle Gaylor's northern shore about a quarter mile farther. A creek leading uphill from Middle Gaylor leads to Upper Gaylor. There is a trail junction here. The left path leads around Middle Gaylor Lake. The right path follows its connecting stream to Upper Gaylor Lake.

Follow the stream up through lovely meadows dotted with glacial erratics. Everyone agrees that hiking in Yosemite is sublime. On this trail, you will enjoy a feast of treats that reinforce that opinion. Views west into the heart of Yosemite are superb.

You reach Upper Gaylor Lake after 1.7 miles. It is a rocky bowl (glacial cirque) with almost no vegetation around it. If you like bare rock (you do, of course), then you will be quite at home sitting here with the snow-capped granite peaks surrounding you and reflected in the Gaylor lakes.

Even after two enchanting alpine lakes, we are not yet done, though. There is more climbing to do, so rest a while and then continue along Upper Gaylor's west bank. At the north end of the lake you will come to a little run-off stream and a trail fork. You want to go north to continue on to the ruins of the Great Sierra Mine.

Leaving Upper Gaylor Lake behind, climb steeply north for another 0.3 miles to a height of 10,760 feet. You will come to an old stone building with three-foot thick walls, its chimney still intact. This is one of the buildings left from the

Great Sierra Mine. Explore the area to see other remains, including some mine shafts.

The mine tapped into the quartz Sheepherder Vein, so named because it was discovered by a sheepherder named William Bruskey, Jr. in 1874. Or rather, he stumbled upon a previous miner's pick and shovel marking the spot. Rocks from the area tested high in silver. Miners flocked to the Tioga and Mono Pass area to strike it rich. Towns sprung up and investors poured money in, but the silver was not forthcoming. The unsuccessful mines were quickly abandoned.

From the mine site, you can look back down along your hiking route to Middle and Upper Gaylor Lakes, Gaylor Peak, and the mountains beyond. This is a great place to savor a snack and the endless views of the Sierra high country before returning along the same route.

Directions: From Highway 120 (Tioga Road) just west of the Tioga Pass entrance, park alongside the north side of Tioga Road. There is an entrance fee to the park.

Tip: You can catch this trail from just outside the park, just east of the Tioga entrance station, by parking in a pullout and walking cross-country to join it. This will enable you to avoid the entrance fee and shorten the hike.

90. Bennettville Trail

EFFORT:	Moderate
LENGTH:	1.5 to 3.5 miles
GEOLOGICAL FEATURE(S):	Mining
LOCATION:	Inyo National Forest

Description: This trail takes you to the site of the historic mining town of Bennettville, named for Thomas J. Bennett, president of the Great Sierra Consolidated Silver Company. When the company bought up several silver mining claims in the area in 1881, it created Bennettville as a company town. In its day, Bennettville was a modern town with a telegraph line and sophisticated mining equipment. The residents were primarily from New England and were responsible for building the old Tioga Road. When the silver mines turned out to be unproductive and were closed in

1889, the town dried up and blew away.

At the trailhead, an informational panel will give you some background on this town and the mine that supported it. Start out by crossing Lee Vining Creek and going right on the trail to a fork. Bear left to go to Bennettville. Climb up above the campground and then down again above Mine Creek. The trail follows Mine Creek to the townsite and on to three lakes. Your introduction to the mining operation will be a tailings pile, mining machinery, and wooden buildings on the right, reached after 0.75 miles. The buildings here, barn, bunkhouse and assay office, are reconstructions. Explore the buildings before continuing.

At this point, you can return to the trailhead for a 1.5-mile trek, or continue southwest on the trail. If you continue, parallel the creek again and you will reach Shell Lake in just over one mile. At 1.7 miles you will come upon pretty Fantail Lake. Along the way, expect flowery meadows and lovely views of White Mountain.

Retrace your steps to return.

Directions: From Highway 395 in Lee Vining, go south to Tioga Road and turn west. Turn right (north) on Saddlebag Lake Road, then left into the Tioga Junction campground. The trailhead is on Junction Campground Road just before site #1. Toilets are available.

91. Tioga Tarns Nature Walk

EFFORT:..Minimal
LENGTH:...0.5 miles
GEOLOGICAL FEATURE(S):...Glaciation
LOCATION:...Inyo National Forest

Description: This is a short, self-guiding loop trail explaining the natural history found in this breathtaking high alpine environment.

Interpretive signs are placed along the trail to let you know what you're looking at. For our purposes, the main thing is to see what the glaciers have wrought. The features you see here will be found all over the high Sierras, so this short trail makes a good introduction. It is also a sweet little diversion if you want to take a lovely walk but don't have time for one of the longer trails in the Yosemite area.

As you know by now, the Sierras have been subjected to a number of glacial periods since their formation, and both Yosemite Valley and Hetch Hetchy are valleys that were carved out by the glaciers. We have seen granite polished smooth, and observed scratches (striations) in the bedrock made by the movement of the ice sheets. We have seen huge boulders that were carried vast distances by the ice and dropped far from their source (erratics). We have seen tons of sediment that were pushed ahead of the glacier to create new land features where none existed before (moraines). On this trail, we will visit a series of small carvings made by the same forces.

Leaving the highway behind, you enter a forest dotted by tiny meadows and diminutive ponds, or tarns. Tarns are small bodies of water that occupy glacially-carved basins, or cirques. There are several of them along this trail. The short loop ends back at the highway's edge before you know it.

Directions: From Highway 395 in Lee Vining, go west on Highway 120 towards Yosemite National Park. The trailhead is just east of Tioga Lake on the north side of Highway 120.

92. Boyden Cavern Family Walking Tour

EFFORT:..Minimal
LENGTH:..N/A
GEOLOGICAL FEATURE(S):................................Caves
LOCATION:....74101 E. Kings Canyon Road, Kings Canyon National Park

Description: Boyden Cavern is located in the deepest canyon in the United States, the spectacular 8,000 foot deep Kings River Canyon, and lies beneath the massive 2,000 foot high marble walls of the famous Kings Gates. The drive into this canyon is both thrilling and a bit scary. It's a long, curvy way down between massive, imposing walls of rock.

Boyden Cavern is a magnificent cave with many varieties of natural speleothems, including rare "shield" formations.

This popular 45-minute tour is suitable for the entire family. The tour begins with a steep five-minute

Kings Canyon Chevron Folds

walk to the cave entrance and from there visitors travel deep within, where the temperature is a constant 55° F. Groups follow a well-lighted and hand-rail equipped trail as guides point out many natural formations. Reservations are not required. Tours leave approximately every hour on the hour.

Popular features include The Pancake Room, a stalactite group called the Upside Down City, the Bat Grotto where bats spend summer days sleeping, and a flowstone formation called Mother Nature's Wedding Cake. The Drapery Room contains massive drapery-style stalactites, long soda straws and twisting crystalline helictites. As usual, the cave guide will point out cave formations that appear to resemble familiar, everyday objects such as the Taco Shell formations, the Baby Elephant and Mom stalagmites, and the Christmas Tree. There is also a subterranean stream and many other unique features.

Directions: From Sacramento or Stockton, take Highway 99 south to Fresno, then Highway 180 east into Kings Canyon National Park. Follow Highway 180 to the bottom of the canyon where the road meets the Kings River. The parking lot is just off the road next to the bridge. The cave is open daily May through October. There are picnic tables near the parking lot. There is a fee for the tour.

93. Zumwalt Meadow Trail

EFFORT:	Minimal
LENGTH:	1.0 miles
GEOLOGICAL FEATURE(S):	Glaciation, Erosional Features
LOCATION:	Kings Canyon National Park

Description: This scenic trail offers a lush meadow, wildflowers, spectacular views of the granite cliffs, and the South Fork Kings River. It is a self-guiding 18-stop nature trail with brochures at the trailhead. The meadow is located on the south side of the river, and the trail will take you along its edge and into the surrounding forest. From the parking area, cross a footbridge to begin the loop.

You will enjoy the views of some of the largest rocks in the park, Grand Sentinel at 8,504 feet high, and North Dome at 8,717 feet. Pinecones litter the landscape where, in season, lupine blooms in a pink profusion.

Zumwalt Meadow was originally carved by a river. Later, it was subjected to the sculpting power of a glacier that was as much as 1,600 feet deep and modified the shape of the valley into the characteristic U. As the glacier advanced, widening the canyon, it also pushed enough rock and sediment through the canyon to create at least thirty moraines. One of these formed a natural dam which blocked the flow of the river. A lake formed behind it. Eventually, that lake filled with sediment to become Zumwalt Meadow.

The trailhead is located on the northeast side of the parking lot. As you start out on the trail, Grand Sentinel stands tall across the river. Head towards the South Fork of the Kings River, which is lined with cottonwoods, willows, alders and sugar pines. You will walk through a forest of incense cedar and ponderosa pine.

At stop #4 you will find bedrock mortars used by the native Monache Indians to grind acorns from black oaks into meal.

After stop #5, cross over the river on a bridge and turn left at a junction with River Trail. Look across the river to see North Dome and notice its sheer wall. This was created by the passing glacier that shaved off the side of the grand monument. Continuing, you will come to the site of a destructive avalanche which occurred in the winter of 1968, the result of heavy snowfall. Just past stop #6, you will encounter a fork. This is the beginning of the loop trail. Bear right to go counterclockwise in the order of the numbered stops.

Pass into the shade of Grand Sentinel and a forest of white fir. On your right, a cliff rises up. On your left is the moist meadow, visited by numerous songbirds and dotted with wildflowers in early summer. Deer and black bear also visit the meadow. At the base of the cliff is a talus pile, created by rocks falling from the cliff face. The trail has been routed through the talus pile at the meadow's edge.

As you come to the western end of the meadow, you will encounter a trail junction. Turn left to continue the loop. Walk along the south side of the meadow with the river on your right. When you return to the beginning of the loop, turn right to return to the parking area.

Directions: From Cedar Grove Village, go east on Highway 180 4.5 miles to Zumwalt Meadow parking area.

94. Crystal Cave

EFFORT:..Moderate
LENGTH:...1.5 miles
GEOLOGICAL FEATURE(S):...Caves
LOCATION:..Sequoia National Park

Description: Crystal Cave was discovered in 1918 by park employees and is named for the extensive crystal formations within. To explore the rich offerings of this beautiful cave, you will need to take a tour offered by the Sequoia Natural History Association, a non-profit educational organization. The standard tour is 50 minutes, and will take you on a half-mile loop through chambers and passageways to view the typical formations—stalactites, stalagmites, drapery, flowstone, cave pearls, and soda straws. This is a living cave, that is, it is wet and still forming.

Once you arrive at the cave parking lot, you will walk a steep half mile trail along Cascade Creek to the cave entrance. For this reason, people in poor physical condition are discouraged from taking the tour.

The tour starts at the Spider Web gate, a metal grate built in a web pattern, which blocks the entrance to the cave. The temperature within the cave is a steady 48° F. Dress accordingly. Backpacks are not allowed in the cave, but cameras are.

Your guide will lead you through the chambers and point out items of interest. This cave began as limestone that was metamorphosed through high temperatures and pressures into marble, then gradually eroded by groundwater. This type of cave is common in Kings Canyon and Sequoia National Parks, but this one is among the most spectacular. It is estimated that there are 10,000 feet of passageways in the cave, maze after maze of tunnels and the occasional expansive chamber, like the Marble Hall, which is 175 feet long and 40 feet high. You will also tour the Organ Room and Dome Room.

After the tour, you will hike back out to the parking area.

Two other tours are offered at Crystal Cave: the Discovery Tour, which is two hours and more in-depth, and the Caving Tour, which can be custom designed and must be reserved.

Directions: From Highway 99 in Visalia, take Highway 198 east through Three Rivers to the Foothills Visitor Center. From Highway 99 in Fresno, take Highway 180 east to Sequoia National Park and the Lodgepole Visitor Center. Purchase tickets at one of the Visitor Centers (not at the cave), and then drive on the Generals Highway to the cave parking lot where there are restrooms and water.

95. Needles Lookout Trail

EFFORT:	Moderate
LENGTH:	5.0 miles
GEOLOGICAL FEATURE(S):	Erosional Features
LOCATION:	Sequoia National Forest

Description: Beginning at a substantial elevation of 8,150 feet, you don't have to do much climbing to get to the overlook. The Needles are dramatic granite formations rising up from the North Fork of the Kern River. The trail winds eastward up and down fairly easily, starting out on an old logging road. After a few hundred yards, the trail narrows to a hiking path, and enters a mixed forest of fir and pine. Climb up to a saddle and then over a hill. Drop down to another saddle, then climb up a series of stairs and ledges along a steep ridge to the lookout tower.

If you have chosen a clear day, your reward will be spectacular. You look down into the Kern River canyon, over to Dome Rock to the southwest, Olancha Peak to the west, and Mt. Whitney northeast. The Kern River flows about 3,000 feet below at the bottom of the canyon. Return by the same route.

Directions: From Porterville in Tulare County, go east on Highway 190 for 40 miles. Turn south on the Western Divide Highway (107). About a half mile south of the Quaking Aspen Campground, take Needles Road (Forest Road 21S05) east for about 3 miles to the end where you will find the trailhead. Access is free.

THE EASTERN SIERRAS

On the eastern side of the Sierra Nevada Range, in the rain shadow of the mountains, everything looks different. Here, the land is a desert. Not much precipitation occurs, and because of sparse tree cover, much of the rich volcanic history of the area is sitting on display like a museum exhibit.

The Long Valley Caldera is responsible for much of the landscape in the Eastern Sierras and for many of the sights we will visit in this region. In Figure 5, you can see the major eruptions and the extent of this volcanic field, which includes Mono Craters, Inyo Craters, Obsidian Dome, Devil's Postpile, Hot Creek, and several other features.

Here on the east side of the mountains, the Sierra Nevada province gives way to the Basin and Range. Technically, a couple of the locations we will visit are in the Basin and Range, such as Mono Lake. But, as you can see on the map, this feature is clearly part of the Long Valley Caldera region, so we are treating all of the associated locales together for the sake of continuity.

The caldera was created about 750,000 years ago by an enormous eruption which emptied a huge magma chamber underground, causing the surface to sink more than a mile into a depression measuring 10 by 20 miles. A series of smaller eruptions ensued over the next few hundred thousand years. The center of the caldera rose in response to new magma filling in below, creating a resurgent dome, a broad, dome-shaped highland of post-caldera lava domes that stand above the surrounding lower lands.

The Inyo Craters are one of the most recently active eruptive centers in the region, dating from about 600 years ago. The only known younger eruption was Negit Island in Mono Lake, believed to be only 250 years old. We will be visiting these youngsters as we explore the Eastern Sierras. Mammoth Mountain on

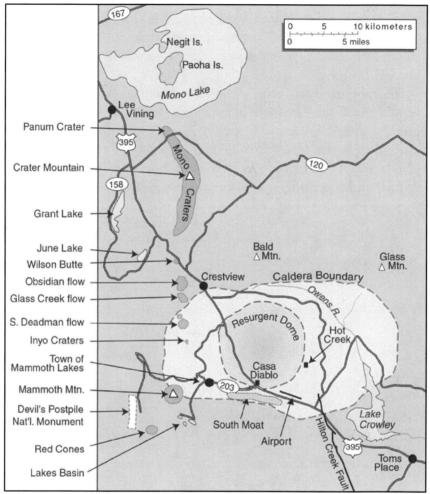

Figure 5 — Long Valley Caldera

the southern edge of the caldera is older. It is believed to have originated about 180,000 years ago with its first eruption, and will likely erupt again in the future.

One of the early major events associated with this caldera was the extrusion of the Bishop Tuff about 760,000 years ago. Approximately 150 cubic miles of ash flows occurred in Long Valley. Airborne ash from this huge event fell as far east as Nebraska. The Mono Basin, Owens Valley, and parts of the Sierras were covered in 600 to 3,000 feet of ash. The blankets of ash, which fell over 580 square miles of California and Nevada, subsequently solidified into the pinkish igneous rock known as the Bishop Tuff. This deposit of hardened volcanic ash is so famous and important to geologists that geology students throughout the United States are familiar with this rock, and often make pilgrimages to the area to observe it for themselves.

Some of the heat underground has been tapped by the Casa Diablo Geothermal Plant, which was built in 1984. Wells 600 feet deep reach into the geothermal field to produce electricity. You can tour the plant if you are interested. You can also experience some of that hot water firsthand at the Hot Creek Geothermal Area where it reaches the surface in warm pools you can soak in.

Earthquakes occur daily in this area, most of them small and uneventful, but frequent reminders of the volatility of the earth beneath our feet. Most of the quakes are centered near the junction of Highway 395 and Highway 203.

As you can imagine, there is plenty to see in the Mammoth Lakes and Bishop areas—volcanoes, obsidian flows, hot springs, oh, my! Let us begin.

96. South Tufa Trail

EFFORT:...Minimal
LENGTH:..1.0 miles
GEOLOGICAL FEATURE(S):...................Volcanism, Erosional Features
LOCATION:...Mono Lake Tufa State Reserve

Description: Situated at the base of the Eastern Sierras, Mono Basin is associated with the Long Valley Caldera, with ample evidence of volcanic activity. Today, the basin contains Mono Lake and its strange growths of tufa. Tufa towers such as these occur in one other place in California, at the Trona Pinnacles in the Mojave Desert.

As you wend your way through the tufa towers, you will get the sensation of being on another world. These irregular bumps and spires rise up all around you like bizarre sand castles.

The towers were once underwater, but the level of the lake has been drained over the years as water from surrounding creeks was diverted to southern California. By 1981, the lake level had dropped 45 feet and the salinity had doubled. In 1994, a lawsuit found that the lake ecosystem had been damaged by the water diversions. The Audubon Society and the Mono Lake Committee have worked tirelessly to stop the drain on the lake, and have been successful in their efforts. The water is no longer being diverted, and the lake has risen

12 feet from its low point. Today, Mono Lake is an 8 by 13 mile body of salt water, a most fetching shade of greenish blue. For the last several years, the lake level has remained stable.

Mono Lake is old for a lake, maybe as old as one million years. About ten million years ago, as the Eastern Sierras were lifted, Mono Basin moved correspondingly down, eventually becoming a catch basin for several streams running down the eastern side of the Sierras. The lake has no outlet, so any minerals running into it are trapped there. As a result, the water of the lake is three times saltier than the Pacific Ocean.

Even though the salty water cannot support a varied marine population, it is an important ecosystem for the state's migrating birds. The California gull nests here on the lake's islands in huge numbers. You may also see eared grebes, loons and many other types of birds which feed on the lake's brine shrimp and alkali flies. The brine shrimp here are peculiar to Mono Lake; they live here in huge numbers, but are found nowhere else on earth.

Tufa is formed through a reaction between calcium carbonate in fresh groundwater or spring water and the briny lake water, because of the abundance of chloride, carbonate, and sulfate in the lake. The resulting material is aragonite, a calcium carbonate mineral that forms commonly in areas of hot springs. Recent research has suggested that algae also contribute to production of tufa by extracting carbon dioxide and thereby reducing calcium carbonate solubility.

You can make your own trail among the towers, so you can spend

Mono Lake *(Courtesy U.S. Geological Survey)*

as little or as much time as you like admiring them. This trail is an interpretive trail which will explain the formation of the tufa towers and the lake's food chain. A paved path starts at the payment booth and heads towards the lake. About halfway along, the pavement ends and a wooden boardwalk completes the trail to the shore of the lake, making this section of the trail wheelchair accessible. The remainder of the trail, going right along the lakeshore, loops through the formations and back to the parking lot, and can only be made on foot.

In addition to the mineral deposits, there is volcanic activity on display here as well. Black Point is the low, black hill on Mono Lake's northwestern shore. It is a volcano that erupted approximately 13,000 years ago during the last ice age. At the time, Mono Lake was 900 feet deeper than it is today, and completely submerged Black Point's eruption. The weight of hundreds of feet of water is responsible for its flat top. Now exposed by the receded shoreline, Black Point is an excellent specimen of an underwater volcano on display.

The islands within Mono Lake are also volcanic, relatively recent additions to the lake's topography. The black island in the northern half is Negit, a volcano that first erupted 1,600 years ago and flowed as recently as 270 years ago.

The youngest member of the Mono Basin volcanic family is Paoha,

the white island in the middle of the lake, which formed only 300 years ago. An unusual volcanic formation, Paoha looks quite different from the classic cinder cone of Negit Island. White and rolling, it resembles the sediment that covers that bottom of Mono Lake. Paoha is, indeed, exposed lake-bottom sediment, pushed up over the surface of the lake in a volcanic upheaval that lacked the momentum to fully erupt. Although there have been a few small lava flows on the north end of the island, Paoha has yet to let go in a full-scale eruption. Still, steam vents and fumaroles on the island indicate its potential for future activity.

Before or after your hike, you may want to visit Mono Lake Vista Point 12 miles north of Lee Vining on Highway 395. From that vantage point you can see the Mono Basin for what it is, a depression with streams draining into it. Another good place to view Mono Lake is on the Rim Trail atop Panum Crater to the south. The next hike will take us there.

Directions: From Highway 395 in Lee Vining, travel 5 miles south. Go east on Highway 120 for 5 miles to the turnoff for the South Tufa Area/Mono Lake Tufa State Reserve. Turn left and go 1 mile to the parking area. There is a small entrance fee, restrooms, and a couple of picnic tables in the open sun.

97. Panum Crater — Rim & Plug Trails

EFFORT:...Minimal	
LENGTH:...1.0 miles	
GEOLOGICAL FEATURE(S):.......................................Volcanism	
LOCATION:..Inyo National Forest	

Description: This route takes you around the rim and then down into Panum Crater, a young, rhyolitic volcano located in the Mono Craters area of the Long Valley Caldera. The trail offers majestic views of the Sierra Nevada and Mono Basin. Panum Crater is the youngest mountain on the American continent, and the last of the Mono Craters to erupt, only 640 years ago. Mono Craters began erupting about 40,000 years ago, producing 21 peaks. Their dramatic, unglaciated shapes indicate that most of them erupted during the 12,000 years since the last ice age. They form a string along the east side of Highway 395 south of Mono Lake, looking somewhat like a moonscape

with their light gray pumice and ash-covered flanks.

The structure of Panum Crater is easily seen in the aerial view shown in the accompanying photograph. It is a tephra ring around an inner rhyolitic plug dome which rises above the rim in the center of the crater sort of like a castle surrounded by a moat. The moat is dry, though, so we can walk into it and over to that castle of volcanic rock.

The intriguing landmark you see today was created in a two-step process. First, magma rising underground came into contact with groundwater, flashing it into steam and causing a huge steam-driven explosion. This produced the crater

Panum Crater
(Courtesy U.S. Geological Survey)

and the debris thrown out around it. After that, the magma slowly rose to the surface, emerging as viscous rhyolitic lava above the vent. The lava hardened and was pushed up and apart by further emerging lava until a substantial pile of volcanic debris stood inside the crater.

Wear a hat and sunscreen and carry water. There is no shade on the Rim Trail.

From the parking lot, head up the loose gravel trail past the signboard to the rim of the crater. From the crater rim, you will have excellent views of the rest of the Mono Craters to the south. Mount Lewis and Mount Gibbs can be seen in the Sierras to the west. Look between Mount Gibbs and Lewis to see two lateral moraines near the mouth of Bloody Canyon.

The crater has a diameter of 4,000 feet, and is littered with pumice ash, lapilli, obsidian, and granite ejecta. At the rim you will encounter a sign which directs you right for the Rim Trail and left for the Plug Trail. We have chosen a route which combines the two for the optimum experience of this crater, although you may choose to do both trails completely if you have time. There will be no surprises along this trail because you can see exactly where you will be going along the entire route. However, the views will change and your proximity to certain features will bring them more sharply into focus.

Go right to follow the Rim Trail, a wide gravel and sand path which contains volcanic material, including lots of obsidian. Find some good samples and observe the conchoidal fractures in the black glass. If you're old enough to remember broken glass of the old Coke bottles, you'll recognize the concentric half-rings that typify a conchoidal fracture. Native Americans took advantage of this natural fracturing pattern to fashion sharp arrowheads. Obsidian was highly valued and extensively traded among tribes.

Be on the lookout for breadcrust bombs, chunks of lightweight rock with surface cracks. These were formed by molten lava flying into the air and cooling to form an outer skin around still hot centers. As the lava within cooled, the surface cracked in a fashion similar to a crusty French bread or Dutch crunch rolls.

Look up on the plug from the south rim and locate a chunk of rock with alternating dark and light stripes on it. This is flow banding, evidence of the course the lava took while liquid. Another good example of this can be found on the north side of the crater sitting just beside the trail.

As you circle the crater in a counterclockwise direction, you will come upon superior views of Mono Lake and the South Tufa Area. From this vantage point, you get a feeling for what the Mono Basin is all about. You can also observe the layout of the tufa formations in a way that is impossible walking among them. They form arcing chains in a pattern that is clearly not random. Since the tufa is built upon natural spring water emerging from the lake bed, the pattern represents the location of faults where the water escaped from underground.

From here you also get good views of Mono Lake's two islands, Negit (the black one) and Paoha (the white one). Both are the result of volcanic eruptions. More details about Mono Lake, its islands, and history can be found in the description of the South Tufa Trail (previous hike).

On the east side of the rim where the trail dips briefly, you can observe birds flying over the low point from their nesting area on the plug dome. From this low point, you will climb somewhat steeply, a process made more difficult by the loose gravel of the trail. On the north edge of the crater, you will go steeply down, your feet sinking into the sand with each step. You will almost be skiing down this slope.

As you reach the northwest corner of the crater, the rim trail goes steeply uphill to the high point. It's a tiring climb, and there is an alternative. A narrow path leads down and south from here. Take that one and drop into the ring at the bottom of the crater. These two trails will meet up back where you began. You will enjoy the new perspective inside the crater, walking alongside the inner plug. There is some vegetation down there, and you may be in the shade of the crater itself, depending on the time of day. Continue along the west side of the dome and then up, out and back to the Rim Trail. This completes the circuit. Turn west and go back down the slope to the parking area, where you can dump the sand out of your boots before leaving.

Directions: From Highway 395 south of Lee Vining, take 120 east 3 miles and then turn left on a dirt road to Panum Crater (there is a small sign). The road is suitable for passenger cars. Continue about one mile to the parking area. There are no facilities. Access is free.

98. Obsidian Dome

EFFORT:...Minimal
LENGTH:...0.5 miles
GEOLOGICAL FEATURE(S):..Volcanism
LOCATION:..Inyo National Forest

Description: From Highway 395, if you are paying attention, and if the exit sign for Obsidian Dome Road means something to you, you can look west and see the high piles of boulders which make up this mile-wide, 300-foot high glass flow. Better yet, if you pull off the road and drive less than a mile, you can walk right up to it.

The formation was made from highly viscous rhyolite lava that was forced up through a small opening, creating a sort of mushroom shape aboveground. The dome is the cap of the mushroom and the stem is the lava in the throat of the eruption. This eruption took place between 1,000 and 5,000 years ago, cooling too quickly to allow crystals to form. It is composed of flow-banded obsidian and rhyolite.

From Obsidian Dome Road, walk uphill on the dirt 4WD road through a forest to a massive, sparkling jumble of boulders. As you near the boulders, you will see that they are primarily black glass, obsidian, a glassy form of rhyolite. You'll see bands of non-glassy rhyolite interspersed with the obsidian. The patterns in the rocks are stunning.

The variation of size and abundance of gas bubbles present created the differing colors and textures as the lava solidified. The pure glass pieces had very little gas.

While we were admiring the gas bubble depressions in the glass, another visitor was climbing up to the top of the flow. If you climb, be very careful. A fall could result in serious cuts. This fellow made it to the top without mishap, while his companion below hollered up, "Do you see the dome?" "No!" he hollered back. He was standing on it, of course.

Wander the perimeter of the flow until you are ready to return the way you came.

Directions: From Highway 395 and Highway 203, drive north on Highway 395 to just past Deadman Summit. Take the Obsidian Dome Road/Bald Mountain Road exit. Go west on dirt Obsidian Dome Road for 0.7 miles. A 4WD dirt road takes off to the left. If you have the proper vehicle, you can drive right up to the obsidian flow. Otherwise, pull safely off the

Obsidian Dome, *(Courtesy U.S. Geological Survey)*

road to park. Another access point for 4WD vehicles can be found taking the Glass Creek Road exit from U.S. 395 west and, after a mile, bear left. Access is free. There are no facilities.

99. Inyo Craters Trail

EFFORT:..Minimal
LENGTH:...0.7 miles
GEOLOGICAL FEATURE(S):.......................................Volcanism
LOCATION:...Inyo National Forest

Description: This short trail leads to three fascinating, young volcanic craters. Two have lakes in them. The Inyo Craters are one of the most recently active eruptive centers of the Long Valley Caldera, dating from about 500 to 600 years ago.

There are three main craters—North, South, and the crater at the summit of Deer Mountain. There are several associated smaller craters and domes in the chain that runs along a north-striking fault system and extends northward to the Mono Craters.

227

Inyo Crater *(Courtesy U.S. Geological Survey)*

The Inyo Craters were created by hydrothermal explosions when the rising magma underground met groundwater, creating a steam explosion that blew off the overlying crust and threw debris outward. This was not a lava eruption.

From the parking area at 8,000 feet, head out on a trail shaded by pine trees. You will climb about 300 feet along the way to the rim. The trail passes between two picnic tables just as you emerge from the forest, approaching a slight rise towards the edge of a huge pit in the ground. When you reach the south crater rim after a mere quarter mile, use the viewing platform to look inside the 600-foot wide hole, over 200 feet deep. The steep sides are only sparsely vegetated, so this crater is much easier to view than the north crater. At the bottom is a murky-looking turquoise lake.

Walk along the rim to a second viewing area. This area was closed when we visited because the edge of the crater had eroded back to start gobbling up the railing's feet. As a matter of fact, one plastic warning sign lay far below inside the crater. Either it fell in, or some rude person threw it. Either way, let this be a caution to keep back from the lip of the crater.

Continuing around to the north side of the south crater, you will suddenly notice that there is another crater on your right. You are standing on the narrow rim between the craters. Turn back and walk east and then north along the rim of the north crater. It is forested and inhabited by many birds and small animals. You can't see the crater's features as well, but you can see how large it is. It is also about 600 feet in diameter, and is somewhat shallower than the south crater at 150 feet deep.

The trail heads up steeply about 400 yards to the north towards the top of Deer Mountain and the Summit Crater. It has no lake in it. We will leave it up to you to decide if it is worth the struggle. There are good views from up there, and we know how the high points beckon.

Return by the same route.

Directions: From Mammoth Lakes on Highway 203 (Main Street), turn right where it becomes Lake Mary Road and proceed to Mammoth Scenic Loop (Forest Service Road 3S23). Turn right onto it and drive to a dirt road signed for Inyo Craters on the left. Follow this dirt road and the signs for 1.5 miles to the trailhead. The road is passable for all vehicles in good weather. Access is free. There are no facilities.

100. Mammoth Consolidated Gold Mine

EFFORT:	Minimal
LENGTH:	0.5 miles
GEOLOGICAL FEATURE(S):	Mining
LOCATION:	Inyo National Forest

Description: This is a self-guided walking tour of the remains of a historic mining camp established in 1927. Tour the old buildings left from the activity surrounding the operation of the Mammoth gold mine. On display are bunkhouses, a cookhouse, manager's office, assayer's office, ore processing equipment, and the mine adit. A brochure is available at the Mammoth Ranger Station.

Long before becoming a ski resort, the Mammoth area supported intensive mining. Known as the Lake Mining District, it was established in 1877 when gold and silver were discovered. This strike came to be known as the Mammoth Lode. A twenty-stamp mill was in operation by 1878 and the towns of Mammoth City, Mill City, and Pine City sprang up.

The six-foot Knight water wheel that powered the stamp mill was shipped around Cape Horn from Europe.

Directions: From Highway 395, exit on Highway 203 towards Mammoth Lakes. Continue on Lake Mary Road southwest. Turn off at Coldwater Campground and park in the Duck Pass Trailhead parking lot.

101. Mammoth Crest Trail

EFFORT:..Difficult
LENGTH:..5.5 miles
GEOLOGICAL FEATURE(S):..Volcanism
LOCATION:..Inyo National Forest

Description: This hike will take you to the magnificent Mammoth Crest through a colorful volcanic landscape, then to the summit of a cinder cone with a total elevation gain of 1,425 feet. Lots of big rocks and bald mountains reveal themselves on this trail.

Heading generally north, the trail is routed above the Woods Lodge cabins through a mixed pine and fir forest. You will climb up some long switchbacks, then emerge into the open to a surprising view of Lakes Mary and George. As you continue to climb, the views get better.

After about a mile, you will duck back into tree cover and come to a trail junction at 1.25 miles. The left path goes to Crystal Lake, the right to the Mammoth Crest. Go left if you want to visit the lake. It's only about a quarter mile to it, and it will be a lovely rest stop before you begin the grueling part of this day hike.

Otherwise, head right towards the Mammoth Crest and begin climbing, sometimes steeply, until you emerge at a level patch with amazing views. All of the peaks of the surrounding ranges are within your view, from the mountains of Yosemite to Mammoth Mountain, the White Mountains, Red and Gold Mountain, Crystal Crag, and several of the area's lakes. Stop walking to take it in or you may trip yourself up.

The trail continues to climb as the tree cover dwindles, and the landscape starts to get really interesting. You are entering young volcanic terrain with pumice, loose cinders and sparse vegetation.

After 2.5 miles you reach a sign announcing that you are entering John Muir Wilderness. Then you arrive at the top of a ridge and descend on the other side. The volcanic landscape surrounds you. There is a classic red cinder cone to the west and red lava rock at your feet interspersed with the Sierra Nevada granite.

At a fork in the trail, you will take the right arm. The main trail continues left, but our destination is the cinder cone. Let those others head for the lakes; we are in it for the rocks. Make your way up the slope as it rises steeply up the side of the cone. This is the rough part of this hike, a slow climb in open sun.

The summit of the cone is 10,480 feet and worth every gasp it took to reach it. What spectacular views! All of the mountains sit solidly around you in a 360-degree panorama. The view around your boots is also entertaining with its myriad of lava colors.

Return the same way after a good rest.

Directions: From Mammoth Lakes, head west to the intersection of Highway 203/Minaret Road and Lake Mary Road. Go straight on Lake Mary Road for almost 4 miles to a fork signed for Coldwater Campground. Bear right to stay on Lake Mary Road. Continue past Lake Mary to a junction where a road leads off to the left signed for Lake George. Turn left and pass Lake Mary Campground. At the next junction, go right towards Lake George, continuing to the lake and trailhead parking lot. Do not take the road on the right to Woods Lodge, but you will find the trailhead beside it. Access is free. There are restrooms near the trailhead and a picnic area at Lake George.

102. Devils Postpile & Rainbow Falls Trail

EFFORT:..Moderate
LENGTH:...5.0 miles
GEOLOGICAL FEATURE(S):....................Volcanism, Erosional Features
LOCATION:.....................................Devils Postpile National Monument

Description: Located in Ansel Adams Wilderness, this national monument was established in 1911 to preserve the geological formation known as Devils Postpile, as well as the magnificent Rainbow Falls. Like many sites in the Sierras, the postpile exhibits a history of assault by the transforming forces of fire and ice.

The postpile is a remarkable basalt column formation about sixty feet high sitting at an elevation of 7,600

Devils Postpile *(Courtesy National Park Service, Wymand W. Eckhardt)*

revealing this splintered cliff face to the world. This is one of the finest examples of basalt columns you can see anywhere.

You will find the trailhead beside the ranger station. Pick up a park brochure there before setting out. It has a map which you may want to use to create your own hiking route, especially if you are taking advantage of the shuttle service and don't need to return to the same trailhead. We will be taking the most popular out and back trail to the postpile and continuing to the waterfall. If you only want to see the waterfall (impossible to imagine), there is a shorter hike (3 miles round-trip) from a trailhead in Red's Meadow, just before the pack station on the right.

feet. The columns formed when basaltic lava erupted in the valley of the Middle Fork of the San Joaquin River about 100,000 years ago. The valley was filled with lava about 400 feet thick, which cooled at a uniform rate from both the top and bottom. As the lava cooled, it shrank and cracked into these geometric shapes. The columns were exposed 10,000 years ago when a glacier flowed down this river gorge and scooped away one side of the postpile,

The trail is wide and well-marked, and the way to the postpile is easy and level. Fortunately, most people can make the less than half-mile trek to the postpile without difficulty. You will walk around a meadow blooming with wildflowers in summer. At a signed trail fork, go left for the postpile.

Other nearby evidence of recent volcanic activity includes Soda Springs on a gravel bar north of the postpile. Gases from deep in the earth combine with groundwater to produce carbonated mineralized springs. The iron in the water stains the gravel a rust color.

When you reach the postpile, walk along its base and marvel at the symmetry that nature exhibits. Each column has from three to seven sides, polygons that occur with some frequency in nature, from salt crystals on the floor of desert playas to mud cracks in a dry pond.

Those columns standing up straight are in place as they formed. Those on the edges which are bowed and angled towards vertical have moved over time. Amazingly, many of the bowed columns have not broken, as the movement occurs so slowly that the basalt has time to adapt and bend. At the bottom, lots of broken column pieces lie in a jumbled pile. Many good examples in this talus slope are immediately beside the trail, so you can get an intimate view of them. Take advantage of several split log benches to sit and admire the formation.

When you are ready, return to the left side of the postpile to take the steep uphill trail to the top. Once you are standing on the flat top of the columns, you will be amazed. It looks like a hexagonal tile floor, each "tile" highly polished and scratched by glaciers. The evidence of scraping ice is easy to read on this surface.

Look around the hill behind this floor, and you will see more exposed sections of the basalt formation. You will also see a trail heading up, signed for Rainbow Falls. Take this trail even if you are not going to the waterfall. It circles the back of the postpile formation and comes around the other side back to the main trail. On the way, you will see more columns and the south side of the pile is quite interesting. Coming down on this loop, turn left to continue to the falls.

Walk south on the trail through lodgepole pine and red fir to Rainbow Falls located on the Middle Fork of the San Joaquin River. Watch for the small Belding ground squirrel and Steller's jays. The trail slopes gently downhill over its entire length. After about a mile from the start of your hike, you will cross a creek on a log bridge. The trail parallels the river bank, coming close enough in a couple of places to give you lovely views of the water and, in autumn, the yellow leaves of aspen and cottonwood. A lightning-sparked forest fire in 1992 burned out many of the trees along the trail. Their blackened trunks cover the hillsides. One memorable dead tree trunk stands beside the trail, its interior completely gutted by fire, leaving only a shell.

You will pass a trail junction where the left arm goes to Reds Meadows. Continue straight for the falls. Across the river are the volcanic formations known as the Buttresses, exposed basalt which is believed to be the oldest volcanic rock in the Monument area. This basalt is different from that of the postpile in that it has abundant pyroxene crystals.

Cross another plank bridge over Boundary Creek. You will enter Ansel Adams Wilderness for a short while, then cross back into monument land. At a junction with Fish Creek Trail, turn right and descend a dirt and log stairway. You will hear the tumult of the waterfall off to the right before you see it, and then you will reach the viewing area above the falls. It is an exquisite 101-foot drop over volcanic rock, which, in the right light, produces rainbows in its mist. When we were here, we saw a rainbow from the second viewing platform just above this first one.

The rock of the waterfall cliff is different from the basalt of the columns. That will be immediately apparent. This is andesite and rhyodacite, light gray and fine-grained, exhibiting horizontal thinly-spaced joints giving a platy appearance.

Walk down to the second platform and take a look, then continue down a long, steep flight of granite stairs to the base of the falls, where the continuous mist creates an inviting habitat for moss and ferns. Using the numerous rocks in the river, you can walk out on a gravel bar to a well-positioned tree trunk at the edge of the waterfall's emerald pool. This makes a perfect spot to sit and watch the falls, the spray gently raining down on you. We were here in October when the volume of water is not at its height, but the waterfall was still running voluminous and magnificent. Along the right side of the main fall, the water skips down a natural stone staircase in a delicate descent to the river below.

You can continue another half mile to Lower Falls, if you are inclined to extend your trek. Otherwise, hike back the way you came. There is also an option of hiking back on another trail to Red's Meadow at the junction we passed on the way out, where the shuttle also stops. There is a store and restaurant there if you haven't packed a lunch. There is a hot spring near Reds Meadow, attesting to the continuing volcanic activity in the area. Allow extra time for the transportation to and from the trail if you are taking the shuttle. We ended up spending four hours on this trail. There was a lot to see.

Directions: Some of the roads traversing the Sierras are closed in winter, so check road conditions if you are coming in spring or fall. From U.S. 395, take the Mammoth Lakes exit and proceed to the Mammoth Mountain Inn (where a woolly mammoth statue stands beside the road). From June to September, you will have to take a shuttle bus to the postpile and pay a fee for the trip from 7:30 a.m. to 7:30 p.m. The bus runs every 20 minutes, starting at

8:00 a.m. Buy tickets at Mammoth Mountain Inn, which is the departing point. If you come off-season or very early in the morning or in the evening, you can drive to the trailhead. Proceed past Mammoth Mountain Inn and past Minaret Vista Point. Continue seven miles to an intersection and turn right, then another quarter mile to the parking lot. The trailhead is next to the ranger station. Access is free. There are restrooms.

103. Red Cones Trail

EFFORT:...Moderate
LENGTH:...6.0 miles
GEOLOGICAL FEATURE(S):...Volcanism
LOCATION:...Inyo National Forest

Description: On a section of the John Muir Trail, you will climb about 1,000 feet to reach the Red Cones, two young cinder cones which are two of the many volcanic features in the Mammoth Lakes area. There is an optional scamper to the top of one cone. There are many hiking trails in this area, and there are other routes to the cones. You might want to study a map to determine the best use of your day. An alternate route can be started from Horseshoe Lake, for instance, off of Lake Mary Road, which is a longer hike, but will give you an excellent swimming hole when you're done.

From Reds Meadow Pack Station, take the trail south through a sparsely wooded area towards Rainbow Falls. You will shortly reach the John Muir/Pacific Crest Trail junction.

Continue uphill on a sandy, pumice-covered trail. There was a major fire here in 1992, and the damage is quite apparent. This has allowed some of the lower-growing plants such as lupine to thrive. If you hike this trail in summer, you will be rewarded with wildflower blooms.

After two miles, you cross Boundary Creek and go up a wooded hillside. After three miles, you reach Crater Creek along Crater Meadow and the base of the northern cone. This eruption is the most recent in the Devils Postpile area, and is younger than the event which created the postpile. The cones, less than 10,000 years old, formed after the last ice age, and have therefore never been glaciated. A basalt lava flow that issued from the base of the southern cone extends down

Crater Creek to within one mile of the Middle Fork of the San Joaquin River

You will easily identify Red Cones from any of the viewpoints in the area. They are the conical peaks protruding from the forest, two symmetrical mounds, reddish in color.

If you want to make the effort, you can climb to the top of the northern cone. You will notice several trails worn by others who have come before you. The 9,000-foot perch at the top will give you fantastic views of Mammoth Mountain, the Mammoth Crest, and the Ritter Range.

Whether or not you climb the cinder cone, retrace your steps on the return trip.

Directions: Some of the roads traversing the Sierras are closed in winter, so check road conditions if you are traveling then. From U.S. 395, take the Mammoth Lakes exit and proceed to the Mammoth Mountain Ski Area, right, and park there. From June to September, you will have to take a shuttle bus to area trailheads and pay a fee for the trip. The bus runs every 20 minutes, starting at 8:00 a.m. Buy tickets at Mammoth Mountain Inn, which is the departing point. If you come off-season or very early in the morning or in the evening, you can drive to the trailhead. Proceed past Mammoth Mountain Inn and past Minaret Vista Point. Continue past the Devil's Postpile exit to Reds Meadow Resort. Access is free.

Red Cones *(Courtesy U.S. Geological Survey)*

104. San Joaquin Ridge Trail

EFFORT:..Moderate
LENGTH:..4.6 miles
GEOLOGICAL FEATURE(S):...................Volcanism, Erosional Features
LOCATION:..Inyo National Forest

Description: The trail is a rough dirt road atop the San Joaquin Ridge with unequaled views in all directions and great wildflower displays in summer. Be prepared for thin air, terrific views, windy exposures, and a gain of 1,080 feet in elevation.

Before starting on the trail, take a few minutes to munch on the view from the vista, one of the best viewpoints around and an awesome place to begin a hike. The information at the viewpoint will identify the major features on the horizon. Look west to see the spiky Minarets, Banner Peak, and Ritter Peak. Below is the upper San Joaquin River drainage. It is a wide, sweeping, fabulous view that will prepare you for the sort of breathtaking journey you are about to undertake.

From the Minaret Vista, the trail is a blocked jeep road passed on the right as you drive the entrance road to the vista parking lot. Walk back to this road to begin, and head north. There is also a path east of the restroom which will take you downhill to the trail if you don't want to walk on the road.

The San Joaquin Ridge marks the Sierra Divide, the border between water runoff to the east and runoff to the west. You will be walking over volcanic soil with chunks of light-colored pumice from eruptions that occurred about 20,000 years ago.

The Minarets, those pointy peaks to the west, are the remnants of an ancient lava flow. Their sawtooth appearance was caused by the repeated cycle of freeze and thaw, winter after winter, which cracked the rock, chipping away at it over time.

At a fork, bear left, continuing on the 4WD road. Where Mountain View bike trail branches off right, you continue on the road called "Hard Corps" trail. This same road will be our route for the duration of the hike. As you gain some height, you will begin to get those promised westward views. You'll also have the company of some colorful blooms alongside the trail.

After 1.25 miles, the trail starts to climb steeply for about a quarter mile before leveling off. A little farther along, at a fork, continue on the Hard Corps trail by bearing left. Begin climbing again, pushing on to the 2-mile mark, and earn views to both east and west. You are walking along the knife-edge in an incredibly dramatic location, and you will feel that drama in your lungs.

Up ahead you will see your destination, Deadman Peak, the high point you will enjoy shortly. In 1868, a headless man's body was found near Deadman Creek, which gave its name to Deadman Pass, which is below Deadman Peak.

The Ritter Range sprawls to the west and Long Valley lies below to the east. As you push on to the summit, take your time to enjoy this top of the world feeling (and catch your breath). Deadman Peak tops out at 10,255 feet. Your views here are endless and unobstructed. Sit down for a while and enjoy it.

The way back is the same, only in reverse.

Directions: From Mammoth Lakes on Highway 203, turn right onto Minaret Road and proceed past Mammoth Mountain Inn heading west to Minaret Summit. Turn right on Minaret Vista access road and park in the large Vista parking area. Access is free. There are restrooms.

105. Hot Creek Trail

EFFORT:..Minimal
LENGTH:...2.0 miles
GEOLOGICAL FEATURE(S):.................................Geothermal Activity
LOCATION:...Inyo National Forest

Description: This trail follows Hot Creek to the Hot Creek Geothermal Area, a spot where hot water bubbles up through fissures, and warm pools provide a spa-like swimming experience. There is plenty of boiling water in the area as well, so be extremely cautious when coming into contact with water.

Magma not far beneath the surface provides the heat for these features. This magma occupies the area under the huge Long Valley Caldera. Most of the hot springs originated on August 24, 1973 in a single event which produced at least five springs, two of them starting out as geysers. The geyser activity dwindled off almost immediately, but the hot springs remain productive. There is no real evidence to explain the appearance of these springs, but some have suggested that a small earthquake 25 miles southeast might be responsible. The springs erupted almost immediately following that seismic activity.

At the parking lot you will find changing rooms, bathrooms, and interpretive panels. You can get an overlook of the trail from the parking area before setting out. You are headed for the lovely steaming pools down below.

Walk down a paved trail into the volcanic canyon, then across a bridge to the north side of Hot Creek. Turn left and follow the dirt path towards the hot pools. The creek water is not hot, and it serves to cool the hot pools to a temperature which can be enjoyed by bathers. The mixing of cold snowmelt and hot spring water produces a wide range of temperatures in Hot Creek, and provides for warm swimming year-round.

The benefits of geothermal activity around Hot Creek extend beyond the naturally warm swimming hole. The nearby geothermal plant produces electricity, and the Hot Creek Fish Hatchery uses the warm spring waters to maintain its artifi-cial environment at optimal conditions for raising young trout.

The canyon is narrow and full of interesting rock formations. Pay close attention to the rocks on the trail. Hydrothermal activity has altered the rhyolite in the canyon, producing a bleached appearance. You will see evidence of intense folding in the colorful bands of the metamorphics. Sulfur deposits and moss add splashes of color as well.

If you want, take a soak in one of the hot pools, but be cautious to avoid coming into contact with scalding water. Return by the same path.

Directions: On Highway 395 east of Mammoth Lakes, continue south to the Hot Creek Fish Hatchery exit. Turn left and proceed 3 miles on Hot Creek Hatchery Road, past the Fish Hatchery to the Hot Creek Geothermal Area. Turn left into the parking lot. Access is free.

106. Big Pine Canyon Trail

EFFORT:..Difficult
LENGTH:..13.0 miles
GEOLOGICAL FEATURE(S):................................Glaciation
LOCATION:..John Muir Wilderness

Description: You know you're going to have to work if you want to touch a California glacier. There is nothing equivalent here to Alaska's Mendenhall where you hop off the cruise ship onto glacial ice. This narrow, rocky trail takes you into the John Muir Wilderness and on to one of the largest glaciers remaining in the Sierras, the Palisade Glacier. This is a serious trail, climbing 3,000 feet from Big Pine Canyon to three glacial lakes named First, Second, and Third. However, there are several possible destinations along this trail for less determined hikers. An easy and rewarding 3-mile trip can be made by visiting two pretty waterfalls along North Fork Big Pine Creek. All of these destinations will be out and back hikes.

Pass a locked gate at the end of the road and walk beside Big Pine Creek past summer homes. The road tapers off to a footpath and climbs up a hill. You will come to a bridge over the creek at just over a quarter mile and your first point of interest. The cascade here is First Falls. Take a moment to enjoy it before passing over to the other side of the creek and continuing to a junction. Turn right for North Fork Big Pine Creek. Switchback steeply up the main trail until you meet up with a road at 0.6 miles. Turn right onto the road and cross the creek on a bridge. Soon you are at another junction with two of the routes heading for the second waterfall. Upper Trail heads right and climbs above the road. For the easier route, take the road left for a level path with spur trails leading off left, providing stream access.

Second Falls will soon come into view as the trail narrows and routes you uphill. At 1.5 miles, you reach a junction with Upper Trail. You can go left on the trail to the top of the falls if you wish. Just beyond that you will enter a meadow beside the creek which, in season, will have wildflower displays.

If Second Falls was your final destination, you can return the same way or take Upper Trail back down to the previous junction. It would have been a steep uphill climb to the falls, but will be downhill from here and will provide some alternative scenery.

If you are going for the long haul, continue beyond the falls and through the flowery meadow. After 2.7 miles, you will pass a trail leading left to Big Pine Creek Wilderness Ranger Camp, a stone building which once belonged to actor Lon Chaney.

Emerge into a sunny stretch of trail with intermittent lodgepole pines and granite outcrops. Ford the stream at four miles and again shortly thereafter. Switchback uphill to a trail junction. Take the left fork. This route takes you to First through Seventh Lakes. Thankfully, the trail reenters tree cover and passes a side trail to the left which leads to a camping area on the shore of First Lake, a lovely glacial tarn.

At 4.5 miles you reach a viewpoint above First Lake at 10,000 feet in elevation. Continuing, you will reach Second Lake about 100 feet higher at 4.75 miles. There is a picnic area here overlooking Second Lake. Glacial erratics will be apparent nearby.

After passing Third Lake, you will climb to a meadow with sweeping views of the icefield. Big Pine Lakes area contains several more lakes, all glacial tarns. You will see many signs of glaciation along the way, such as striations on the rocks along the creek. After six miles, you will see part of the Palisade Glacier, and a newly-formed moraine.

Return via the same path.

Directions: From Highway 395 near Big Pine, take Glacier Lodge Road west about 11 miles to the end, just past the entrance to Glacier Lodge where there is trailhead parking. Access is free.

Appendix A — Thematic Index

Appendix B — Geologic Time Scale

Eon	Era	Period	Epoch	Years Ago
PHANEROZOIC	CENOZOIC	Quaternary	Holocene	10,000 years ago
			Pleistocene	1.6 mya
		Tertiary		
		Neogene (subperiod)	Pliocene	5 mya
			Miocene	24 mya
		Paleogene (subperiod)	Oligocene	38 mya
			Eocene	55 mya
			Paleocene	66 mya
	MESOZOIC	Cretaceous		138 mya
		Jurassic		205 mya
		Triassic		240 mya
	PALEOZOIC	Permian		290 mya
		Carboniferous		
		Pennsylvanian (subperiod)		330 mya
		Mississippian (subperiod)		360 mya
		Devonian		410 mya
		Silurian		435 mya
		Ordovician		500 mya
		Cambrian		570 mya
		Precambrian Time		
PROTEROZOIC (87 percent of geologic time scale)				2.5 bya
ARCHEAN				4.55 bya

Glossary of Geology Terms

Aa – a Hawaiian word used to describe rough, jagged lava. So named because if you fall down on it you're likely to cry out "Ah! Ah!" See Pahoehoe.

Adit – a nearly horizontal entrance to a mine.

Agate – a semi-precious stone prized by rockhounds. It is composed of bands of chalcedony, a type of cryptocrystalline quartz, which means that the crystals are too small to be seen even with a microscope. Agates are formed in the vesicles of volcanic rocks.

Alluvial – any material or process associated with transportation or deposition by a stream. "Alluvium" refers to the material (sand) and alluvial refers to the process. Alluvial is pretty much interchangeable with the word "fluvial."

Alluvial Fan – a very large, fan-shaped deposit of sand and gravel at the base of a mountain in the arid west. The fan is formed when a stream courses down the steep mountain and then hit the plains below. The stream loses all of its energy and dumps its load of sand, silt and gravel. When there are numerous alluvial fans that blend together, the resulting deposit is called a bajada.

Alpine – the name given to any environment that resembles the Alps, a high, mountainous area above the tree line with a cold climate.

Ammonite – a beautiful, coiled mollusk that was predominant in the Mesozoic seas. The fossil shells are so abundant and diverse that the Mesozoic was subdivided into smaller pieces of time based on this one animal. A modern example of an ammonite is the chambered nautilus.

Andesite – a fine-grained volcanic rock that is in between basalt and rhyolite in chemical composition. Andesite has more quartz and light-colored feldspars than basalt, but less than rhyolite. It is sort of a gray, indistinct kind of rock.

Angle of Repose – the maximum angle at which material such as soil or loose rock remains stable.

Arête – a narrow, saw-toothed mountain ridge formed when cirques (see below) are carved out on either side of the ridge by glaciers.

Badlands – an area where loose sediments with minimal vegetation erode easily by contact with water. Generally, badlands form where deposits of shale have eroded so much that there is hardly any actual rock left. Because of the presence of a variety of minerals, badlands are often multi-colored and have names like "Artist's Palette." Dinosaur fossils have often been found in badland areas. Probably the most well-known of all the badlands is in North Dakota, around Mount Rushmore.

Bar – the name for the sand and gravel that is deposited on the inside bend of a winding river or stream.

Batholith – large (huge!) volume of igneous rock that cooled slowly underground at great depth. Whole mountain ranges are formed from a single batholith. The name comes from the Greek bathos (depth) and lithos (stone). In order to qualify as a batholith, the igneous mass must be so deep into the ground that the bottom cannot be found and have an area of surface exposure greater than 100 square kilometers (that's about 70 square miles).

Bedrock – a general term for the solid rock that underlies the soil and other unconsolidated material or that is exposed at the surface.

Bench – a shelf-like or ridge-like cut in rock.

Brachiopod – an extinct mollusk abundant in the Paleozoic that looks a lot like a clam with bilaterally symmetrical shells. Their muscles worked the opposite of clams, however, so that when brachiopods relaxed (died) their shells shut instead of opening. That means that when you find a fossil brachiopod, you usually find both shells together clamped shut.

Chevron Fold – a dramatic feature where rocks are folded so sharply that they form a zig-zag pattern, similar to a chevron shape. Chevron folds are a sign of intense deformation.

Cinder Cone – a conical elevation formed by the accumulation of ash or cinders (pyroclastic ejecta) around a volcanic vent. A cinder cone can't form unless a main volcano is in the area.

Cirque – a bowl-shaped depression open in front, caused by glaciation, and sometimes containing a round lake, or tarn.

Cleavage – the property of a mineral that determines how it splits along planar surfaces which are determined by the particular crystalline structure of the material.

Cross-Bedding – sedimentary strata that cross at an angle with each other. The most dramatic cross beds form from the migration of wind-formed dunes (Checkerboard Mesa in Zion National Park, Utah). Also known as inclined bedding or current bedding. Cross-bedding is useful to geologists who are trying to reconstruct depositional environments, because they offer a clue as to what direction was upstream (or upwind).

Delta – a body of alluvium, nearly flat and fan-shaped at or near the mouth of a stream where it enters a body of relatively quiet water, usually a lake. Deltas are named for their shape, because the shape is supposed to resemble the Greek letter delta. A classic delta is the Mississippi delta, of course, but Stockton, California also boasts a large delta that starts at Stockton and continues to Antioch on its way to the San Francisco Bay.

Depression – any relatively sunken part of the Earth's surface, especially a low-lying area surrounded by higher ground. In the environmental world, depressions are good places to investigate for soil and groundwater contamination, because humans typically view depressions as large trash containers.

Detritus – the general term for loose sediment, sand, gravel, silt and clay. The term is particularly used for small rock fragments derived from larger rocks.

Drift – a term applied to all detrital material (clay, sand, silt, boulders) transported by a glacier and deposited directly by or from the ice, or by running water emanating from the glacier. Generally applies to Pleistocene glacial deposits.

Dune – a low mound, ridge, bank, or hill of loose, windblown, granular material (generally sand), either bare or covered by vegetation, that is capable of movement from place to place but always maintaining its characteristic shape. This dry description does not convey how breathtakingly beautiful dunes can be, especially in the late afternoon sun with shadows in their folds. Dunes are very difficult to trudge through, however. The Algodones Dunes, located in Imperial County about 20 miles west of Yuma, Arizona, are the most spectacular dunes in California, and have been the site of a large number of Hollywood films.

Erratic – a rock or rock fragment, often very large, that is distinctly out of place. The erratic is usually carried by glacial ice, or less commonly, by floating ice, and subsequently deposited at some distance from the outcrop where it originated.

Exfoliation – breaking or peeling off of concentric sheets (like an onion) from bare rock surfaces by physical or chemical forces.

Facies – part of a rock body as differentiated from other parts by composition or appearance. Also, igneous facies is a type of igneous rock that is somewhat abnormal compared to the larger mass of which it is a part.

Fault – a fracture in a body of rock, with displacement of the rocks on either side relative to one another. Rocks on one side of the fault have either moved up, down, or sideways relative to rocks on the other side.

Fault Scarp – a cliff formed by a fault. The most dramatic fault scarp in the United States is the Grand Teton Mountains in Wyoming. A good local example is the Berkeley Hills that formed on one side of the Hayward Fault.

Flood Plain – the nearly level plain that borders a stream and is subject to inundation under flood stage conditions unless protected artificially, such as by levees. People sometimes build on the flood plain, but as every geologist knows, the flood plain ultimately belongs to the river.

Fluvial – of or pertaining to rivers; produced by river action (see *alluvial*).

Fold – a bend in strata or any planar structure, usually because of deformation. Folds show up very well in the bedded cherts around San Francisco, as well as in outcrops along highway 14 near Lancaster.

Frost Weathering or Wedging – the disintegration of rock brought about by freezing and thawing. This is a tremendously important mechanism of weathering in mountainous areas. As water gets into the small cracks and macropores in a rock, it freezes and subsequently expands, pushing out against the rock. During the day, the ice converts back to water and then at night freezes again and starts the process all over again.

Fumarole – a hole or vent in the earth's crust through which gases and fumes emanate, usually in volcanic areas, often in late-stage volcanism. You can observe several fumaroles at Lassen National Park.

Fusilinid – tiny football shaped microfossils that have been highly studied because of their association with oil-producing rocks.

Geomorphology – the science that studies the general configuration of the earth's surface; specifically the study of the classification, description, nature, origin, and development of landforms and their relationship to underlying structures, and of the history of geologic changes as recorded by these surface features.

Glacier – a large mass of ice formed by the compaction and recrystallization of snow that moves slowly downslope due to its own weight. Glaciers are one of the three agents of erosion (the other two being wind and water) that are responsible for the spectacular scenery in Yosemite and elsewhere in the Sierra Nevadas. Although the really large glaciers of the past ice ages have long since receded from California's landscape, smaller glaciers still ring the summit of Mt. Shasta and the high mountains in the Sierras.

Glacial lake – a lake created by glacial ice that forms a dam, holding the water in place. Glacial lakes are usually associated with continental ice sheets, the broad, deep sheets of glacial ice that covered much of the United States during the ice age (as opposed to Valley or Alpine glaciers, the type that formed in Yosemite).

Glaciation – the formation, movement, and recession of glaciers or ice sheets; geologic processes of glacial activity.

Glaciofluvial deposits – material moved by glaciers and subsequently sorted and deposited by streams flowing from the melting ice. Materials are commonly stratified.

Granite – one of the most recognized igneous rocks, consisting primarily of quartz and potassium feldspar with crystals that are easily visible to the naked eye. Granite may be very pink or almost white, depending on the amount of pink potassium feldspar present in the matrix. Granite that cooled very slowly underground will have relatively large crystals while granite that cooled more quickly will have smaller crystals.

Grüs – an accumulation of angular, coarse-grained fragments resulting from the disintegration of granite. You'll know you're walking on grüs, by the crunch underfoot.

Hanging Valley – a valley carved by a tributary glacier that flowed into a main, or "trunk" glacier. The smaller valley is higher in elevation because the main glacier had greater erosive power than the smaller, tributary glacier.

Hornito – a small mound of spatter formed by lava thrown up through the ceiling of a lava tube.

Ichthyosaur – an extinct marine lizard shaped something like a porpoise or a shark, but more like a whale in size, that lived in the oceans of the Middle Triassic to Upper Cretaceous periods.

Igneous – rocks solidified from a melt. The melt is usually associated with volcanic activity on the surface, but occurs abundantly underground as well.

Kame – a low mound, ridge, or hummock deposited by streams flowing out of glaciers. Kames are more commonly encountered in the eastern United States where large continental ice sheets formed.

Lahar – a volcanic mudflow.

Lakebed – the flat to gently undulating ground that underlies a lake or former lake. Generally composed of fine-grained sediment. Several ancient lakebeds exist in Central California; in fact, the entire Great Valley itself was once covered by a lake, or a series of lakes.

Lake Plain – a nearly level surface marking the floor of an extinct lake filled with well-sorted generally fine-textured sediments that are commonly stratified.

Landform – any physical, recognizable form or feature on the earth's surface, having a characteristic shape and range in composition, which is produced by natural causes.

Lapilli – volcanic ejecta of small size.

Lateral Moraine – a ridge-like moraine deposited at the side margin of a valley glacier.

Lava – fluid rock that issues from a volcano or fissure in the earth, or the solidified rock which results after cooling. If the fluid rock is underground and not on the surface, it is referred to as magma.

Limestone – a sedimentary deposit made out of calcium carbonate. Limestone mainly forms in the ocean from the millions of marine skeletons and shells that rain down from the shallower waters every day. Over time, the ocean bottom is buried and subject to heat and pressure, and eventually becomes limestone. The origin of limestone is readily apparent in many rocks in which the fossils are abundant and easily seen. Some limestone rock, however, was formed from a limey mud and fossils are not apparent. Limestone that was formed in fresh water (such as a lake) is called travertine.

Magma – naturally occurring molten rock material within the earth (see *lava*, which is the name given to magma that occurs above the surface).

Metamorphic – type of rock that has been changed from another, preexisting rock due to heat, temperature, and chemically active fluids associated with burial underground. Limestone, for example, metamorphoses into marble, and shale into slate. The heat and pressure the rock is exposed to is enough to change the rock, but not enough to melt it.

Monzonite – a granular plutonic rock containing equal amounts of orthoclase (potassium feldspar) and plagioclase. Monzonite has less quartz than granite but more than gabbro.

Moraine – a general name given to unsorted silt, sand, gravel, and cobbles deposited by glaciers. Various types include ground moraine, lateral moraine, recessional moraine, etc., all of which refer to what was going on with the glacier at the time of deposition. A *lateral moraine*, for example, is material that was deposited on the side of a glacier, while a *recessional moraine* was deposited during a pause in a glacial retreat. A *ground moraine* is also known as a bottom moraine, and refers to material that was carried along the bottom of a glacier. A *terminal moraine* marks the farthest advance of a glacier and can be a hill of fairly significant size. Moraines can be huge deposits if formed from large continental ice sheets. In Minnesota, a popular ski resort is built on a terminal moraine.

Moraine Kame – an end moraine that contains numerous kames. A kame is a low ridge of glacial deposit that formed as a delta at the glacial front by meltwater streams.

Obsidian – volcanic glass, usually black. If you get a small enough piece you'll see that it is actually opaque rather than black. Obsidian can be recognized by its conchoidal fracture, which is the semi-circular breakage pattern that all glass exhibits (think of a broken glass coke bottle, if you're old enough).

Ophiolite Suite – a piece of the oceanic crust that has ended up on the continent through the action of plate tectonics. The suite consists of a base unit of gabbro that formed from the initial magma chamber, vertical sheeted dikes that formed as the magma moved upward in the crust, and a top layer of pillow basalt, which formed as the magma extruded out onto the oceanic floor and was cooled by oceanic waters.

Orogeny – the process of mountain building.

Pahoehoe – a Hawaiian word used to describe smooth, ropy lava. See (AA).

Pillow Basalt – basalt that was extruded initially at an oceanic trench. As the basalt emerged, the waters of the ocean cooled and rounded the magma, forming "pillows" that are seen on land today. Pillow basalts are the top sequence in an ophiolite suite.

Phenocryst – the name given to visible crystals that are larger than the surrounding crystals in an igneous rock.

Physiographic Province – a region of which all parts are similar in geologic structure and climate and which has consequently had a unified geomorphic history; a region whose relief features and landforms differ significantly from that of adjacent regions.

Playa – broad, desert plain in an undrained basin, occasionally filed with a lake. The most famous playa in the U.S. is the Great Salt Lake and surrounding area. In California, playas are most common in the southern desert regions. As the water evaporates in these basins, evaporite minerals such as salt deposits are left behind.

Pluton – a body of igneous rock that has formed beneath the surface of the earth by consolidation from magma.

Plutonic – igneous rocks formed at great depth beneath the earth's surface.

Porphyry – rocks containing conspicuous phenocrysts in a fine-grained ground mass, representing two stages of cooling. The larger crystals formed slowly and then, as conditions changed, the remaining crystals formed quickly.

Post-Glacial - refers to the Holocene (i.e., present time).

Pumice – a porous, lightweight volcanic glass pitted with gas bubble vesicles.

Radiolarians – numerous marine protozoa with complex silica-based skeletons. Layers of sea-bed deposits are often composed of such skeletons.

Rain Shadow – The dry side of a mountain range that results when air loses its precipitation as it moves across the range. The windward side of a mountain range is typically wet while the lee side is dry.

Roche Moutonnée – a resistant knob of rock left behind after a glacier carved its way around it. This is a French term meaning "sheep rock," named for the common shape such features take. Fannette Island in Emerald Bay at Lake Tahoe is a roche moutonnée.

Roof Pendant – older rocks atop a batholith.

Sand Dune – (see Dune)

Scarp – a line of cliffs, usually formed by faulting.

Sea Stack – an isolated pillar of rock, separated from the mainland scarp by wave erosion.

Sedimentary – type of rock formed from sediments deposited by the action of wind, water or ice. Examples of sedimentary depositional environments include lakes, streams, oceans, glaciers, or sand dunes.

Serpentinite – California's state rock, metamorphic, consisting of serpentine minerals derived from the alteration of previously existing mantle materials olivine and pyroxene.

Shale – a sedimentary rock exhibiting bedding, usually soft and easily broken into its constituent layers.

Shield Volcano – a broad, gently sloping volcanic cone of flat, domical shape, covering several tens or hundreds of square miles, built chiefly of overlapping basaltic lava flows.

Skarn – rock composed almost entirely of lime-bearing silicates, derived from limestone or dolomite.

Slate – a fine-grained metamorphic rock.

Soil Creep – the gradual, slow, downhill movement of soil on a steep hillside. The actual movement is imperceptible to the human eye but is evidenced by trees bending in the downslope direction.

Spattercone – a particularly messy volcanic vent or fissure. These are general low with steep sides created by the spatter of a lava fountain.

Stratified – sedimentary rocks that have been formed, arranged, or laid down in layers.

Stratovolcano – a volcanic cone, generally large, characterized by alternating layers of lava and pyroclastic materials.

Stream terrace – one of a series of platforms in a stream valley, flanking and more or less parallel to the stream channel, originally formed near the level of the stream, and representing the dissected remnants of an abandoned flood plain, stream bed, or valley floor produced during a former state of erosion or deposition.

Striations – lines and grooves scratched into bedrock by rocks carried at the base of glacial ice. Striations are considered proof of glacial movement over the bedrock.

Strike-Slip Fault – a fault in which the rock mass on either side of the fault moves parallel to each other (rather than up or down).

Subduction – in plate tectonics, the process of the edge of one tectonic plate sliding beneath another.

Subduction Zone – the area along which subduction takes place. Deep oceanic trenches occur along subduction zones.

Summit – the topographically highest point on a mountaintop or hill, exhibiting a nearly level surface.

Tafoni – any rock that has weathered so that it has a honeycomb structure. The name comes from Sicily where impressive honeycomb structures have formed in the coastal granite.

Talus – rock fragments, usually large and angular, that have piled up at the base of a scarp, cliff, or steep slope.

Tarn – the lake which occupies a cirque, a mountain basin carved out by a glacier. Tarns come with a guarantee of alpine beauty.

Terrain – topography, or the character of rock in a geographic region.

Terrane – a fault-bounded grouping of rocks characterized by being stratigraphically or structurally distinct from the surrounding rocks. Generally referred to as "suspect" terrane.

Topography – the configuration of a surface with the relative position and elevation of the natural or man-made features of an area.

Transform Fault – a strike-slip fault characteristic of oceanic ridges, along which the ridges are offset.

Trilobite – extinct Paleozoic marine arthropod whose dorsal skeleton consisted of three distinct parts (hence the "tri" in trilobite), namely, the cephalon (head), thorax (body), and pygidium (tail). The closest living relative of the trilobite is the modern horseshoe crab.

Tufa – also known as travertine, a type of sedimentary rock composed of calcium carbonate or of silica, deposited from solution in the water of a spring or lake or from percolating groundwater. In other words, freshwater limestone. Dramatic tufa towers are found in and around Mono Lake, and at Trona Pinnacles in southern California.

Tuff – a rock formed of compacted volcanic fragments, generally smaller than 4 mm. in diameter. Tuff often occurs in small, distinct layers and is very useful for dating events. The hypothesis that dinosaurs became extinct because of a meteor impact is based on the occurrence of a rare earth metal found in a distinct tuff layer that is almost worldwide.

Ultramafic – igneous rock that contains almost no quartz or feldspar, but is instead composed of mantle-type minerals such as dunite, perodite, amphibolite, and pyroxenite.

Volcano – c'mon, everyone knows what a volcano is. Okay, it's a vent in the earth's crust that provides a conduit for magma to reach the earth's surface. Also used to describe a mountain which erupted in the past.

Volcanic Plug – what is left of the volcano after the outer part has eroded away leaving behind the central plug. Volcanic plugs can be recognized because they are usually a large, contorted monolithic mass of solidified igneous rock for which no other reasonable explanation exists.

Xenolith – a preexisting rock which has been incorporated into an igneous flow. The xenoliths in the Sierra Nevadas are easily seen as large rectangles of dark basalt incorporated into the lighter colored granite.

Resource List

United States Geological Survey (USGS) California
Placer Hall
6000 J St.
Sacramento, CA 95819-6129
(916) 278-3000
Fax (916) 278-3045

California Department of Conservation
801 K Street, MS 24-01
Sacramento, CA 95814
(916) 322-1080
Fax (916) 445-0732

California Department of State Parks and Recreation
P.O. Box 942896
Sacramento, CA 94296
(916) 653-6995
Toll Free (800) 777-0369
Fax (916) 657-3903

National Parks and Monuments

Devils Postpile National Monument
P.O. Box 3999
Mammoth Lakes, CA 93546
Summer (760) 934-2289

Golden Gate Natl. Recreation Area
Fort Mason, Building 201
San Francisco, CA 94123-0022

Visitor Information (415) 561-4700
Fax (415) 561-4750

Lassen Volcanic National Park
P.O. Box 100
Mineral, CA 96063
(530) 595-4444
TDD (530) 595-3480

Lava Beds National Monument
Indian Wells Headquarters
Tulelake, CA 96134
Fax: (530) 667-2737
Headquarters (530) 667-2282
Info (530) 667-2282
  ext. 232

Pinnacles National Monument
5000 Hwy. 146
Paicines, CA 95043
Info (831) 389-4485
Fax: (831) 389-4489
Headquarters (831) 389-4485,
  ext. 0

Point Reyes National Seashore
Point Reyes, CA 94956
Fax: (415) 663-8132
Visitor Information (415) 464-5100

Redwood National & State Parks
1111 Second St.
Crescent City, CA 95531
Fax: (707) 464-1812
Headquarters (707) 464-6101

Sequoia and Kings Canyon National Parks

47050 Generals Highway
Three Rivers, CA 93271-9700
Fax: (559) 565-3730
Info (559) 565-3341

Yosemite National Park

Superintendent
P.O. Box 577
Yosemite National Park, CA 95389
Fax (209) 372-0220
Information & Headquarters
   (209) 372-0200
Visitor information (TDD)
   (209) 372-4726

National Forest Offices

El Dorado National Forest

100 Forni Rd.
Placerville, CA 95667
(530) 622-5061
TTY (530) 642-5122
Info (530) 644-6048

Inyo National Forest

351 Pacu Ln., Ste. 200
Bishop, CA 93514
(760) 873-2400
TTY (760) 873-2538

Klamath National Forest

1312 Fairlane Rd.
Yreka, CA 96097-9549
(530) 842-6131
Fax (530) 841-4571
TDD (530) 841-4573

Lassen National Forest

2550 Riverside Dr.
Susanville, CA 96130
(530) 257-2151
TDD (530) 257-6244

Los Padres National Forest

6755 Hollister Ave., Ste. 150
Goleta, CA 93117
(805) 968-6640
TTY (805) 968-6790

Mendocino National Forest

825 N. Humboldt Ave.
Willows, CA, 95988
(530) 934-3316
TDD (530) 934-7724

Modoc National Forest

800 W. 12th St.
Alturas, CA 96101
(530) 233-5811
TDD (530) 233-8708
Fax (530) 233-8709

Plumas National Forest

159 Lawrence St.
P.O. Box 11500
Quincy, CA 95971
(530) 283-2050
TTY (888) 822-3119

Sequoia National Forest

900 W. Grand Ave.
Porterville, CA 93257
(559) 784-1500

Shasta-Trinity National Forest

3644 Avtech
Redding, CA 96002
(530) 226-2500

Sierra National Forest
1600 Tollhouse Rd.
Clovis, CA 93611
(559) 297-0706
TTY (559) 322-4925

Six Rivers National Forest
1330 Bayshore Way
Eureka, CA 95501
TTY and Voice (707) 442-1721

Stanislaus National Forest
19777 Greenley Rd.
Sonora, CA 95370
(209) 532-3671
TTY (209) 533-0765

Tahoe National Forest
631 Coyote St.
Nevada City, CA 95959
(530) 265-4531
TDD (530) 478-6118

Bureau of Land Management

California State Office
2800 Cottage Way, Ste. W-1834
Sacramento, CA 95825-1886
(916) 978-4400
TDD (916) 978-4419

BLM Field Offices:

Alturas Field Office
708 W. 12th St.
Alturas, CA 96101
(530) 233-4666

Arcata Field Office
1695 Heindon Rd.
Arcata, CA 95521-4573
(707) 825-2300

Bishop Field Office
351 Pacu Ln., Ste. 100
Bishop, CA 93514-2471
(760) 872-5000

Eagle Lake Field Office
2950 Riverside Dr.
Susanville, CA 96130
(530) 257-0456

Folsom Field Office
63 Natoma St.
Folsom, CA 95630
(916) 985-4474

Hollister Field Office
20 Hamilton Crt.
Hollister, CA 95023
(831) 630-5000

Redding Field Office
355 Hemsted Dr.
Redding, CA 96002
(530) 224-2100

Surprise Field Office
602 Cressler St.
Cedarville, CA 96104
(530) 279-6101

Ukiah Field Office
2550 N. State St.
Ukiah, CA 95482
(707) 468-4000

Sierra Nevada Recreation Corporation
P.O. Box 78
Vallecito, CA 95251
(866) 762-2837
Fax (209) 736-0330
E-mail: caverns@caverntours.com

Selected Bibliography

Harden, Deborah R. *California Geology*, Prentice-Hall, Inc., Upper Saddle River, New Jersey, 1998

Hill, Mary, *California Landscape: Origin and Evolution*, Berkeley: University of California Press, 1984.

Kane, Phillip S., *Through Vulcan's Eye: The Geology and Geomorphology of Lassen National Park*, Red Bluff: Walker Lithograph, 1998.

Kious, W. Jacquelyne and Robert I. Tilling, *This Dynamic Earth: The Story of Plate Tectonics*, U.S. Geological Survey, 1996.

McPhee, John, *Assembling California*, New York: Farrar, Straus, and Giroux, 1993.

Oakeshott, Gordon B., *California's Changing Landscapes: A Guide to the Geology of the State*, New York: McGraw-Hill Publishing Company, 1978.

Sharp, Robert P., *A Field Guide to Southern California*, Dubuque, Iowa: Kendall/Hunt Publishing Company, 1994.

About the Authors

Robin Johnson is a computer professional for a major West Coast supply distribution facility, where she is a software designer and webmaster. She has worked as a newspaper journalist and has published numerous short fiction and nonfiction works in literary journals, nationally—distributed magazines, and technical publications as a freelance author.

Dot Lofstrom, is a Registered Geologist with a B.S. in geology from Southwest Missouri State University and an M.S. in geology from University of Missouri – Columbia. She has been practicing geology for 17 years in the states of Arizona and California in both the public and private sectors. She developed the Environmental Technology program at Arizona Western College in Yuma, Arizona, and is currently working in the hazardous waste management field. She has taught HAZMAT classes to students and professionals in the U.S. and overseas in the Philippines and India.

Both are avid hikers, and enjoy the varied trails of California and the desert Southwest.